Daily Devotions

. . .with Calvary Chapel Pastors

compiled by:
Mark Maciel

KNi Printing

Anaheim, CA.

Cover Design by: Gregg Zamora

Library of Congress Catalog Card Number: 98-75386

ISBN 0-9668433-0-4

Printed in the United States of America

ACKNOWLEDGEMENTS

To my senior pastor, Jeff Johnson, for all his support and for the example that he has shown through the Word.

To Patricia and Tricia, my wife and daughter, the two special girls in my life who have shown me the Lord in their lives through their prayers and support.

To Julie Simpson, Debbie Schmidt, Sue Allen, Olga Anderson, Brenda McDonough, and my wife Patricia. Thanks for all the typing and editing you have done. May the Lord bless you for all your time and diligent work.

To the Lord, Jesus Christ, for the encouragement of His Word. To Him be all the glory and honor and praise.

FORWARD

"Daily Devotions" is a collection of messages from various Calvary Chapel pastors. These mini-sermons are being placed every week in church bulletins around the country in: Parson to Person, Shepherd to Sheep, Maranatha Matters, etc.

These words of encouragement are meant to help us, as Christians, see our absolute need for an intimate relationship with our Lord. Without this, the joy and power of God's Holy Spirit cannot be experienced fully!

Mark Maciel has compiled these brief Old and New Testament messages in hopes that your devotional time may be more meaningful and inspirational -- to stir your soul, and give you food for thought to start your day. Remember. . . morning by morning, new mercies we see . . . *"My voice shalt thou hear in the morning, O LORD; in the morning will I direct my prayer unto thee, and will look up," (Psalm 5:3).*

Agape,

Pastor Jeff Johnson
Calvary Chapel of Downey
Downey, California

January 1

NEW YEAR!

As we face the beginning of a New Year, it is a time of looking back, and looking ahead. Generally, we are hoping to do better and improve over the past. That is why it is a time of resolutions, but we all know what a joke they are. That longing for improvement comes from God. All of us are aware that we could do better, and be better. The problem is, it is not in the scope of our power to do, or to be, any better than we are. That is why the resolutions fail. Does that mean that I have to always be frustrated with my failure to live up to my own desires? No, if we seek the strength and help of the Lord, by His grace and the power of His Spirit, we can be all that He wants us to be!

Chuck Smith, Senior Pastor
Calvary Chapel Costa Mesa
Santa Ana, California

January 2

DON'T BE LATE

*". . . of the times and seasons, brethren, you have no need
that I should write unto you. For you yourselves
know perfectly that the day of the Lord
so comes as a thief in the night!"*
I Thessalonians 5:1,2

So knowing the time, it is high time to awake out of sleep, to cast off the works of darkness, and put on the Lord Jesus Christ! The night is far spent, the day is at hand *(Romans 13:11,12,14)*! Who knows, this could be the year the Lord returns!

May we be wise virgins, having our lives trimmed and our hearts full of the Holy Spirit. Remember, the five that went in unto the Lord were ready! Are you ready? The foolish virgins were not ready and were left behind *(Matthew 25:1-10)*.

Thank God for our *"blessed hope"* that purifies us and keeps us ready. So if He's to come this year, we won't be late.

Looking up for our redemption draws near!

Jeff Johnson, Senior Pastor
Calvary Chapel of Downey
Downey, California

January 3

FROM SELF RELIANCE TO SERVANTHOOD

*"Now Moses was tending the flock of Jethro his father-in-law,
the priest of Midian. And he led the flock to the back of the
desert, and came to Horeb, the mountain of God. And the
angel of the LORD appeared to him in a flame of fire from the
midst of a bush. So he looked, and behold, the bush was
burning with fire, but the bush was not consumed. Then
Moses said, 'I will now turn aside and see this great sight, why
the bush does not burn.' So when the Lord saw that he turned
aside to look, God called to him from the midst of the bush and
said, 'Moses, Moses!' And he said, 'Here I am.'"*
Exodus 3:1-4

Moses, after a flash in the pan try at being God's man of
the house *(Exodus 2:11-15)*, has settled for being a simple
shepherd -- not even tending his own sheep. Yet the sight
of an unnatural occurrence sparked a response in Moses.

As Moses drew near the burning bush, God called to him.
The night for Moses was ending. This man of God had
come through the training of tending the flocks of others
and was ready to shepherd the nation of Israel, the flock of
God. Is it time for you to turn aside and see what the Lord
would have for you to do?

*"Call to Me, and I will answer you, and show you great and
mighty things, which you do not know."*
Jeremiah 33:3

Rick Kiscadon, Senior Pastor
Calvary Chapel Alamogordo
Alamogordo, New Mexico

January 4

PRESSING FORWARD

As we enter this year with promises and resolutions which most of us have already broken, I like what the Apostle Paul stated:

"That I may know Him, and the power of His resurrection, and the fellowship of His sufferings, being made conformable unto His death; if by any means I might attain unto the resurrection of the dead. Not as though I had already attained, either were already perfect: but I follow after, if that I may apprehend that for which also I am apprehended of Christ Jesus. Brethren, I count not myself to have apprehended: but this one thing I do, forgetting those things which are behind, and reaching forth unto those things which are before, I press toward the mark for the prize of the high calling of God in Christ Jesus."
Philippians 3:10-14

As we serve Him this year, let Jesus apprehend our hearts so that He has our undivided attention. That we might forget those things which are in the past and press forward to those things that God has called us to do as we look for the prize of His high calling.

Mark Maciel, Assistant Pastor
Calvary Chapel of Downey
Downey, California

January 5

THE CROSSROADS OF LIFE

". . .Choose you this day whom ye will serve; whether the gods which your fathers served that were on the other side of the flood, or the gods of the Amorites, in whose land ye dwell; but as for me and my house, we will serve the Lord."
Joshua 24:15

At the end of his life, Joshua said these final words in faith to men and women who stood at the crossroads. Under Joshua's leadership, God had brought them into the Promised Land. He showed them His goodness, His mercy, and His provision -- what great things God had done! And now Israel stood at the crossroads. Their past, their future, at an intersection.

You are at a crossroads. In one sense, every single day of your life you are standing at a crossroads; you are at an intersection where your past meets your future. That is what *today* really is. Standing at that intersection, you must make certain choices. As you move ahead with tomorrow, will it be dictated by yesterday, or will you move freely through the open doors God has provided for the future?

Maybe you have failed in the past -- that's the past. God's given you a will, and He's given you a choice. Don't lay it aside and say, "Oh well, whatever happens, happens." Come on! Free choice is too valuable a gift to throw away. Decide today, ". . .*as for me and my house, we will serve the Lord."*

Tim Hamilton, Senior Pastor
Calvary Chapel of Lake Arrowhead
Lake Arrowhead, California

January 6

FREE AT LAST!

*"For sin shall not be master over you, for you
are not under law, but under grace."*
Romans 6:14

Can you think of a greater promise than this one? Is there anything that a child of the Holy One would rather hear than sin shall not be his master? This is a truth to rejoice in, *"sin shall not be master over you."* Let the fullness of what we are promised sink in. Sin shall not -- not maybe -- but definitely will not have dominion over us.

That evil master had his power over us taken away when we were purchased out of the slave market of sin that held us captive and ruled over us. No longer do we answer to that master, but to a new one. We answer to the One who purchased and freed us from such a cruel ruler, and gave us a new life and freedom in Him. So go forward into today realizing that you no longer have to answer to sin and it's solicitations, but you are free and no longer under its rule.

James Wenger, Assistant Pastor
Pacific Hills Church
Aliso Viejo, California

January 7

JESUS IS JEHOVAH

The following list of scriptures offers definite proof that Jesus is Jehovah God. This list is very useful in witnessing to those who believe otherwise.

1. ISAIAH 41:4b: *". . . I, the LORD, am the First; and with the Last I am He."*

2. ISAIAH 44:6: *"Thus says the LORD, the King of Israel, and his Redeemer, the LORD of hosts; 'I am the First and I am the Last; besides Me there is no God."*

3. ISAIAH 48:12: *". . . I am He, I am the First, I also am the Last."*

4. REVELATION 22:13: *"I am Alpha and the Omega, the Beginning and the End, the First and the Last."*

5. REVELATION 1:8: *"I am Alpha and Omega, the Beginning and the Ending,' saith the Lord, 'which is and which was and which is to come, the Almighty."*

6. REVELATION 2:8: *". . . These things saith the First and the Last, which was dead, and is alive."*

QUESTION: Who was dead and came to life? It was Jesus, of course. He is the *"I Am."* Case closed!

Joe Guglielmo, Senior Pastor
Calvary Chapel of Manitowoc
Manitowoc, Wisconsin

January 8

THE PRIORITY OF PRAYER

"And it came to pass, as He was praying in a certain place,
when He ceased, that one of His disciples said to Him, 'Lord,
teach us to pray as John also taught his disciples.'"
Luke 11:1

Again and again, we find Jesus praying and one of His disciples was so deeply impressed with the way Jesus prayed, he asked Him to teach them to pray. He did not ask the Master to teach them <u>HOW</u> to pray, he simply said teach us to pray. We need to ask the Lord to teach us to pray, not how to pray. It is not a matter of not knowing how, but a matter of not praying. We don't spend enough time in prayer.

He also mentioned that John the Baptist had taught his disciples to pray. We usually think of him as a prophet and a martyr, yet the disciples remembered him as a man of prayer. Prayer was a priority in the life of Jesus, and in the life of John the Baptist, and it should be a priority in our life.

If Jesus, being who He was, found it necessary to pray, we should not think that we can go on without prayer. Some people think they can survive in this world without prayer. Without an established prayer life, they will be lacking spiritually, eventually fail and, unfortunately, will wonder why. Jesus spent much time in prayer, and so should we.

Joseph Prudhomme, Senior Pastor
Calvary Chapel of Solano County
Fairfield, California

January 9

READY, AIM . . . FIRE!

In the early morning darkness of January 8, 1991, an Iraqi Scud missile streaked high over the Saudi Arabian desert. It was bound for the allied coalition forces sent against Iraqi leader Saddam Hussein. But as the Scud raced across the night sky, it was fixed in the invisible spotlight of American radar. A 17 foot long rocket called the Patriot was sent rushing up to meet it. Three miles above the earth, the Patriot destroyed the Scud turning it into a huge orange fireball.

Such an incredible weapon to use against powerful enemies. Victorious warfare requires knowing who your enemy is, and which weapons he's vulnerable to. In this, we need to be careful to know just who is our real enemy, as Paul says.

"We wrestle not against flesh and blood, but against principalities, against powers, against the rulers of the darkness of this world, against spiritual wickedness in high places."
Ephesians 6:12

Spiritual enemies require spiritual weapons. Our most important weapons include God's Word, and prayer. God's Word can target any incoming deception and destroy it in mid air!

"For the weapons of our warfare are not carnal, but mighty through God to the pulling down of strongholds."
2 Corinthians 10:4

Rich Cathers, Senior Pastor
Calvary Chapel of Fullerton
Fullerton California

January 10

KEEP THE GOAL IN SIGHT

"Since we are surrounded by so great a cloud of witnesses, let us lay aside every weight, and the sin which so easily ensnares us, and let us run with endurance the race that is set before us, looking unto Jesus, the author and finisher of our faith, who for the joy that was set before Him endured the Cross, despising the shame, and has sat down at the right hand of the throne of God."
Hebrews 12:1,2

Christianity is like running a race. A short time into the race your body is saying, "Slow down, let's rest for a while." The body, left to itself, would drop out, bail out, or fall out. Yet with the goal in sight, and fixed in the mind, the body is beat into submission and the race is run to completion.

If you suffer from temporary spiritual fatigue, don't feel alone. Some of the "heavies" of the Bible did too: Elijah, David, and Paul, just to name a few. Get off the curb, put one foot in front of the other, and don't lose sight of the goal -- Jesus.

Bill Stonebraker, Senior Pastor
Calvary Chapel, Honolulu
Honolulu, Hawaii

January 11

MOMENTS TO REMEMBER

". . . do this in remembrance of Me."
1 Corinthians 11:24b

Sweat poured down my face as I mowed the lawn in the hot, Arizona sun. Glancing toward the house, I spied our three small children toddling toward me with an ice cold drink and cookies, while mom smiled at us from the door. "Rest with us awhile, daddy," they begged. They pulled me to a makeshift table where we reclined in the freshly cut grass.

It was one of those special family moments, an unforgettable time filled with laughter, caring, and sharing. Their love was truly sweeter than the refreshments. We passed around the cookies and sipped from the same chilled glass — somehow reminding me that I would be sharing the communion service at church the next day. I had the perfect illustration!

"Jesus enjoyed similar times with His disciples," I told the congregation the following morning. "He knew He'd be leaving them soon, and He wanted them to reflect on those special times they shared together. He did not want them to forget the laughter, their heartwarming talks, and joyful fellowship. Most importantly, He wanted them to remember what He was about to do for them on the Cross."

Several years later, I was asked to share that same communion message at another church service. "What illustration?" I asked. Ironically, I had to be reminded of that special af-

(Continued)

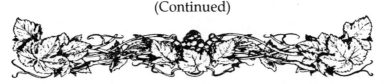

ternoon with my kids and how it tied into remembering Jesus' love for us — the very thing I vowed I would never forget! This is why the Lord has us gather frequently at His table: He knows we are prone to forget those wonderful things He has done for us.

John Bonner, Senior Pastor
Calvary Chapel Conference Center
Twin Peaks, California

January 12

SAFETY - - NOT NECESSARILY IN NUMBERS

"The fear of man bringeth a snare: but whoso putteth his trust in the LORD shall be safe."
Proverbs 29:25

What a lesson we have in this verse! How often do we fall into sin because we are more concerned with what man thinks, than what God thinks? Like Aaron, in the wilderness making the people a golden calf, or like Peter, afraid of a maiden and some soldiers denying Jesus. We, too, lose much when people, not God, are our primary care.

Fear of man will keep us from being saved, from witnessing, from being used by God and more. The only solution is the obvious one spoken here: Trusting in the Lord will keep you safe. Safe to share His love without shame. Safe to live for Him in an ungodly world. Safe to be His witness. Safe from the lies of the devil, the pull of and the lure of the flesh. Do you know this verse? Memorize it today! It will keep you well all the days of your life!

Jack Abeelen, Senior Pastor
Morningstar Christian Chapel
Whittier, California

January 13

REPENTANCE EQUALS RELATIONSHIP

"Come now, and let us reason together, saith the LORD:
though your sins be as scarlet, they shall be as white as snow;
though they be red like crimson, they shall be as wool."
Isaiah 1:18

Salvation is a choice, according to the grace of God, and there are no barriers that can keep me from experiencing the love of Christ once that grace has been offered. Corporately, there may still be the veil that blinds the Jew, but individually, as grace is offered and the heart believes, that veil is removed.

True repentance must be exercised to experience that love relationship with Christ Jesus.

God says that it's yours for the asking! Take a look at Romans 11 and II Corinthians 3.

Jack Trent, Assistant Pastor
Calvary Chapel of the Finger Lakes
Farmington, New York

January 14

LOVE

"And now abide faith, hope and love, these three;
but the greatest of these is love."
I Corinthians 13:13

What is it about love that makes it the greatest abiding attribute of life? Could it be that love requires of itself that which is not required of faith or hope? Both faith and hope are conditioned upon an expected response from the object of their placement. Therefore, they are highly conditional, whereas, love is not. Love is a sovereign choice on the part of the one who loves, rather than the one loved.

But we can, and do, place complete faith and hope in others without the slightest trace of love. In fact, we might even hate them. So it seems to me that love may or may not be the motive behind either faith or hope. They may be given without any regard to love at all.

Contrarily, love by its very nature must express itself by investing both faith and hope in the one loved. The worthiness of the one loved to have either faith or hope placed in them is never in consideration. Love expressed toward such a one is known as charity. Charity just may be the best concept we have of expressing God's love.

Dave Sweet, Senior Pastor
Calvary Chapel of Paradise
Paradise, California

January 15

GOD'S MAJORITY RULES

"Be strong and courageous; do not be afraid nor dismayed before the king of Assyria, nor before all the multitude that is with him; FOR THERE ARE MORE WITH US THAN WITH HIM. With him is an arm of flesh; BUT WITH US IS THE LORD OUR GOD, to help us and to fight our battles."
II Chronicles 32:7,8

The mighty kingdom of Assyria had assembled its vast forces against the tiny kingdom of Judah to squash it like an ant. To make a modern day comparison, this would be like the nation of Russia invading Israel, or Mike Tyson squaring off with Pee Wee Herman for a bout.

Logically, the tiny kingdom of Judah didn't stand a chance. But if we remember that Assyria represents the arm of the flesh, and Judah the arm of the Lord, we instantly recognize that the victory is Judah's. For an arm of the flesh, no matter how muscular, how sophisticated, how clever, how intelligent, is still an arm of the flesh. All of man's brawn and brains, be it muscle or chemical, nuclear, or biological warfare of today, has all the power of a clogged peashooter, when fighting against God's anointed. Remember, 1 + God = the majority, or better yet, you + God = the majority.

"You will keep him in perfect peace whose mind is stayed on You, because he trusts in You."
Isaiah 26:3

Rick Kopp, Senior Pastor
Calvary Chapel of the Lewis-Clark Valley
Lewiston, Idaho

January 16

NO SNAPSHOT, PLEASE!

*"Being confident of this very thing, that He who has
begun a good work in you will complete it
until the day of Jesus Christ."*
Philippians 1:6

I was so excited to show off my family! I pulled out my wallet and said, "Here's Karen, Joshua, Jessica, Jeremiah, and Jordan." But no sooner had I said that, then I had to add, "But this is an old picture. They look different now."

As I left that encounter, the thought came to me — snapshots really aren't current. I began to realize that not only did my family and I look different; we were different. That picture was taken twelve months ago. We've grown up and matured since then.

I thought of how people take snapshot images of each other. They snap mental images of people and carry that image of them in their wallets or pocketbooks. And that snapshot is all they see. But the moment it was snapped, the person goes on living, changing, growing. It's not fair to hold people to the snapshots we take of them.

What if all we had was a snapshot of Jesus on the Cross -- dead -- is that the current story? May I suggest, keep the camera rolling. God is working, and completing what He has started in us.

Bruce Koczman, Senior Pastor
Calvary Chapel Four Winds
Red Bank, New Jersey

January 17

SACRIFICIAL BODY BUILDING

"Therefore, I urge you, brothers, in view of God's mercy, to offer your bodies as living sacrifices, holy and pleasing to God—this is your spiritual act of worship."
Romans 12:1

The believer is to be devoted to God in worship and service. Anything less than total devotion to Him is short of God's glory, and it is sin. Therefore, when talking about the believer's relationship to God, scripture is strong in its exhortation. Without wavering, scripture urges total devotion -- spiritual as well as physical. In Romans 12:11, we are called to present our bodies to God as a living sacrifice. Many profess their devotion to God, however, it does not manifest itself in their actions or in the use of their bodies. The one thing upon earth that is abused more than anything else is man's body. Man abuses, neglects, and ignores his body in many different ways. It can be by overeating or undereating, by becoming inactive or too active, or by stress (which manifests itself by cursing, arguing and fighting). Taking drugs (even prescription) or alcohol puts incredible toxins into the body. Many care for the external part of their bodies through exercise and sports, but abuse the internal. This list could go on and on. But if there is an exhortation in scripture that must be heeded by Christian believers, it is the exhortation of the next two verses.

"Do not conform any longer to the pattern of this world, but be transformed by the renewing of your mind. Then you will be able to test and approve what God's will is --
His good, pleasing and perfect will."
Romans 12:2

(Continued)

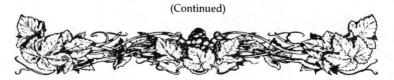

The believer is to present his body as a living sacrifice to God. God is not interested in man's spirit alone; He is also vitally interested in man's body.

"Or do you not know that your body is the temple of the Holy Spirit who is in you, whom you have from God, and you are not your own? **For you are bought at a price: therefore glorify God in your body and in your spirit, which are God's.** *"*
I Corinthians 6:19,20

His interest could not be any stronger or clearer. This is seen by contrasting the world's view of the body with God's view. The believer is to present his body to God. The dedication is not to be made selfishly; doing your own thing. It is not to be made to others -- living for family or employer. Our dedication is not to material things -- houses, land, property, money, cars, possessions, profession, recreation, retirement, luxury, power, recognition, fame.

God requires our body to be offered as a sacrifice to Him. Old Testament believers sacrificed animals to God. The believer is to make the same kind of sacrificial offering to God, but with one profound difference. The believer's offering is not to be the sacrifice of an animal's flesh and blood, but an offering of His own body as a living sacrifice.

Chuck Kelly, Senior Pastor
Calvary Chapel Bullhead City
Bullhead City, Arizona

January 18

CONFESSION

*"If we confess our sins, He is faithful and just to forgive us our
sins and to cleanse us from all unrighteousness."*
1 John 1:9

How many of us hold onto sins that we think God cannot
forgive? Or perhaps have repetitious sins that we no longer
confess because we think those particular sins have no hope
for cleansing? God wants us to confess for a reason -- to
cleanse us from all of the junk we hold onto. Won't you
trust Him today for a new cleansing, and a brand new fresh
start?

> Johnny Garcia, Assistant Pastor
> Calvary Worship Center
> Colorado Springs, Colorado

January 19

AN IMITATION OR THE REAL THING?

"For God did not call us to uncleanness, but in holiness."
1 Thessalonians 4:7

Paul was concerned for the spiritual well being of the church in Thessalonica. Immoral lifestyles were the norm. He wanted to see the believers grow in their faith, but knew the uncleanness of the worldly society around them could hinder that. So he encouraged them to lead a holy life.

The Greek word for church "ekklesia" literally means a calling out. If we are in Christ, we are called out of the uncleanness of this world, into His holiness.

Les Prock, Senior Pastor
Calvary Chapel North Hill
Milton, Washington

January 20

THE BLESSEDNESS OF BROKENNESS

"How blessed is he whose transgression is forgiven, whose sin
is covered! When I kept silent about my sin, my body wasted
away through my groaning all day long. I acknowledged my
sin to Thee, and my iniquity I did not hide; I said
'I will confess my transgressions to the Lord;'
and Thou didst forgive the guilt of my sin."
Psalm 32:1,3,5

Psalm 1 proclaims the blessedness of the man who avoids
the counsel, causes, and comforts of this world and instead
chooses to delight himself in the Law of the Lord, to meditate there day and night. Surely this is the happy life, the
blessed life. Which of us has yet attained to it? How glad
I am that this was not the last beatitude in the Psalms.
David now tells us that there remains yet another blessedness for all who have fallen short of the first psalm's promise; it is the blessedness of brokenness before the Lord.

The only sins that the Lord can't cover in our lives are the
ones that we try to cover ourselves. From the first fall in
the garden of Eden, until this present day, the Lord cries
out to us as a heartbroken father, "Where are you? Come
out from your hiding." He desperately desires to end the
distancing effect of our lies, and draw us near to Himself
once again. The truth sets us free. Honesty opens the door
to Him. He is a consuming fire. You can't hide <u>from</u> His
fervent love. Hide <u>in it</u>!

Bruce Mumper, Senior Pastor
Calvary Chapel of Fresno
Fresno, California

January 21

BLESSINGS

There are faces I remember,
Some have changed, and some have grown.
Some are bitter, some are better,
As they reap from seeds they have sown.

All of these faces had their moments,
Of serving the Lord,
And answerin' His call,
Now some are listless, some are lovely,
With your life, He's blessed us all.

You've got memories worth repeating,
After tens of years of planting seeds.
Times of wounding, times of healing,
Always seeking first, obeying His lead.

The memories are still in the making,
You're keeping it simple, loving your Lord.
You know we often stop and think about you,
With your life, He's blessed us all.

Mike Stangel, Senior Pastor
North Shore Christian Fellowship
Haleiwa, Hawaii

January 22

SEEK THE HOMELAND

"These all died in faith, not having received the promises, but having seen them afar off were assured of them, embraced them, and confessed that they were strangers and pilgrims on the earth. For those that say such things declare plainly that they seek a homeland."
Hebrews 11:13,14

In the first part of Hebrews 11, various attributes of faith are mentioned of former people from the Old Testament. They "<u>offered</u> to God;" "<u>pleased</u> God;" "<u>moved</u> with godly fear;" "<u>obeyed;</u>" "<u>judged Him faithful.</u>" Yet, these all died in faith, **not having received the promises.** Wow! We think, "But they were obedient Lord! They pleased you Lord!!" How often do we base our decisions of obedience to the Lord on the results it might produce?

What we see with our physical eyes isn't the criteria for faith. What we see with our spiritual eyes is. Having seen them afar off, they were **assured** of them, **embraced** them, and **confessed** the larger reality: that they were strangers and pilgrims on the earth. Be encouraged. Walk in faith now, regardless of what you see as the results. Seek the homeland!

Jack Kier, Senior Pastor
Calvary Chapel Northwest
Acworth, Georgia

January 23

WALKING WITH GOD

"And Enoch walked with God and
he was not, for God took him."
Genesis 5:24

Walking with God. What does that mean to you? What does the Bible say about our walk as Christians?

"Walk worthy of the Lord, to please Him in all respects,
bearing fruit in every good work and increasing
in the knowledge of God."
Colossians 1:10

"I entreat you to walk in a manner worthy of the
calling with which you have been called."
Ephesians 5:1

We should all walk in a way that would match our position. Because of who you are, this is how you are to behave.

"This I say therefore, and affirm together with the Lord, that
you walk no longer just as the Gentiles (heathen) also walk in
the futility of their mind being darkened in their understanding
excluded from the life of God, because of the ignorance that is
in them because of the hardness of their heart."
Ephesians 4:17,18

If you think the Christian life is like a walk in the park, you are probably still walking in the dark. Come into the Light.

Glenn Kravig, Assistant Pastor
Calvary Chapel of Downey
Downey, California

January 24

COMMITMENT

"Let no man despise thy youth; but be thou an example of the
believers, in word, in conversation, in charity,
in spirit, in faith, in purity."
I Timothy 4:12

We shouldn't allow people to discourage us as we serve the Lord. There are people, even Christians, who will tell you: "You are not qualified, you're too young, it's not your ministry, don't get involved." Or even, "You read your Bible too much." No matter what people say to try to discourage you, stay committed to the One who called you!

Mark Maciel, Assistant Pastor
Calvary Chapel of Downey
Downey, California

January 25

BECAUSE YOU SAY SO

"When He had left speaking, He said to Simon, 'Launch out into the deep and let down your nets for a draught.' And Simon answered and said to Him, 'Master, we have toiled all night and caught nothing: nevertheless at thy word I will let down the net.'"
Luke 5:4,5

Simon was a professional fisherman. When Jesus told him to go out and cast his nets again after a night of fruitless labor, Simon could have put up an argument based on his professional expertise. Instead, he replied," . . . *nevertheless at Your word I will let down the net."*

It wasn't because Jesus gave a good argument. He didn't even try to. Jesus simply told Simon to do it and, by obeying despite the apparent futility of it, Simon witnessed the power of the Lord in action.

When the Lord tells us to do something, our response should be that of Simon's. We ought to never think that we know more than the Lord does in any situation. Even if we think what God tells us to do seems futile or impossible. We ought to have enough respect and trust in the Lord to believe that He can accomplish what He has told us to do. If we will be like Simon and obey the Lord, regardless of how futile His direction might seem to us, we will see the power of God in action in our lives.

Ernest Finklea, Senior Pastor
Calvary Chapel of Durango
Durango, Colorado

January 26

THE DISCIPLE'S PRAYER

"In this manner, therefore, pray: Our Father in heaven, hal-
lowed be Your name. Your kingdom come. Your will be done
on earth as it is in heaven. Give us this day our daily bread and
forgive us our debts, as we forgive our debtors. And do not lead
us into temptation, but deliver us from the evil one. For Yours
is the kingdom and the power and the glory forever. Amen."
Matthew 6:9-13

I suppose this is the most famous prayer ever uttered. Yet
it is clear that Jesus was teaching His disciples how to pray.
I've read this prayer, prayed this prayer, and so many times
I've never realized what it was I was praying. So I sat down
and paraphrased it and personalized it. As I pray through
it now, I realize that so much of what troubles my heart is
that I have not approached the Lord as in this prayer. Here
I offer to you my paraphrase — may it transform your prayer
life as it has mine.

In this manner, therefore, pray:
Our Father in heaven, hallowed be Your name. "Heavenly Father, you are so holy, and you always do right in all your
works and ways."

Your kingdom come. Your will be done on earth as it is in heaven.
"Oh, holy Dad, I only want to be in your presence, and for
Your presence to be felt here in the world. Please conform
my life to Your plan, I yield to You!"

Give us this day our daily bread. "Give me only those things
this day which will cause growth in my life towards you
both spiritual and physical."

(Continued)

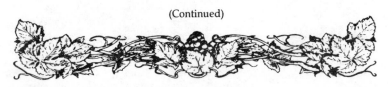

And forgive us our debts, as we forgive our debtors. "Holy Dad, I give You all those things that would hinder me from growing closer to You, and I let go of anything others owe me, as this would hinder Your love from operating through me."

And do not lead us into temptation, but deliver us from the evil one. For Yours is the kingdom and the power and the glory forever. Amen. "Loving Father; keep me from the things that would stumble me, and render me in bondage to the devil. Father, all I desire is for You to be glorified in my life, and for Your power to work through me for Your glory forever. So be it!"

Dale Lewis, Senior Pastor
Calvary Chapel of Merced
Merced, California

January 27

THE LORD IS FAITHFUL

". . .I will never leave thee, nor forsake thee."
Hebrews 13:5

Throughout the Word of God, we see that the Lord never tries to hide the failures of His people. They are exposed for our benefit, so that we may learn from them.

One man who stands out that we can all relate to is the Apostle Peter. In Luke 22:33, we find him boasting of his faithfulness to the Lord. However, as we read on in the chapter, we find that he failed the Lord in a big way.

Most of us have felt like Peter at one time or another. The good news is that Peter wasn't left to suffer in his failures. It is not God's desire that we remain in a state of suffering. In the Gospel of John, Chapter 21, we read that after Jesus died and rose from the dead, He sought out Peter to call him into the ministry.

Why would God want to use Peter now? He had proven himself to be a complete failure. Because the Lord had a plan for Peter, just as He has a plan for you and me. We find that Peter learned some very important lessons in his failures. We have all learned some very important lessons in life through our failures, also.

Peter was no longer a self-sufficient, boasting, prideful man. He was now a broken, humble man and he was ready to trust only in the Lord for his strength. Peter found the right place to live . . . in the Lord's strength.

(Continued)

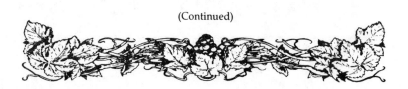

Someone once said, "Christians are known to forget what they should remember, and remember what they should forget." Isn't that the truth? I pray that today we would remember that God is faithful, even when we are not, and that God has a plan for our lives. He promises that to us even if we do not see it right now. Let us look to God for forgiveness and strength and learn from our mistakes.

"In Thee, O Lord, I have taken my refuge; let me never be ashamed; In Thy righteousness deliver me. Incline Thine ear to me, rescue me quickly; be Thou to me a rock of strength, a stronghold to save me. For Thou are my rock and my fortress; For Thy name's sake Thou wilt lead me and guide me. Thou wilt pull me out of the net which they have secretly laid for me; For Thou are my strength."
Psalm 31:1-4

Mike Morris, Senior Pastor
Calvary Chapel of the High Desert
Hesperia, California

January 28

CRUCIFY THE WORLD

*"But God forbid that I should glory, save in the Cross of
our Lord Jesus Christ, by whom the world is crucified
unto me, and I unto the world."*
Galatians 6:14

What shall I boast about? That we no longer live for the
world. If we are living for the world and its rewards, then
we get what we deserve. But if we sow to the things of the
Spirit, then it's the things of the Spirit that we receive. We
are to be dead to the things of this life and alive to God. The
symbol of Christianity is a cross, not a Lazy-Boy recliner.
Let us live with the fact that it's the Cross that I died on, too,
with Christ and, if dead, then alive with Christ. I must live
as one who has ceased from works that produce death, but
live for those things that bring life.

Chick Chikeles, Senior Pastor
Calvary Chapel Saint Paul
Saint Paul, Minnesota

January 29

ESCAPE HATCH

"Watch and pray, lest you enter into temptation.
The spirit indeed is willing, but the flesh is weak."
Matthew 26:41

First: We Must Watch. This has the idea of being on guard, to be paying attention to what is going on. Put another way, if you are paying attention to the road, you can avoid the potholes.

Second: We Must Pray. So often we resemble the disciples in Gethsemane, sleeping when we should be praying. Even those who are not "physically asleep," are many times "spiritually asleep" in their prayer lives. This is not talking about those emergency prayers we offer in temptation (although we should do that, too!), but this is about having a healthy prayer life that helps keep you out of temptation.

Third: We Must Depend on Him. Even as Jesus shares this truth with them, He reminds them they cannot do it on their own, for the flesh is so weak - we need to depend on Him to be able to stand in our weakness (*see Galatians 5:16-25*).

Temptation . . . the daily commercials for sin that is aired in our hearts. Someone once said that we always have one of three relationships with temptation: We are in a temptation, coming out of a temptation or going into a temptation. It is a constant battle that we face on this earth. In Matthew 26, Jesus tells His disciples an extremely important truth: We don't have to go through every temptation. Let me say that again, we can avoid some of the temptations of life.

(Continued)

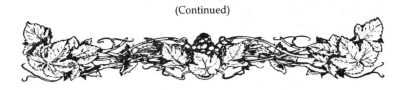

In this account, Jesus is facing the greatest temptation of His life, and is deeply in prayer about it, but the disciples are sleeping. Jesus wakes them up and tells them (and us) that if we watch and pray we can avoid entering into temptation.

Have you been beaten up with temptation this week? I encourage and challenge you that not only can you keep from falling into the temptations, but by being spiritually watchful, prayerful, and dependant, you can even escape going through many of the temptations that would come your way. I pray that this will be true of us, starting today!

Jim Suttle, Senior Pastor
Calvary Chapel of Roswell
Roswell, New Mexico

January 30

THINK ON THESE THINGS

<u>What Things?</u>
"Whatever things are true, whatever things are honest, what-
ever things are just, whatever things are pure, whatever
things are lovely, whatever things are of good report;
if there be any virtue, and if there be any praise,
think on these things."
Philippians 4:8

<u>Why?</u>
Because our thoughts mold our actions.
"For as he thinketh in his heart, so is he."
Proverbs 23:7a

<u>How?</u>
If Christ is in my thoughts, all good things are there. Make
Him your companion and He will help you. He will give
you your thoughts, tastes, and desires.

Brian Phillips, Assistant Pastor
Calvary Chapel of the Finger Lakes
Farmington, New York

January 31

HANG UP THE GLOVES

*"'You will not need to fight in this battle. Position yourselves,
stand still and see the salvation of the LORD, who is with you,
O Judah and Jerusalem!' Do not fear or be dismayed; tomorrow
go out against them for the LORD is with you."*
II Chronicles 20:17

While God said He would fight for the people of Judah, He
also called them to take their position so they might see His
salvation. The king had prayed and asked for God's help.
God answered with a promise and a command. The point
is this: God does His part; we must do ours. Our part is to
diligently follow Him.

We see a perfect example of this when Jesus told the disciples to pray that the Father would compel laborers to enter into the harvest of lost souls. Just days later, he sent
them out to preach in the cities and villages of Galilee. They
became the answer to their own prayers. When we pray
and ask the Lord to do something, we must be willing to
become the answer to that prayer. And if we aren't, then
our prayer is insincere, and the best place to start is with a
request that God would change our hearts.

Lance Ralston, Senior Pastor
Calvary Chapel Coram Deo
Oxnard, California

February 1

REMEMBER -- TRIALS BUILD PATIENCE

*"Though He slay me, yet will I trust in Him; but I will main-
tain mine own ways before Him."*
Job 13:15

Several years ago, our church went through a major division that affected many lives, especially myself, my family,
and the leadership of the church. That same week, my dad's
father, Grandpa Ray, passed away at the age of 90 years
young! My dad had called and asked if I would come to
the funeral in East Los Angeles on Brooklyn Avenue to share
God's Word with our families. Because of the division and
problems in our church, I told my dad I would not be able
to attend. My dad said he understood.

I thank God for my wife, who took it upon herself, and made
flight arrangements, talked with our remaining elders of
the church who agreed with her that we should go, and
that they would take care of the situation at the church. My
dad, bless his heart, gave me this verse in Job that has, since
then and other trials now passed, helped me tremendously!
We all know James' famous passage — in *James 1:2*, *"Count
it all joy when you fall into various trials."* Job's message causes
me to fully understand when he says: *"Though He (God)
would slay me* (literally - put me to death) *yet will I trust* (wait,
hope, be patient) *in Him."* By knowing these verses, through
the power of God's love, I can count it all joy!!

Bob Ortega, Senior Pastor
Calvary Chapel of Las Cruces
Las Cruces, New Mexico

February 2

LABOR OF LOVE

"Except the LORD build the house, they labor
in vain that build it . . ."
Psalm 127:1a

Please note in this Psalm that "they" labor. As husband and wife, we need to be building our home together. The most important thing a father can do for his children is to love their mother. Is your house a home?

"For we are laborers together with God: ye are God's
husbandry, ye are God's building. According to the grace
of God which is given unto me, as a wise master
builder, I have laid the foundation, and another
buildeth thereon. But let every man take heed how
he buildeth thereupon. For other foundation
can no man lay than that is laid, which is Jesus Christ."
1 Corinthians 3:9-11

Rick Clarke, Assistant Pastor
Calvary Chapel of the Finger Lakes
Farmington, New York

February 3

WHAT MIRACLES ARE MADE OF

*"And when Jesus went out He saw a great multitude; and He
was moved with compassion for them, and healed their sick.
When it was evening, His disciples came to Him, saying, 'This
is a deserted place, and the hour is already late. Send the
multitudes away, that they may go into the villages and buy
themselves food.' But, Jesus said to them, 'They do not need to
go away. You give them something to eat.' And they said to
Him, 'We have here only five loaves and two fish.' He said,
'Bring them here to Me.' Then He commanded the multitudes
to sit down on the grass. And He took the five loaves and the
two fish, and looking up to heaven, He blessed and broke and
gave the loaves to the disciples; and the disciples gave to the
multitudes. So they all ate and were filled, and they took up
twelve baskets full of the fragments that remained. Now those
who had eaten were about five thousand men,
besides women and children."*
Matthew 14:14-21

Miracles! We see Jesus, in each of the gospels, performing
the miracle of feeding five thousand men from five loaves
and two fish. If we were to count women and children, the
total could have been more than twice that. After Jesus
blessed the food and broke it, the people ate and were filled.
Curiously, twelve baskets were left over. Who were they
for, and why were there twelve? As we devote our lives to
serving God and others, we sometimes do not seem to have
the time to meet our own needs. Mark 6:31b, which directly precedes the story of the loaves & fishes, tells us *"For
there were many coming and going, and they did not even have
time to eat."* Jesus knew his disciples needs!

(Continued)

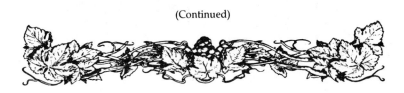

In a crowd of people, few know what is really going on. In church services, sometimes the announcements are made, bulletins are passed out and someone will say:

"Men's Breakfast . . . yesterday? No one told me!"

I am convinced that as the food was passed out, only a few people, along with the disciples, knew that something very unusual was happening with the loaves and the fish. The crowds may have thought Jesus had a cave full of food hidden somewhere. They also may not have cared about who Jesus was, or the miracles of healing the sick. They just wanted their bellies filled. On the following day, *John 6:26* tells us, *"Most assuredly, I say to you, you seek Me, not because you saw the signs, but because you ate of the loaves and were filled."*

Only those who are close to Jesus see the miraculous! And so today, as we are about our Father's business, we also see His miracles, power, and glory. Others who focus on themselves miss out. In the Beatitudes, Jesus said *"Blessed are the pure in heart for they shall see God."* Just as Jesus knew His disciples' needs and provided for them, you can trust that He knows yours.

Mike Kestler, Senior Pastor
Calvary Chapel of Twin Falls
Twin Falls, Idaho

February 4

THE FEAR OF THE LORD

*"The fear of the Lord is the beginning of knowledge; fools
despise wisdom and instruction."*
Proverbs 1:7

Knowledge, as the Bible describes it, means more than just "knowing things," or the accumulation of information. Our intellectual capacities and accomplishments don't impress God, nor do they really help us to fulfill our potential or purpose for which God created us. God created us to know Him first, and "stuff" second. He intended that we would experience intimate fellowship with Him, and that we would honor and glorify Him. So, the "knowledge" so often referred to in the Bible, particularly in the Proverbs, has to do with our relationship to God, not mental achievement -- what we know about Him and His ways. Furthermore, once we gain this knowledge in spiritual things, what do we do with it? Does it make us self-righteous and prideful? Or, does it cause us to humbly bow before our Maker, yielding our lives to Him?

The beginning of this relationship is found in a proper perspective. We must fear the Lord. That is the starting point. As we get to know God, and as we grow in our understanding of Him and His ways, it is always necessary that we fear Him. That is, we are to stand in reverential awe of Him. He is the Sovereign Creator of the entire universe! That includes us. He deserves our worship and complete and humble surrender. Our very breath is in His hands. True knowledge, knowledge that really matters, is that which begins with fearing the Lord. That is the knowledge that

(Continued)

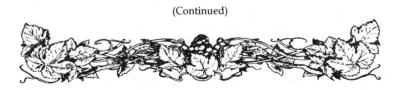

should govern our lives, and it is the base upon which all our relationships should rest. This is what safeguards us from seeking to be our "own god." It protects us from being deceived and controlled by our own pride and sinful nature.

The fear of the Lord keeps us humble. It ensures that we remain teachable. It is foolish to despise wisdom and instruction. God has much to teach us, and we have much to learn! God desires to instruct us in His ways. His intention is to equip us with wisdom so that we become skilled in Godly living, thus fulfilling part of His purpose for our lives. To reject Him or His wisdom and instruction is the height of folly, because in so doing, we fail to become who He created us to be.

Jon Sanne', Senior Pastor
Calvary Chapel of Olympia
Olympia, Wastington

February 5

LOVE LETTER

Dear Christian Parents:

As I watch the news and speak with parents, I am troubled and concerned! As a parent, I am sure that you, too, sense the frustration of not having enough time, of having too many pans on the stove -- some boiling over! What's a parent to do as we see many kids today reaching out for direction and guidance in strange ways?

Recently, as I was reviewing some notes I had prepared on Ephesians chapter 6, and the Book of I Samuel, God reminded me that, *"Faith comes by hearing and that of the word of God."* I believe what Malachi 4:6 says *"... and He shall turn the heart of the fathers to the children and the children to their fathers."*

I believe this part of Scripture will help to bring this prophecy to reality, if we have ears to hear and apply His Word. May God bless and equip you as you sit down with your family and read about the Lord's strategy for victory and success in parent-child relationships.

Jeff Johnson, Senior Pastor
Calvary Chapel of Downey
Downey, California

February 6

SERVICE ADDICTION

"You know that the household of Stephanas were the first
converts in Achaia, and they have devoted themselves to the
service of the saints. I urge you, brothers, to submit
to such as these and to everyone who joins
in the work, and labors at it."
I Corinthians 16:15,16

What a commendation coming from the Apostle Paul!
"They have devoted themselves to the service of the saints," he
says.

The idea behind it is that they've given themselves <u>completely</u> to it! They've ADDICTED themselves to serving
and ATTENDING to the needs of their Christian family!

Jesus Himself is our model for this kind of attitude! It's
what He LIVED for! In *John 13:12-17*, we find Him washing His disciples feet, for crying out loud! Removing their
sandals, and then cleaning the dirt and grime from between
their toes!

Jesus not only came to die for us, He DIED to come for us!
All that He enjoyed in heaven, He left behind to come and
serve! That is the heart of God, His children! SERVANT
LEADERSHIP. May it be your desire to be addicted to the
service of God's kingdom.

Robert Fountain, Senior Pastor
Calvary Chapel of Miami Beach
Miami Beach, Florida

February 7

CHRIST GIVES US A NEW LIFE

*"And the Lord God formed man of the dust of the ground, and
breathed into his nostrils the breath of life;
and man became a living being."*
Genesis 2:7

As God made man in His image, and His breath entered
man's body, he became a living being. This is what takes
place when we make a decision to give our lives to Christ
today. When Christ becomes our Lord, we no longer are
separated from Him, but His Spirit fills us and gives us a
new life!

*"Therefore, if anyone is in Christ, he is a new creation; old
things have passed away; behold, all things have become new."*
II Corinthians 5:17

Are you ready for a new life today?

Louie Cruzado, Assistant Pastor
Calvary Chapel of Downey
Downey, California

February 8

DIVINITY

"For God so loved the world, He gave. . . ."
John 3:16

<u>DIVINE LOVE</u> is always giving. It's motive and intent is to bless -- to make another's life better, richer.

<u>DIVINE LOVE</u> is unselfish, unconcerned about what it will get in return. It is willing to be taken advantage of -- it is unconditional.

<u>DIVINE LOVE</u> cannot be mustered up by human desire, we are too selfish by nature. It must come from God, for the Bible says:

"God is Love and everyone who loves
is born of God, and knows God."
1 John 4:7

Kelley Taylor, Senior Pastor
Calvary Chapel of Everett
Everett, Washington

February 9

PRICELESS LOVE

The death of our precious Lord, Jesus Christ, is not a subject I enjoy studying. When I think of what Jesus willingly did for me, it sometimes makes me want to run and cry. To think of Him willingly enduring the taunts of those puny little men who dared to mock the King of the Universe. To see how they ordered Him beaten and whipped. Then, finally, to see Him choose to lay down upon that cross as they drove the spikes through His hands and His feet. Beyond all the pain He felt, He willingly took the weight of all my sin heaped upon His back.

All for me. All to pay for my sin.

It doesn't seem to make sense to me that someone would love me so much. I know what I'm really like and it isn't always very nice. To know that He is aware of all my short-comings, all my selfishness, all my sin, and still chooses to love me -- still chooses to willingly go to the Cross and die in my place -- how can I respond to love like that?

The apostle Paul wrote it best how to respond:

> *"For ye are bought with a price: therefore glorify God*
> *in your body, and in your spirit, which are God's."*
> *1 Corinthians 6:20*

Rich Cathers, Senior Pastor
Calvary Chapel of Fullerton
Fullerton, California

February 10

THE LOOK OF LOVE

*"Beloved, let us love one another; for love is of God; and
everyone that loveth is born of God, and knoweth God."*
1 John 4:7

Quite a few years back there was a popular song entitled,
"Looking For Love In All The Wrong Places." Many today
still strive trying to find love everywhere but where true
love is.

Won't you experience "True Love Today" in a relationship
with Jesus Christ?

Tony Falcione, Assistant Pastor
Calvary Chapel of the Finger Lakes
Farmington, New York

February 11

AGAPE LOVE

"The LORD said to me, "'Go, show your love to your wife again, though she is loved by another and is an adulteress. Love her as the LORD loves the Israelites, though they turn to other gods and love the sacred raisin cakes."
Hosea 3:1

Hosea 3:1 is one of those areas of scripture that displays so vividly the depth and devotion of God's love. In the midst of our unfaithfulness, God's redemptive hand reaches out to buy back what He already owns. What the world calls worthless, God dies for with a love that sees value with the heart, and not the eyes. God calls us to see others in this same invisible realm of eternity, through the lens of Christ's shed blood. It is only then that the twisted and tortured figure of a harlot can become a beautiful and innocent bride.

It was bad enough that God instructed Hosea to go and buy back his wife from the consequences of her harlotry. But then he instructs him to love her as He loves Israel. Many of us can muster up a facade of feigned love, but this is not the love God seeks. His love is sincere and honest. It is willing to pay the price, even when the cost far outweighs the perceived value of the merchandise.

Pray that God would fill you with the agape love that He has for us. The love that saw more value in us than in His own life. The love that was willing to sacrifice everything to purchase what it already rightfully owned.

Bob Coy, Senior Pastor
Calvary Chapel Ft. Lauderdale
Ft. Lauderdale, Florida

February 12

FORGIVEN TO FORGIVE

*"And be kind to one another, tenderhearted, forgiving one
another, even as God in Christ forgave you."*
Ephesians 4:32

Forgiveness is indeed difficult when you have been unjustly
wronged. Forgiveness, however, requires a proper attitude.
"Forgiving one another, even as God forgave you." How has He
forgiven us? His forgiveness toward us is free, unconditional, and with great mercy. When we have a clear understanding of what Christ has forgiven us, we must forgive
others. A willingness to forgive is a manifestation of Christ's
love, and His love is the basis for all of our relationships in
Christ.

Al Pittman, Assistant Pastor
Calvary Worship Center
Colorado Springs, Colorado

February 13

A WORK IN PROGRESS

I get so frustrated when Christians don't become what I want them to become. Then Philippians 1:6 shed a whole new light on it.

"Being confident of this very thing, that He who began a good work in you will complete it until the day of Jesus Christ."
Philippians 1:6

I have always applied that verse to myself because I know that God is still working on me. But it also applies to my fellow Christians that I become so frustrated with because they aren't being the kind of Christians I think they should be. Often I forget that God is not finished with them yet, but I can be confident of this very thing -- that He will complete His work in their life too, in His timing.

This was a lesson Samuel learned when he went to the house of Jesse to anoint the next king of Israel. Samuel was attempting to pick the king based on outward appearances, but God looks at the heart, and David was who He chose.

I judge from outward appearances because I can't see into a person's heart, but God can. As Samuel was wrong, so am I. All the pressure, all the frustration, I feel towards my Christian brothers and sisters is now relieved and I am released to love and accept them as Christ has done for me. It's wonderful to be back to loving God and His people.

Kent Nottingham, Senior Pastor
Calvary Chapel Tallahassee
Tallahassee, Florida

February 14

RESPOND! DON'T REACT!

*"Finally, be ye all of one mind, having compassion one of
another, love as brethren, be pitiful, be courteous; not rendering
evil for evil, or railing for railing; but contrariwise blessing;
knowing that ye are thereunto called,
that ye should inherit a blessing."*
1 Peter 3:8,9

How often do we do this? Is it done as husband and wife?
Is it done as parent to child? Is it done in the work place?
God honestly wants us to walk in a manner that is pleasing
to Him. Jesus said:

*"But I say unto you which hear, love your enemies, do good to
them which hate you, bless them that curse you, and pray
for them which spitefully use you."*
Luke 6:27-28

This oppression in relationships may come in many different forms, such as arguments, tension, and stress, to name a
few. Yet He always points to us individually and how we
need to <u>respond</u>:

*"Therefore whatsoever ye would that men
should do to you, do ye even so them. . ."*
Matthew 7:12a

May the Lord bless you as you bless others.

Rick Johnson, Assistant Pastor
Calvary Chapel of Downey
Downey, California

February 15

EVERLASTING LOVE

". . .Yea, I have loved thee with an everlasting love. . ."
Jeremiah 31:3

It is so easy to fail and become ensnared in some sin for a season, even while putting out an effort to walk with God. We become heavily burdened and discouraged when this happens. Our understanding of God can become distorted. Even as Christians, we can suddenly find ourselves trapped, believing a major misrepresentation of who our Heavenly Father really is.

The truth is that God loves us with an unchanging everlasting love. Because Jesus Christ died on the Cross and shed His blood for our sins, God is able to look at us as though we had never sinned. In a positional sense, He sees us clothed in the righteousness of God the Father in Jesus Christ the Son. We must hold this truth before us. We will discover His yoke to be easy and His burden light as we go on in our efforts to match our practice to our position. Our efforts will become a joy rather than a frustrating grind. We will find that fellowship with God is delightful beyond all telling!

Danny Bond, Senior Pastor
Pacific Hills Church
Aliso Viejo, California

February 16

LOVE AT FIRST SIGHT

Remember your first love,
Think of how He looked at you,
Looked at you,
Before you could say or do,
The Father was in love with you

He's still in His first love,
Still loves to look at you,
Looked at you,
Whatever you say or do,
The Father's still in love with you.

As a new believer in Jesus, so often the most amazing thing of all is to sense -- for the first time ever -- God's love. Yet, as we continue to grow in the Lord, we must not lose sight of His love. Though we may leave our first love for Him, there is no such thing as the Father leaving His first love for us. He loves us, He loves us, He loves us. That's good news!

Mike Stangel, Senior Pastor
North Shore Christian Fellowship
Haleiwa, Hawaii

February 17

BOUND WITH CHRIST

"But above all these things put on love,
which is the bond of perfection."
Colossians 3:14

Plato said, "The fairest (best) bond is that which most completely fuses and is fused into the things which are bound."

Love is what holds the things of Christ together in our lives. We cannot hold the image of Christ without it. Without it, the image is incomplete.

Les Prock, Senior Pastor
Calvary Chapel North Hill
Milton, Washington

February 18

THE GREAT DIVIDE

"Teach me thy way, O Lord; I will walk in thy truth:
unite my heart to fear thy name."
Psalm 86:11

Psalm 86 is a prayer David poured out in great distress and turmoil. Arrogant and ruthless men were seeking his life. David does three things that are valuable for us to note. First, he calls out to the Lord to guard and protect him (vs. 1-2). Next, He stops to consider and praise the Lord, for He is. . . kind, forgiving, abounding in love, compassionate, slow to anger, great, and does marvelous deeds, and is the one and only God (vs. 5, 15). And then, in the midst of this craziness and stress, he prays, *". . . unite my heart to fear thy name."* Another translation says, *"Give me an undivided heart."*

I do not have, as far as I know, arrogant and ruthless men seeking my life. But yet, it seems that much lesser things cause me distress and turmoil. What a blessing it is to have this Psalm. When difficult situations come, praying for the Lord to guard me comes rather quickly. Praising and remembering His greatness and goodness towards me requires a bit more unction from the Holy Spirit. But how wonderful it is to see David, not only focused on thinking about his God, but also praying that his heart would not be distracted from his God by the circumstances.

Peyton Jones, Assistant Pastor
Calvary Chapel of Huntington Beach
Huntington Beach, California

February 19

JESUS IS AMAZING

"Then they went into Capernaum, and immediately on the Sabbath He entered the synagogue and taught. And they were astonished at His teaching, for He taught them as one having authority, and not as the scribes."
Mark 1:21,22

It is interesting how many times, in all four Gospels, that words such as "amazed, astonished" and "overwhelmed" are used to describe people's response to Jesus' teaching and ministry. There are several things about which we ought to be amazed, too.

We need to be amazed just by the gift of life itself. None of us have any guarantee that at 3 o'clock this afternoon we're still going to have this gift of life. Life is always a gift of God, and we should receive it with amazement and thanksgiving and be grateful stewards of it. It is amazing that God loves us! Now behavioral scientists do not agree on a great many things. But one of the things they all agree on, is that the greatest human need is to be loved. God has created us with a need to be loved, and a need to love others. The good news is, "GOD LOVES US."

We also ought to be amazed about His grace, forgiveness, and power -- the power that enables us to live the way He created us to live since we can't do it on our own. Any way you look at it - Jesus is amazing!

Chuck Wooley, Senior Pastor
Calvary Chapel Palm Springs
Cathedral City, California

February 20

GUARD YOUR HEART!

I have always enjoyed watching the news, keeping up on current events, sports, etc. But nowadays, watching some of the news is almost a compromise for a Christian.

I won't list the horrible variety of things that are termed *news* today, but I would encourage you to watch or guard your heart, for it is the wellspring of life *(Proverbs 4:23)*. We must avoid every kind of evil *(1 Corinthians 14:10)*, be innocent about what is evil *(1 Corinthians 16:19)*, and walk in our houses with blameless hearts, not setting our eyes on any evil thing *(Psalm 101:2,3)*.

We can't watch the news and, at the same time, obey these verses. Instead of watching the bad news, read the Good News!

Dan Marks, Assistant Pastor
Calvary Chapel of Downey
Downey, California

February 21

CALVARY COUPLES

"Mercy and truth have met together;
righteousness and peace have kissed."
Psalm 85:10

Righteousness can only be peace with truth. Righteousness is walking in perfect truth, it knows no error. Righteousness is God Himself, outside of Him there is none righteous, no not one! As far as righteousness goes, man could have never known Him.

But, *". . . righteousness and peace have kissed!"* A match made on Calvary. The righteousness of Jesus Christ has given us peace with God — Jesus is our peace! Truth could never change and remain Truth, He met Mercy. Another Calvary Couple! The Flawless One invites the wretched to be intimate with Him. This would require Mercy, that Truth would remain.

What a glorious testimony — that God has given us eternal life. That life is in His Son who alone is the way for us, who are sinners, to be freed from sin and to have eternal life with Him! Have you kissed "Righteousness" today? Do you know His peace in your life? Receive His mercy, so His truth can be established in you! Hug Him with your whole heart, give Him only the treasure of your life! You and Jesus, another Calvary Couple!

Chris Fredrich, Senior Pastor
Calvary Chapel of Orange Park
Orange Park, Florida

February 22

LOVE ONE ANOTHER

"....Love one another fervently with a pure heart."
1 Peter 1:22b

One of the most difficult experiences in life is having pure, honest, and sincere relationships with others. When I was young, I found the easiest way to solve this problem was to be alone. Shunning involvement with others isolated me from hurt. Yet, how empty and introverted that life-style was.

Praise God that Jesus has taken us from our self-centered existence and *". . . is working in us that which is pleasing in His sight,"* to love one another.

"A new commandment I give to you, that you love one another;
as I have loved you, that you also love one another. By
this all will know that you are My disciples,
if you have love for one another."
John 13:34,35

Bill Stonebraker, Senior Pastor
Calvary Chapel of Honolulu
Honolulu, Hawaii

February 23

JESUS -- THE MODEL EXAMPLE

The Apostle Paul stated that Christ was the perfect example of how to treat others.

"If there be therefore any consolation in Christ, if any comfort of love, if any fellowship of the Spirit, if any bowels and mercies, fulfill ye my joy, that ye be like-minded, having the same love, being of one accord, of one mind. Let nothing be done through strife or vainglory; but in lowliness of mind let each esteem the other better than themselves. Look not every man on his own things, but every man also on the things of others."
Philippians 2:1-4

If we see each other through the eyes of Jesus, we will be able to demonstrate a lot more love (agape) toward each other . . . but only if we put on the mind of Christ.

"Let us therefore, as many as be perfect, be thus minded: and if in anything ye be otherwise minded, God shall reveal even this unto you. Nevertheless, whereto we have already attained, let us walk by the same rule, let us mind the same thing."
Philippians 3:15-16

Mark Maciel, Assistant Pastor
Calvary Chapel of Downey
Downey, California

February 24

DEDICATED TO THE ONE I LOVE

"Coming to Him as . . a holy priesthood, to offer up spiritual sacrifices acceptable to God through Jesus Christ."
1 Peter 2:4,5

"Then . . . take some of its blood and put it on the tip of the. . . right ear of his sons, on the thumb of their right hand and on the big toe of their right foot."
Exodus 29:20

If you are a Christian today, did you know that in God's eyes, you are a priest? It's true! Pastors and spiritual leaders are not the *"priests"* for the church today, but every Christian is -- we all have access to God's presence.

With that in mind, we now look back to how a priest was to be dedicated to the Lord in Exodus. In being recognized as a priest, there would be an offering for his sin, and a burnt offering to declare his entire life to the Lord. But there was also a unique consecration a priest had to go through. A sacrifice was made, and then the blood was placed on:

>The right ear--dedicating everything he heard to the Lord.
>The right hand--dedicating everything he'd do to the Lord.
>The right foot--dedicating everywhere he'd go to the Lord.

Maybe such a transaction needs to take place between you and the Lord. Because you, too, are a priest of the most high God, your life should be dedicated to Him in everything you hear, and do, and everywhere you go.

Jim Suttle, Senior Pastor
Calvary Chapel of Roswell
Roswell, New Mexico

February 25

DOING ALL THINGS FROM YOUR HEART

*"For I say to you, unless your righteousness surpasses
that of the Scribes and the Pharisees, you
shall not enter the kingdom of God."*
Matthew 5:20

The Scribes and the Pharisees were the spiritual leaders at the time of Christ. With the normal man looking up to these men, how could their "righteousness" ever surpass that of these spiritual leaders? These religious leaders spent their days studying scripture and trying to keep every law.

What the Lord was saying, however, was that although the Scribes and Pharisees <u>seemed</u> to be doing everything right, they had a problem in their hearts. Their righteousness was only on the outside, seen by men. The Lord was looking at their hearts.

Listen to what Jesus says in Matthew 23:27, *"Woe to you, Scribes and Pharisees, hypocrites! For you are like white-washed tombs which on the outside appear beautiful, but inside they are full of dead men's bones and all uncleanness."* He went on to say a lot more to these religious men, warning them about their hypocrisy.

Are you aware that God is more interested in what is going on in your heart than the outward display of your flesh? The Lord instructs Samuel in 1 Samuel 16:7, *"Do not look at his appearance or at the height of his stature, because I have rejected him; for God sees not as man sees, for man looks at the outward appearance, but the Lord looks at the heart."*

(Continued)

There are many people who go to church and are even involved in ministry where the question may be asked: "Are they living their lives for the Lord, or to be seen by the men around them?" No matter what we do as Christians, we need to do it from our hearts, and for the glory of God only.

Let's start our day today by committing ourselves to the Lord. Let's not have a secret agenda of our own. Let's pray that the Lord will guide and direct us in all that we do.

Jesus said, "*. . . I seek not mine own will, but the will of the Father which hath sent me,*" *(John 5:30).* Can you make that your prayer, today?

> *"Whether, then, you eat or drink or whatever you do,*
> *do all to the glory of God!"*
> *1 Corinthians 10:31*

Mike Morris, Senior Pastor
Calvary Chapel of the High Desert
Hesperia, California

February 26

WHICH FIRE?

Scripture is very clear about the fires of testing, and the fires of judgment, which result from solicitation of evil. In Amos, chapters 1 and 2, we find God noting specific sins we can enter into that result in a devouring fire.

There is a connection between lust and burning *(Romans 1:27)*. Is it possible for a person to commit adultery and not be burned *(Proverbs 6:27-29)?* An ungodly man digs up evil and then "fires" away at another's expense *(Proverbs 16:27)*. Make no mistake about it, there is that natural burning process that takes place during any temptation *(James 1:13-15)*. There is a suffering in the flesh *(1 Peter 4:1-2)* whenever we choose to please self and not God *(Hebrews 11:25)*.

Yes, fiery darts *(Ephesians 6:16)* are a part of our daily combat. However, this fiery trial is not some strange thing that only some Christians face *(1 Peter 4:12)*; it's a par for our personal purging process *(1 Peter 1:7)*. God's holy fire cleanses *(Matthew 3:11)*; the flesh's whole fire corrupts *(Galatians 6:8)*. One fire enhances life, the other brings destruction. The only thing that God's fire consumes is sin *(Hebrews 12:29)*.

Ray Viola, Senior Pastor
Koinonia Fellowship
East Rochester, New York

February 27

A LOVE THAT GOD HATES

*"Love not the world, neither the things that are in the world.
If any man love the world, the love of the Father is not in him.
For all that is in the world, the lust of the flesh, the lust of the
eyes, and the pride of life, is not of the Father, but is of the
world. And the world passeth away, and the lust thereof:
but he that doeth the will of God abideth forever."*
1 John 2:15-17

God loves us so much that He gave Himself for us so that
we would be forgiven, saved, and freed from the penalty,
power, and one day, the presence of sin, Satan, and the
world! What a great salvation we have been given, and a
blessed hope we possess! So, why would we even enter-
tain the thought of loving any of the things belonging to
this world? God forbid! May we always hate the love and
things of this world and do the will of God.

Tim Hearron, Assistant Pastor
Calvary Chapel of Downey
Downey, California

February 28

O LORD, REVIVE US

"For thus saith the high and lofty One that inhabiteth eternity, whose name is Holy; I dwell in the high and holy places, with Him also that is of a contrite and humble spirit, to revive the spirit of the humble, and to revive the heart of the contrite ones. "
Isaiah 57:15

Watching the evening news surely ranks as one of the most depressing things we can do. As we see the usual assortment of atrocities, is there any doubt that we are living in a world that has forgotten God, that rejects the message of Jesus Christ? We live in Satan's domain, and that fact can cause us great distress, especially when television reinforces that reality night after night. As pilgrims in a hostile land, how can we survive without despairing at the darkness all around us? But if we lose heart <u>now</u>, how will we make it in the future?

In Isaiah 57:15, our Lord promises to revive all who come humbly to Him. You hear a lot about revival these days: in fact, it seems to be happening all the time in some churches! Yet, what is true revival? Scripture makes the steps to true revival easy and direct.

Revival begins with a fervent desire <u>to be right with God</u>. Such desire can only come from Heaven as God, through the convicting work of His Holy Spirit, shows us our sins and places within our hearts a longing for His forgiveness. In *Psalm 85:6*, David cries out, *"Wilt thou not revive us again: that thy people may rejoice in thee? "* He knew where his help would come from.

(Continued)

Revival brings with it an intense desire <u>to see God</u>. This, too, must come right out of the Lord's hand. We often hope that God will work in our lives at some point in the future. And, yet, why wait? We need that miracle today. Genuine revival longs to see God at work in every single situation, NOW, not just in the future.

True revival brings with it a deep sense of <u>humility before the Lord.</u> When we see God as He really is, we also get a clear picture of ourselves ... and we don't like what we see. As the prophet Isaiah said, *"Woe is me, for I am undone; because I am a man of unclean lips,"* (Isaiah 6:5).

And true revival starts in <u>the house of God</u>. Can we claim Him as our Savior if we don't long to see His face at every available opportunity? Can we claim to be His children if we don't have an intense desire to please our Father, to be right with Him in every way possible? We do not need to live in the despair that plagues this world. Our Lord promises, *". . . to revive the heart of the contrite ones."*

Steve Mays, Senior Pastor
Calvary Chapel of South Bay
Torrance, California

February 29

KNOWING WHEN TO KEEP IT CLOSED

"Even so the tongue is a little member and boasts great things.
See how great a forest a little fire kindles!"
James 3:5

Has your tongue ever gotten you into trouble? If anyone has ever been an "open mouth, insert foot" kind of guy, it's me! How we wish we didn't stumble so much with our words. If anything could help us get in line and use discretion with our tongue, hopefully just the fear of doing damage to someone and possible vexing our own spirit would be enough to help keep our mouth closed. How we need a coal from God's altar to touch these unclean lips *(Isaiah 6:6,7)*. Be slow to speak my dear brethren, and let your silence be your wisdom!

Work on it today, He's strengthening you to do so. Remember, Jesus is bigger than your mouth.

John Schaffer, Senior Pastor
First Love Calvary Chapel
Whittier, California

March 1

FRUITFUL LABOR

"For to me, to live is Christ and to die is gain. If I am to go on living in the body, this will mean fruitful labor for me. Yet what shall I choose? I do not know! I am torn between the two: I desire to depart and be with Christ, which is better by far; but it is more necessary for you that I remain in the body. Convinced of this, I know that I will remain and I will continue with all of you for your progress and joy in the faith, so that though my being with you again your joy in Christ Jesus will overflow on account of me."
Philippians 1:21-26

Does our remaining here on earth bring joy to those we are in contact with? Is others faith in Jesus encouraged because of our fruitful labor? Is our labor fruitful or am I just fruitlessly laboring? Tough questions that deserve tough answers. You see, it would be easier to die for Christ and gain Heaven now. The hard thing to do is live for Him now and be an encouragement and a faith builder, and someone who causes others joy to be overflowing. For me, to live, is to live for Christ.

Chick Chikeles, Senior Pastor
Calvary Chapel Saint Paul
Saint Paul, Minnesota

March 2

REGULATE THE FLESH

*"Therefore, if you died with Christ from the basic principles
of the world, why, as though living in the world, do you
subject yourselves to regulations."*
Colossians 2:20

Living in the world is Paul's reference to lives lived natu-
rally -- after the flesh. These regulations are imposed to
curtail the indulgences of the flesh. The goal being to live
a more spiritual life. But the life of the Spirit is not one of
disciplining the flesh against sin. It is a life that reckons
the flesh dead to sin.

Les Prock, Senior Pastor
Calvary Chapel North Hill
Milton, Washington

March 3

BE YE TRANSFORMED

"But now ye put off all these; anger, wrath, malice, blasphemy,
filthy communication out of your mouth. Lie not
to one another, seeing that ye have put off the
old man with his deeds."
Colossians 3:8,9

Paul's epistles contain his written testimonies of lives that
he had seen changed by the power of Jesus Christ. The
changes occurred because the people had a relationship
with Him. *"And such were some of you..."* were the words
Paul used in *1 Corinthians 6:11* to acknowledge lives that
were truly TRANSFORMED.

Transformed hearts manifest themselves in transformed attitudes, actions, and speech.

Bob Lawren, Assistant Pastor
Calvary Chapel of the Finger Lakes
Farmington, New York

March 4

SINLESS PERFECTION

"For our citizenship is in heaven, from which we also eagerly
wait for the Savior, the Lord Jesus Christ, who will transform
our lowly body that it may be conformed to His glorious body,
according to the working by which He is able even to
subdue all things to Himself."
Philippians 3:20,21

There is no promise in the Scriptures that a Christian, in
this life, will ever reach the place where he will no longer
sin. Sinless perfection and complete sanctification await
the coming of the Lord Jesus Christ. At that time, we will
be delivered from our *"lowly body of humiliation and sin."*
Then, and only then, the transformation will be complete!
We shall soon be like our Savior, for we shall see Him as
He is. Let us all wait *eagerly* for that awesome Day!!

Pancho Juarez, Senior Pastor
Calvary Chapel Montebello
Montebello, California

March 5

A BANQUET FOR THE POOR

*"And He also went on to say to the one who had invited Him,
'When you give a luncheon or a dinner, do not invite your
friends or your brothers or your relatives or rich neighbors, lest
they also invite you in return, and repayment come to you. But
when you give a reception, invite the poor, the crippled, the
lame, the blind, and you will be blessed, since they do not have
the means to repay you; for you will be repaid at the
resurrection of the righteous.'"*
Luke 14:12-14

In our society, we are taught from an early age to desire recognition and pay-back for all that we do. We strive to be number one, and second place is a loss. In these verses and many others in the Word, Jesus teaches us to not seek repayment or acknowledgment, but rather to reach out to those who have no means to repay!

In a society where pity has been substituted for compassion, we gather with friends and loved ones to talk about how bad things are for the poor and the crippled around the world, but do we get involved helping those who cannot repay? Our Lord gives us a great promise here which we could call "life assurance" that if we reach out to the poor and crippled of this world, He will be the one who will repay and I can think of no better way to receive repayment than by our Lord!!! He calls us to be not only hearers but "doers" of the Word.

Steve Oliver, Assistant Pastor
Calvary Worship Center
Colorado Springs, Colorado

March 6

WHAT ARE WE ACCUMULATING

"He must increase, but I must decrease."
John 3:30

The Jews had come to John, and they just didn't get it. They said to John, *"Everyone is going to be baptized by this Jesus instead of you."* However, John had the proper perspective. He realized that he was just the voice and not the message *(Isaiah 40:3)*, the forerunner and not the Messiah. Jesus is coming again, and we are His voice today. It is our turn to prepare the way.

Today, it seems that the philosophy of most people is exactly the opposite of John's. Many are increasing, and the Lord is decreasing in their lives. We live in an age of much ambition and luxury. Many have become consumed with day-to-day living, and enslaved by the demands of inflated life-styles. In turn, they discover that they have no time for Jesus. John lived very simply and God used him mightily. His life was not complicated by the cares of this world. As Christians, the only thing we should be striving after and accumulating is a deeper relationship with the Lord. Let us evaluate each desire in light of God's Word and lighten the load. May the world fade away and God consume our lives.

Jason Van Divier, Senior Pastor
Calvary Chapel of Lake Forest
Lake Forest, California

March 7

YOU SNOOZE, YOU LOSE

"And when He was at the place, He said unto them,
'Pray that you may not enter into temptation.'"
Luke 22:40

Just shortly before Jesus was about to be crucified, He, Peter, James, and John were on the Mount of Olives. In *Luke 22:40*, Jesus said to them, *"Pray that you may not enter into temptation."* Jesus began praying so intensely, He sweat blood. *"My Father if it is possible let this cup pass from me; yet not as I will, but as thou wilt."* The agony of the Cross, the mockery, the scourging, and worst of all the sin of the world was about to fall upon our righteous Savior.

Were His three faithful friends abiding in His will? No, His disciples were snoring like Larry, Moe, and Curly that day. Jesus asked for their prayers -- just for an hour. Surely if Jesus asked you or I to pray for Him and ourselves, we'd do it, right?

So what happens when we don't obey the Lord? Well, Peter acts it out for us. We read in verse 54 that Peter was following the Lord at a distance. Then he began to blend in with those in the world that opposed Jesus. The next thing you know, he denies ever having known Jesus at all.

Are you blending in with the world or following Him at a distance? Are you awake or asleep? Rise and pray that you may not enter into temptation. Read *2 Peter 1:4-11*.

Ken Shaffer, Assistant Pastor
Calvary Chapel of Fullerton
Fullerton, California

March 8

OPEN FOR BUSINESS

"But the fruit of the Spirit is love, joy, peace, longsuffering,
kindness, goodness, faithfulness, gentleness, self-control.
Against such there is no law."
Galatians 5:22,23

There are primarily two things we do to live out the Christian life. First, we must give a green light to the working of the Holy Spirit, and second, we must have an "open for business" sign in our daily life.

People will demand of us to be gentle even when we're tired. They will ask for answers when we're in tears. But, we still don't have the right to go "out of business" just because we're tired or hurt. Giving the life of Jesus away will ultimately cost us something. But He'll restore us. Oh, may we not just "look good" minus the fruit. But rather, that people will be attracted to Him when they find what is missing in their lives by watching His Spirit work through us.

Chuck Wooley, Senior Pastor
Calvary Chapel Palm Springs
Cathedral City, California

March 9

I REBUKE YOU!

What does scripture say about rebuke? What does it mean? Well, the Word itself, within the context of the Body of Christ, describes a firm, loving, but necessary reprimand due to conduct or behavior that misrepresents Jesus or offends others. It must be noted that the spirit behind any rebuke must be loving, not angry. A classic example is when Paul withstood Peter. There are other uses of the word in unchurched settings such as when Jesus rebuked the elements, or Jesus rebuking a foul spirit.

As a minister of the Word of God, rebuke is as vital as doctrine. Some Judaizers who tried to put the church under a grace-works trip, needed to be rebuked. These things of God need to be spoken about authoritatively. The scriptures tell us that as God's children we should expect rebuke. Like Balaam, you can count on the Holy Spirit to rebuke us for works of iniquity. (As a brief detour, have you ever seen or heard people rebuking the devil? Check out *Jude 9*.) Unfortunately, the word rebuke has become a nasty word, when in reality it is a word that assures us of Jesus' love for us.

Saints, every single one of us need the Lord's rebuke. In fact, if we claim to be wise, we will actually love the instrument through whom the necessary correction comes. Response to the Lord's dealings reveals our true character. Open rebuke is better than secret love, and obtains the favor of the Lord.

Ray Viola, Senior Pastor
Koinonia Fellowship
East Rochester, New York

March 10

A CRY IN THE NIGHT

"Give ear to my words, O Lord, consider my groaning. Heed the sound of my cry for help, my King and my God, for to Thee do I pray. In the morning, O Lord, Thou wilt hear my voice; In the morning I will order my prayer to Thee and eagerly watch. For Thou art not a God who takes pleasure in wickedness; No evil dwells with Thee."
Psalm 5:1-4

What a great blessing it is to know that the Lord listens to us! It is of great encouragement that God, the creator of the universe, hears our cry. He is interested in our meditations and awaits our prayers.

Knowing that God is ready to listen to our prayers should be an encouragement to pray even more. Even as we are comforted by His presence, we are convicted to come into His presence more often. As David asks God to listen to his prayers, he makes a commitment to be faithful to pray. It is a commitment worth making. We are assured that as we lift our voices to the Lord, He will be there to hear us.

Matt DeWitt, Assistant Pastor
Calvary Chapel Church Planting Mission
Vista, California

March 11

A REASON TO DO RIGHT

"He feared God and shunned evil."
Job 1:8

Job fears God and shuns evil. We do many things because of fear. We pay rent so we won't be evicted. We drive within the speed limit so we won't get a ticket. And we try not to sin so God won't punish us. Is that what the Bible teaches? Is fear of God a valid motive not to sin? It was for Job.

We can safely assume that there is a connection between fear and right behavior. We must understand an important distinction. This fear is not superstitious terror of a fickle god who zaps us the instant we do wrong. Rather, it's a deep respect and reverence for God's holy character and awesome power. It's a healthy fear not only of sin's painful consequences, but of sinning against the One who loves us, and on Whom we depend for our very life. If we love Him, we will not want to offend Him. Yes, the fear of God is a good reason to do right. *"Be not wise in thine own eyes: fear the Lord, and depart from evil,"* (Proverbs 3:7).

The measure of our love for God is our obedience.

Glenn Kravig, Assistant Pastor
Calvary Chapel of Downey
Downey, California

March 12

THE COST OF REDEMPTION

"In Him we have redemption through His blood, the forgive-
ness of sins, according to the riches of His grace."
Ephesians 1:7

Salvation is free, we often say. However, we forget that salvation was not free for our Lord. It cost the Son of God
dearly to redeem us. Redemption means to set one free by
the payment of a price. And the price that our Lord had to
pay for us was a terrible one.

Our Lord, kneeling in the garden, sweating great drops of
blood, with the agonizing thought in his mind that he would
have to drink the cup of the wrath of God to its last dregs.
"Father, if there be any other way, take this cup from me." There
was no other way. He suffered for us by paying our penalty on the Cross that day. What was that penalty? The full
wrath of God. You and I have never felt that wrath because
of Jesus.

Somehow that day, our Lord paid the equivalent of <u>ALL</u>
our eternities in Hell. This is indeed a mystery. Martin
Luther himself sat for hours one day not moving a muscle
as if in a trance staring blankly in horror at the thought that
our Lord had paid this immense price for us. As one puri-
tan had said, "It cost more to redeem us than to make us."

Peyton Jones, Assistant Pastor
Calvary Chapel of Huntington Beach
Huntington Beach, California

March 13

FREE MERCY -- NO LIMIT

"Surely goodness and mercy shall follow me all the days of my
life, and I will dwell in the house of the Lord for ever."
Psalm 23:6

Nothing can ever exhaust the endless mercy of God. No
matter how deep your sin, no matter how distant you feel,
no matter how alone you are, no matter how abandoned
you've been, no matter how bitter you've become, no matter how guilty and ashamed you are, nothing can keep you
from the throne of mercy - except your will.

Larry DiSimone, Senior Pastor
Calvary Chapel of the Canyons
Silverado, California

March 14

AGONY'S REWARD

I heard cries of agony
Come from the garden
The night before Calvary

Over on the East side
'Neath the olive tree
Where sweat stained the ground
With drops of blood. . . or me

Looking back - would You do it again?
Seeing how I've treated You since then?
Looking back - is there gain or loss?
Have I thanked You enough for the Cross of agony?
The Cross You bore for the unlovable
Such as me.

Mike Stangel, Senior Pastor
North Shore Christian Fellowship
Haleiwa, Hawaii

March 15

OUR DAY OF VISITATION

*"Now as He drew near, He saw the city and wept over it
saying, "If you had known, even you, especially in this your
day, the things that make for your peace! But now they are
hidden from your eyes. For days will come upon you when
your enemies will build an embankment around you, surround
you and close you in on every side, and level you, and your
children within you, to the ground; and they will not leave in
you one stone upon another, because you did not
know the time of your visitation."*
Luke 19:41-44

These words from the lips of Jesus are especially somber as
we realize the scenario surrounding this speech. He is approaching Jerusalem on Palm Sunday. The crowds have
poured out of the city to meet Him, casting down their garments before Him, paving the road with the branches of
palm trees, as they declared Him to be their Messiah. They
have cried, *"Blessed is He who comes in the name of the Lord."*
We refer to this as the Triumphal Entry, however, Jesus sees
it as a time to mourn. It was not that they did not believe.
It was that they had missed the reason and purpose for His
coming. They wanted a Messiah who would do things their
way. Jesus knew that days later the same voices who cried
praises would call for His crucifixion.

Are we all too often like the crowds? Do we see Jesus approach our lives and welcome Him, only to fall away
as He doesn't work the way we had anticipated? Are there
times when we miss our day of visitation due to the fact
that we, just like those of Jesus' day, want a Lord who follows our plan and purpose?

(Continued)

We need to be a people who cry, "Hosanna, this is the day that the Lord has made, let us rejoice and be glad in it." And we need to be a people who will follow His plan and His purpose, *"looking unto Jesus, the author and finisher of our faith."* Let us recognize not only the time of His visitation but follow His purpose.

Dave Fitzgerald, Senior Pastor
Hosanna Calvary Chapel
Maryland Heights, Missouri

March 16

ARE YOU A "RELIGIOUS" HYPOCRITE?

*"And He spake this parable unto certain which trusted
in themselves, that they were righteous,
and despised others."*
Luke 18:9

Here's how to find out!

Ask yourself these three simple questions:

1. Who are you trusting in for salvation?
2. In whose righteousness are you counting upon
   to save you?
3. Do you "love" and value others, or "despise"
   and look down upon others?

It shouldn't be too difficult to figure it out from here.

Mike Sasso, Assistant Pastor
Calvary Chapel of Downey
Downey, California

March 17

PUT THINGS INTO PERSPECTIVE

"Ah, Sovereign LORD, you have made the heavens and the
earth by your great power and outstretched arm.
Nothing is too hard for you."
Jeremiah 32:17

I saw some really scary pictures awhile back. They were photographs of some kind of strange reptilian-like animals. Most of them had horns or huge jaws that looked like they could destroy anything or anyone in their path. They were not just frightening, but they were ugly too. I began to scan the text to see where these things lived. The text told me they lived in MY neighborhood, and, in fact, they probably lived in my house. As I read on, I realized that these hideous pictures were, in fact, electron microscope photos of dust mites and lice, the kinds of tiny bugs that live all around us every day.

This made me think of how we see the world, and how God sees it. From His perspective, the things that scare us are nothing more than little bugs that will pass away in a few short days. I have discovered that the more I think upon the difficulties of life, the bigger they become. It is only when we ascend into the presence of God through the Word, worship, and prayer, that we can look clearly at our problems and see them in their proper perspective.

Run to the God of the Word for perspective. You will find that truly nothing is too hard for God.

Greg Cull, Senior Pastor
Calvary Chapel Shingle Springs
Shingle Springs, California

March 18

SHARE THE WEALTH

"I know that the LORD secures justice for the poor,
and upholds the cause of the needy."
Psalm 140:12

There are many different ways of responding to folks when they greet us with, "How are you doing?" We can say fine, and usually they move on to something else and everyone is satisfied. But we can also either launch into a full color presentation of all our woes and trials, or we can enthusiastically proclaim how wonderful everything is.

This Psalm give us some assurance to measure our interaction with one another so that we can be an encouragement, yet not conceal it when we need help. Scripture is clear that we are not to carry trials completely on our own, but that God has provided the church family to come along side. But no one can pray and stand with us if they have no idea we are going through difficulty.

This Psalm offers encouragement, too. It assures us that God does uphold those who are poor and needy. Each of us, at one time or another, will find ourselves either in need of comfort and prayer, or in a position to give comfort and prayer. The reason we often miss what God has for us is because we simply don't reach out either to serve, or to be served. Let's not be afraid to be God's instrument in whatever way He desires to use us with one another.

Greg Cull, Senior Pastor
Calvary Chapel Shingle Springs
Shingle Springs, California

March 19

ABUNDANT LIFE IN CHRIST

"We then who are strong ought to bear with the scruples of the weak, and not to please ourselves. Let each of us please his neighbor for his good, leading to edification. For even Christ did not please Himself."
Romans 15:1-3

On a trip to St. Petersburg where I taught at a Men's Conference, I had the opportunity to experience something that I had not encountered in many years. At the close of the conference, I found myself at a hotel unwinding from the weekend, waiting to travel home the next day.

As I sat by myself in the restaurant for dinner, I sensed a deep and dreary emotion from the past that took me several minutes to pinpoint. I was lonely. But not just in a physical sense. It was much more encompassing than my mere status of being by myself. It permeated even my spirit as I sensed my separation from the rest of those around me. I was like a foreigner in a strange land -- not just out of place, but out of sync. I was not at all on the same wave length as those who were searching for some kind of amusement, entertainment, or pleasure.

My waiter kept apologizing that the "girls," usually come on another night and asking if he could get me some kind of alcoholic beverage. I could remember the emptiness of being driven by a self-centered quest for pleasure and taunted by an insatiable appetite for more, yet never being able to reach the goal of contentment and satisfaction.

I realized as I sat in that hotel restaurant that the only thing

(Continued)

separating me from them was the person of Jesus Christ. In Christ, I am no longer compelled to seek pleasure in this life, but I am driven by the divine nature that works within me to please others. In so doing, I find great satisfaction. Jesus put it this way:

> *"Whoever seeks to save his life will lose it, and whoever*
> *loses his life will preserve it."*
> Luke 17:33

As I give my life away to others in service to Christ, I find the abundant life promised by my Lord. But I must be careful that I do not look for my pleasure in the ministry, because the ministry is not for my pleasure, but for God's. If I do only that which pleases me, I miss the opportunities for real joy and satisfaction provided by the Lord.

I am certain that Christ's crucifixion was not pleasurable to His flesh. Yet the Bible tells us that He did it for the joy set before Him. That joy was in the salvation He would bring for you and me. In others-centered abandonment, He poured out His blood to the total and complete pleasure of God the Father. As we pick up our cross, die to self, and seek the pleasure of others, may God the Father find pleasure in us also.

Bob Coy, Senior Pastor
Calvary Chapel Ft. Lauderdale
Ft. Lauderdale, Florida

March 20

CLEANING HOUSE

*"How can I cleanse my way? By taking heed
thereto according to thy Word!"*
Psalm 119:9

David asked God how to cleanse his way, but then answered his own question, *". . . according to thy Word."* Studying God's Word, that's the key! And just as David already knew the answer, we do, too.

Have you ever wondered how long it would take you to read the entire Bible? If you read it out loud at a pace that is easy to understand, you could read Genesis to Revelation in 78 hours. To read the entire Bible in a year, you would find that God's Word could be read cover to cover in *365* days by reading it 12 minutes a day!

It's been said that, "A Bible that's *falling* apart probably belongs to someone who isn't." What's falling apart, you or your Bible?

Neil Matranga, Assistant Pastor
Calvary Chapel of Downey
Downey, California

March 21

THE SUBTLE ART OF RATIONALIZATION

"Therefore to him that knoweth to do good,
and doeth it not, to him it is sin."
James 4:17

Rationalization: Justifying our disobedience to God. Rationalization often comes into play when we choose not to obey God's prompting as well as when we disobey His commands.

Why do we make excuses for our disobedience? Psychologists say it stems from "cognitive dissonance" which occurs when we hold two beliefs that are contradictory to one another. We cannot live with that tension; we will modify one of the beliefs in order to make ourselves more comfortable.

As Christians, we know God's commands. When what we know about those commands conflicts with other desires of our hearts, one of those beliefs or desires has to go. When we choose to rationalize, we are compromising God's truth to obtain our own desires.

"And my God shall supply all your needs according to
His riches in glory in Christ Jesus."
Philippians 4:19

"Hate the evil, and love the good."
Amos 5:15a

Glenn Kravig, Assistant Pastor
Calvary Chapel of Downey
Downey, California

March 22

I'VE HAD IT!

When God saw the wickedness of man on earth in the days of Noah, He literally declared, "I've had it!," *(Genesis 6:3,12)*. He plainly states that man's unchecked flesh corrupted both God's way as well as man's way upon the earth. If I may use this passage in a little different way, I believe we can see hidden in the words, "I've had it" enough inspiration to *". . . be ye angry, and sin not," (Ephesians 4:26)*. If we are going to have productive lives in God's kingdom, our spirit must not strive with God. Additionally, we must say to our ugly, unredeemed, Christ-hating flesh, "I've had it!"

Are you content living with unsurrendered areas in your life? Have you taken all you possess -- your dreams, your future, and past, to Calvary and declared, "I've had it Jesus; take it all, take me, no reservations?" Have you taken those sins which so easily beset us -- your attitudes, your lukewarm service, or sin of the tongue, to Jesus and said, "I'm sick of this Lord, I hate those sins, I've had it!"

You see, it's not until we've had it that we can begin to see the light at the end of the tunnel. Is any sin or habit we hang onto worth the grief or reward of corruption? We all possess an unredeemed body with unredeemed emotions. We are in a civil war *(Galatians 5:16)*. However, it's only as we respond by the grace of God, to the Spirit of God, that the fullness of His fruit comes *(Galatians 5:22-23)*.

Where are you habitually sowing your seed, *(Galatians 6:8)*? I'm afraid too many of us have "jumped the Ark of Christ" and plunged back into Egypt. Oh, we aren't adulterers, or perverted, and we would never think of getting drunk or

(Continued)

cheating on our IRS forms, but we've done worse. We've been lulled into spiritual amnesia, indifference, and a luke-warm walk. Typical descriptions of the nominal American believer.

Jesus went all the way to the Cross. Will you? Will you not declare <u>today</u> as the day when <u>you</u> will stop striving with God? When I think about Calvary and my Lord's total commitment to His Father and to me, I find myself ashamed for complaining, and angry for allowing the little foxes of compromise to spoil the Vine *(Song of Solomon 2:15)*.

I don't know about you today, but I've had it! Will you join me in a holy rebellion? We are in those days of Noah *(Luke 17: 26,27)* and it's later than you think *(I Thessalonians 5:5-11)*.

Ray Viola, Senior Pastor
Koinonia Fellowship
East Rochester, New York

March 23

LONGSUFFERING

"But the fruit of the Spirit is love, joy, peace, longsuffering,
gentleness, goodness, faith, meekness, temperance:
against such there is no law."
Galatians 5:22,23

I was helping my daughter one evening with her home-work, and we were going over the word patience, or longsuffering, in the King James. After we spent a good length of time studying this one particular word, she then had to write a paragraph about it. She drew a blank, and I lost all my patience.

Here I was, after I had just finished explaining how God was so patient (longsuffering) with us, losing my patience with her. All of a sudden I stopped and, deeply convicted, I asked her to forgive me and told her patience is the oppo-site of what dad just did. She understood then.

Steve Everett, Assistant Pastor
Calvary Chapel of Downey
Downey, California

March 24

EYES TO SEE

"I counsel you to buy from me gold refined in the fire, that you may be rich; and white garments, that you may be clothed, that the shame of your nakedness may not be revealed; and anoint your eyeswith eye salve, that you may see."
Revelation 3:18

Sometimes we think we're doing just fine, and then we read something from the Lord that shows us we're not! There's always another angle the Lord can show us about our lives. Are you shortsighted or even blind to something? How would you know if you couldn't see? Ask the Lord today to open your eyes so you may see clearly anything the Lord is trying to show you.

May the Lord take away any spots in our vision that we may see clearly to walk His way.

John Schaffer, Senior Pastor
First Love Calvary Chapel
Whittier, California

March 25

THE UNSURPASSABLE VALUE
OF THE SCRIPTURES

Based on Psalm 19:7-11, the following observations can be made about God and the scriptures:

1. They are perfect, restoring the soul.
2. They are sure, make wise the simple.
3. They are right, rejoicing the heart.
4. They are pure, enlightening the eyes.
5. The fear of the Lord is clean, enduring forever.
6. The judgments of the Lord are true, they are righteous altogether.
7. They are more desirable than gold.
8. By them one is warned.
9. In keeping them there is great reward.

Because of the unequaled value of the scriptures, it would be wise to pour one's life into them; to allow them to guide your every footstep. Conversely, it would be utterly foolish to walk away from them.

Ron Terrall, Assistant Pastor
Calvary Chapel of Downey
Downey, California

March 26

UNDER THE CHISEL

"For we are His workmanship, created in Christ Jesus for good works, which God prepared beforehand that we should walk in them."
Ephesians 2:10

Someone once saw Michelangelo chipping away with his chisel at a huge, shapeless, piece of rock, and he inquired as to what he was doing. Michelangelo replied, "I am releasing the angel imprisoned in this rock."

Isn't it wonderful how Jesus looks at people? He sees not only what a person *is*, but He sees what that person can *become*. He sees not just the *actualities*, but the *possibilities*.

Jesus looked at Simon and saw an uneducated fisherman. But He also saw a *rock*. So, He changed his name from "Simon" which means "shifting sand," to "Peter" which means "rock." Take heart! Jesus isn't finished with you yet. And though the chisel may hurt at times, you are a beautiful sculpture in progress!

Mark Scott, Senior Pastor
Calvary Chapel of College Park
College Park, Maryland

March 27

WHAT ARE YOU WORTH?

"Because you say, 'I am rich, have become wealthy, and have
need of nothing' — and do not know that you are wretched,
miserable, poor, blind, and naked. . ."
Revelation 3:17

Ouch!! Those words sure don't do very much for my self-esteem! Society teaches us that we need to think better of ourselves. The Bible teaches that we need to see ourselves as we really are. Not as good people with minor flaws, but as wretched sinners in desperate need of a Savior.

It is not a good feeling to realize that our sin has made us "wretched, miserable, poor, blind, and naked" in the eyes of a holy God. But it is very good to know that God loves us in spite of what we really are. There is nothing in us that is worth esteeming. Any self worth should come from God, who tells us in His Word what <u>He</u> thinks we are worth.

"Knowing that you were not redeemed with corruptible things,
like silver or gold, from your aimless conduct received by
tradition from your fathers, but with the precious blood of
Christ, as of a lamb without blemish and without spot."
1 Peter 1:18,19

We may be wretched because of our sin, but to God we are worth the sin-less blood of His only Son. Let us esteem only Him!

Todd Lauderdale, Assistant Pastor
Calvary Chapel of Murietta
Murietta, California

March 28

SPECK INSPECTORS

"And why do you look at the speck in your brother's eye, but do not consider the plank in your own eye?"
Matthew 7:3

I have often noticed how easily we all seem to spot faults in others, and not necessarily because they are easy to spot (Jesus likened them to specks). But more often than not, it's because we're looking for them. I've been taken aback by those simple words of Jesus, *"Why do you look?"* It's as though Jesus cuts to the very heart of our motives to show us that the problem lies with our own hearts, not in our brother's eye. If I am having to expend so much energy searching out the faults of others (the specks in their eyes), then I obviously have a greater problem (a plank in my own eye). We must all guard against having a critical, overactive propensity to look at others faults, be they ever so small. For in doing so, we expose our greater problem and need, a need to have Jesus change <u>our</u> hearts.

Joseph Gros, Senior Pastor
Calvary Chapel of Silver City
Tyrone, New Mexico

March 29

GOD'S WORD KEEPS ME FROM SIN

"Thy word have I hid in mine heart,
that I might not sin against thee."
Psalm 119:11

"Thy word is a lamp unto my feet, and a light unto my path."
Psalm 119:105

I love to spend my devotion time in the Psalms. My favorite is Psalm 119, which speaks of "Praise of God's Word" -- 176 verses alone are attributed to the power of God's Word! Verses 11 and 105 are just two of my favorites. I am reminded that sin is still prevalent in my life, and that I am a sinner saved by His grace. Psalm 119 shows me the importance of reading God's Word and hiding it in my heart on a daily basis. The more I have His Word hidden in my heart, the less I will be tempted to sin. God's Word is the pathway for my life. Indeed, if I truly apply His Word on a daily basis, He shall lead me! Jesus said in Matthew 24:35:

"Heaven and earth shall pass away,
but my words shall not pass away."

What a glorious promise of our security in Christ Jesus!

Bob Ortega, Senior Pastor
Calvary Chapel of Las Cruces
Las Cruces, New Mexico

March 30

TWENTY-FOUR SEVEN

*"How precious to me are Your thoughts, Oh God. How vast is
the sum of them! Were I to count them, they would
outnumber the grains of sand."*
Psalm 139:17,18

Somehow someone has figured out that the meaning of this
scripture is that God thinks about us seven times every second! I think the most beautiful aspect of this scripture is
knowing that God is always thinking of us 24 hours a day,
7 days a week! Sometimes, we forget about God, but God
never forgets about us.

Dan Marks, Assistant Pastor
Calvary Chapel of Downey
Downey, California

March 31

MIRACULOUS INTERVENTION

*"I have compassion on the multitude, because they have now
continued with Me three days and have nothing to eat. And if
I send them away hungry to their own houses, they will faint
on the way; for some of them have come from afar."*
Mark 8:23

We need to see that Jesus was totally man and could identify with their hunger. Literally, Jesus was saying, "I know
what it's like to be hungry." There has been a tendency for
us to create a transcendent Jesus, *(Hebrews 13:8)*. Jesus Christ
is the same yesterday, today, and forever. Yesterday, He
saw hungry people! We've had Jesus way up there and not
able to approach Him with our weaknesses. Listen, Jesus
accepts full responsibility for you.

The church, from time to time, may not be able to meet
your needs. The church may fail to satisfy you. The church
may fall short in reaching out and touching you. It is imperfect, filled with imperfect people. It's not the church
that assumes responsibility for your well-being. It is the
Lord Jesus Christ and He always intercepts you where you
need to be intercepted. He does not come to us and say,
"Why are you the way you are?" But, He comes to us and
touches us at the point of need, because He can identify
with us. That's just one more reason that makes it impossible not to love Jesus. For He has totally committed Himself to us.

Chuck Wooley, Senior Pastor
Calvary Chapel Palm Springs
Cathedral City, California

April 1

BALANCING ACTS

*"Iron sharpeneth iron; so a man sharpeneth
the countenance of his friend."*
Proverbs 27:17

To be balanced Christians, we should always be looking
for a "Timothy" and a "Paul" in our lives. What I mean is,
that we should be looking for both people to mentor and
people we can mentor.

An ancient Persian proverb offers the following excellent
advice on knowing who to invest your life into:

He who knows not,
And knows not that he knows not,
He is a fool, shun him.
He who knows not, and knows that he knows not
He is a child, teach him.
He who knows, and knows not that he knows,
He is asleep wake him.
He who knows, and knows that he knows,
He is wise follow him.

Mike Sasso, Assistant Pastor
Calvary Chapel of Downey
Downey, California

April 2

THE WORK IS NOT FINISHED

*"David said to Solomon his son, "'Be strong and of good
courage, and do it: fear not, nor be dismayed: for the Lord
God, even my God, will be with thee; He will not fail thee, nor
forsake thee, until thou hast finished all the work
for the service of the house of the Lord.'"*
1 Chronicles 28:20

Be encouraged today as you experience the joy, sorrow, and
especially the excitement of all that God is doing in your
life. He is faithful to complete His work in you!

Tony Falcione, Assistant Pastor
Calvary Chapel of the Finger Lakes
Farmington, New York

April 3

AWAKEN TO HIS GRACE

"However, to the man who does not work but
trusts God who justifies the wicked, his
faith is credited as righteousness."
Romans 4:5

"Jesus answered, 'The work of God is this:
to believe in the one He has sent."
John 6:29

It is by grace we are saved, by grace we are kept, by grace that we are used, and by grace that we are holy. Salvation is God's work from start to finish and we can add nothing to it. While it is our job to *"work out our salvation with fear and trembling" (Philippians 2:12)*, let us remember that it is *"God who works in us to will and act according to His good purpose" (Romans 8:28)*. In our zeal to please God, let us never lose sight of His grace, His undeserved favor, which is the life-breath of all that we have, all that we are, and all that we are to become. To Jesus be the glory, now and forever.

Roger Scalice, Senior Pastor
Calvary Chapel of Big Bear
Big Bear, California

April 4

EXCITED FOR THE LORD

"Never be lacking in zeal, but keep your
spiritual fervor serving the Lord."
Romans 12:11

Sometimes people are cynical about enthusiasm, but there is nothing wrong with it. There is a joy and excitement that comes from our relationship with God. The initial relationship with Christ is meant to last, and not to peter out. The longer we have been Christians the more enthusiastic we should be. Sadly, the opposite is often the case. It should not be so.

John Corcoran, Assistant Pastor
Calvary Chapel Costa Mesa
Santa Ana, California

April 5

BEING CONTENT IN THE FAITH

*"But godliness with contentment is great gain. For we
brought nothing into [this] world, [and it is]
certain we can carry nothing out."*
I Timothy 6:6,7

Have you ever wonder what it would be like if we could
serve the Lord, and not worry about anything else -- money,
bills, mortgages, car payments, etc?

Like it or not, we have a need for money to take care of our
responsibilities. However, we need to live within our means.
Too many Christians take on more financial burdens than
they afford to, and so sacrifice their peace with the Lord.

All God desires for us is to live one day at a time and live it
in Him! We need to learn to be content in what we have, as
well as what we do not have; knowing He will provide for
our every need. Being content is being thankful in whatever state you may be in. Read *Philippians 4:11-13*.

Don't get caught up in the madness of this society. As Christians, we should find our rest in Him not in our circumstances!

Mark Maciel, Assistant Pastor
Calvary Chapel of Downey
Downey, California

April 6

THE IMPORTANCE OF FORGIVENESS

"And be ye kind one to another, tenderhearted, forgiving one another, even as God for Christ's sake hath forgiven you."
Ephesians 4:32

Sometimes in our thirst for spiritual growth, we explore nuggets of scripture looking for that one truth that will catapult us into the state of maturity. But most often, it's applying the "ABC's" of our faith daily that is the real cause of growth.

One fundamental doctrine that is taught repeatedly in scripture is that of forgiveness. Remember how beautifully Joseph forgave his brothers? That act of Joseph is a correct practical application of Our Lord's teaching found in *Matthew 18:21-35*.

Now before you ho-hum and conclude, "I've read that a hundred times," let me ask you something. Do you have unforgiveness, resentment, or bitterness in your heart toward someone, anyone, right at this moment? The measure of our ability to forgive others is the measure whereby you and I will be forgiven.

Forgive, and you shall be forgiven. Indeed, to be forgiven is a blessed thing, but it's that very act of undeserved forgiveness that sets us free to forgive others. Forgiveness always erases differences and exalts the Cross. Unforgiveness needs to be confessed and repented of.

Ray Viola, Senior Pastor
Koinonia Fellowship
East Rochester, New York

April 7

DEBTOR'S PRISON

*"He will turn again, He will have compassion upon us;
He will subdue our iniquities; and thou wilt cast
all their sins into the depths of the sea."*
Micah 7:19

What if you were in debt to someone for a large amount of
money and he told you that today was the last day to pay
or else he would put you in jail? Then suddenly, from out
of nowhere, a man came and said to you, "Do you want to
be free from this debt?" Your response would be, "What
do I have to do?" And His answer was, "Just serve me and
love your neighbor, and don't do anything that you
wouldn't want someone to do to you. Also, remember my
labor is easy and simple."

Would you accept that deal or reject it?

We were in debt because of sin and God came to die for
those sins and set us free. So, He will remember our sins
no more. For Jesus also said, *"Come to me all that labor."*

Do you accept this or reject this? Think about it!

Manuel Lopez, Assistant Pastor
Calvary Chapel of Downey
Downey, California

April 8

THE HEALING TOUCH

"And Joseph said unto them, fear not: for am I in the place of God? But as for you, ye thought evil against me; but God meant it unto good, to bring to pass, as it is this day, to save much people alive. Now therefore fear ye not: I will nourish you, and your little ones. And he comforted them, and spake kindly unto them."
Genesis 50:19-21

Joseph's brothers had burned him -- big time. As a result of selling him into slavery, he ended up innocently spending years in prison during the prime of his life. In Genesis 50, the tables have turned and Joseph is second in command in Egypt. His brothers are at his mercy -- they are certain he will seek revenge for all the pain they have caused him . How does a Godly person respond?

First, Joseph tells them not to be afraid (v. 19). Obviously, he was not about to explode in anger like they thought he would. He realized anger does not help in times of healing. Next, he shared with them how much God has used this circumstance in all their lives (v. 20). Joseph's perception of life's circumstances included the sovereignty of God.

Finally, he demonstrated his forgiveness toward them (v.21). He *". . . provided for them. . . comforted them and spoke kindly to them."* We can tell those that offend us they are forgiven, but true healing comes when we demonstrate this by again *"speaking kindly to them."*

Mike Stangel, Senior Pastor
North Shore Christian Fellowship
Haleiwa, Hawaii

April 9

FOLLOW THE LEADER

"He is not here; for He is risen, as He said.
Come, see the place where the Lord lay."
Matthew 28:6

You can follow a leader only as far as he can lead you. Others claim to know a way, but death was as far as they were able to go. Jesus claimed to be the way, the truth, and the life. To Him, death was only a rest stop.

There is an empty tomb in Jerusalem that bears silent witness to the truth that Jesus is risen from the dead. Other faiths pay homage to their dead prophet or master; only those who follow Jesus Christ worship a risen Lord.

Les Prock, Senior Pastor
Calvary Chapel North Hill
Milton, Washington

April 10

YOU NEED FRIENDS

Does anyone know your troubles, sufferings, hurts, or pains? Does anyone know about the temptations that are driving you crazy? Have you taken the time to open your heart to anyone lately? Are there things happening inside of you that you know you need to share with someone, but are afraid? Perhaps you failed the Lord miserably lately and now you feel this cloud of doom and gloom following you everywhere you go. What keeps us from opening up to someone? What keeps us from disclosing to others those personal, intimate and, at times, very painful areas of our lives to others? May I suggest a few reasons?

Fear of the reactions of others: "What will they think of me? I'm supposed to be a strong Christian."

Fear of losing respect: "People will think I'm strange. They will think I'm a hard-core pornography addict when I am really not that way." Maybe you're in full-time ministry and X-rated magazines and movies really trip up your life.

Fear of being rejected: "I will lose all my friends. They will all abandon me, no one will ever want anything to do with me!"

Is that how you feel? The truth is that some may think badly about you, some may lose respect for you, some may forsake you forever. But the fact is that not all people are like that. Rest assured that there are some brothers and sisters who will completely understand. Check out what the Proverbs says: "A *friend loves at all times, and a brother is born for adversity,*" *(Proverbs 17:17).*

(Continued)

How can you find this kind of friend: *FELLOWSHIP WITH OTHERS CONSTANTLY!* Meditate on these scriptures:

"They devoted themselves to the apostles' teaching and to the fellowship, to the breaking of bread and to prayer."
Acts 2:42

"Do not be yoked together with unbelievers. For what do righteousness and wickedness have in common? Or what fellowship can light have with darkness?
II Corinthians 6:14

"Let us not give up meeting together, as some are in the habit of doing, but let us encourage one another and all the more as you see the Day approaching."
Hebrews 10:25

"See to it, brothers, that none of you has a sinful, unbelieving heart that turns away from the living God. But encourage one another daily, as long as it is called today, so that none of you may be hardened by sin's deceitfulness."
Hebrews 3:12,13

Today, make a decision to meet a new brother or sister in the Lord. Be open and transparent. Stop being a Lone Ranger Christian because if you remain that way long enough, you will eventually become an open target for the enemy. Satan is looking for someone to devour, and some of his easiest targets are those who have isolated themselves from other Christians. Is that you?

Fidel Gomez, Senior Pastor
Calvary Chapel Tamarac
Tamarac, Florida

April 11

OF SINS

"In Him we have redemption through His blood, the forgiveness of sins, according with the riches of His grace."
Ephesians 1:7

Paul is careful to point out in this passage that it was for the forgiveness of "sins" that we were redeemed. Christ did not just pay for sin in one abstract lump sum. He felt the weight of each and every one of them personally. He bore our sins, Isaiah says. He shouldered up each and every one of them and bore the wrath of His Father in Heaven. In the moment when all of the wrath of God was unleashed upon Him, He cried out, *"My God, my God, why have you forsaken Me?" (Psalms 22:1).*

It is clear that the Son had never felt anything like that before in all eternity past. Paul said, *"He made Him who knew no sin to become sin for us, that we might become the righteousness of God," (2 Corinthians 5:21).* God punished Christ as if He were our sins. At that moment, Christ felt the Father treat Him as an enemy, rather than as a beloved Son. We will never have to feel that. Because He was forsaken and punished, we never will be. Every sin has been individually punished by the Father in His beloved Son. Let us be lost in wonder, praise, and love for Him.

Peyton Jones, Assistant Pastor
Calvary Chapel of Huntington Beach
Huntington Beach, California

April 12

HAPPY RESURRECTION MORNING!

That first Easter morning, Mary was left weeping at the empty tomb. She was like many today who have lost hope; their plan has failed, that which they had hoped in is gone, now they find themselves in hopelessness!

Yet the Bible says if we believe that Jesus <u>died</u> and <u>rose again</u> then we will not sorrow as those which have <u>no hope</u>! For if Christ is not raised our faith is in vain, then we of all men are most miserable.

But the Word of God states, "*. . . but now is Christ risen from the dead.*"

His resurrection substantiates His claim that He is God, and it validates His Cross . . . that we are forgiven! But most of all it continues His work of prayer for us, preparing a place for us, and providing power to us through the Holy Spirit.

Thank God He lives! If you will confess Him as Lord and believe God raised Him from the dead, you too can have resurrection hope!

Jeff Johnson, Senior Pastor
Calvary Chapel of Downey
Downey, California

April 13

ASK AND YE SHALL RECEIVE

*"But if any of you lacks wisdom, let him ask of God, who gives
to all men generously and without reproach,
and it will be given to him."*
James 1:5

The task of witnessing and presenting the Gospel can often be humbling. Questions we are not prepared for can stumble us, and the right words to answer with can seem hard to find. What an encouragement it is to know that it is not all up to us. God is reminding us, gently, that He is our source of wisdom. He wants us to turn to Him, and seek His answers and guidance. God knows exactly which words will touch the heart of the person we are ministering to. As we are reminded to seek God as our source of wisdom, we remember that this is exactly what we are asking the person we are sharing with to do.

Matt DeWitt, Assistant Pastor
Calvary Chapel Church Planting Mission
Vista, California

April 14

WISE UP!

"O that thou hadst hearkened to my commandments!
Then had thy peace been as a river, and thy
righteousness as the waves of the sea."
Isaiah 48:18

We as Christians, have the unique advantage of being given the Word of God (the Manufacturer's Handbook) to look to in leading our lives. These insights from God which contain His ways for life, peace, joy, love, and fulfillment are found in His Word. Unfortunately, many spend little time with it, and even less effort in following it. Yet that is not a new problem as Isaiah's words to the nation of Israel reflect here. God's lament over them breaks your heart. Oh, that you had but paid attention to My Word, you could have had such peace, and your life lived rightly before Me! Will God have to lament one day over you? Or will you heed His Word and live?

Jack Abeelen, Senior Pastor
Morningstar Christian Chapel
Whittier, California

April 15

THE INDESTRUCTIBILITY OF THE BIBLE

*"All flesh is like grass, and that's its glory like the flower of
grass. The grass withers and the flower falls off
but the word of the Lord abides forever."*
1 Peter 1:24,25

Throughout the course of history, man has tried to remove the Bible from the face of the earth. For example, the Roman Emperor Diocletian issued an edict to destroy Christians and the Bible. While many manuscripts of the Bible were destroyed, the complete irradication of the Bible was never seen. In fact, 25 years after Diocletian's edict, Constantine commissioned Eusebius to prepare 50 copies of the Bible, which was financed by the government.

Voltaire stated that in 100 years from his time Christianity would be swept from existence and passed into history. Ironically 50 years after the death of Voltaire the Geneva Bible Society used Voltaire's press and house to print Bibles.

I like what Bernard Ramm has to say about the attacks made against the Bible. "A thousand times over, the death knell of the Bible has been sounded, the funeral procession formed, the inscription cut on the tombstone, and committal read. But somehow the corpse never stays put."

Although the Bible will continue to be attacked by man, let's remember *". . . the word of the Lord abides forever."*

Ron Terrall, Assistant Pastor
Calvary Chapel of Downey
Downey, California

April 16

CALLED TO THE COVENANT

*"For the Word of God is living and active and sharper than any
two-edged sword, and piercing as far as the division of soul and
spirit, of both joints and marrow, and able to judge
the thoughts and intentions of the heart."*
Hebrews 4:12

In 2 Kings 22, Josiah was only eight years old when he became a King. One thing that stood out about this young King was that he heard the Word of God and it moved him to get things right before God. He made a covenant to walk after the Lord, to keep His commandments, and to carry out the words of His covenant. What has the Lord called you to do?

Rudy Cardenas, Assistant Pastor
Calvary Chapel Downey
Downey, California

April 17

ARE YOU WITHERED OR WATERED?

"Blessed is the man who walks not in the counsel of the un-
godly, nor stands in the path of sinners, nor sits in the seat of
the scornful; but his delight is in the law of the Lord, and in His
law he meditates day and night. He shall be like a tree planted
by the rivers of water, that brings forth its fruit
in its season, whose leaf also shall not wither;
and whatever he does shall prosper."
Psalm 1:1-3

I have this plant in my office. I have no idea what kind of plant it is. It's small and green with white streaks running through the leaves. My wife got it for me to add a little color and "atmosphere" which my office desperately needed.

I like plants that look nice, but I'm really not into plants. I pay very little attention to the thing. In fact, I can't even see it when I'm at my desk. It sits behind me on a bookshelf. Needless to say, it doesn't get watered very regularly.

Occasionally, though, the plant does catch my eye while I'm searching my shelves for a book. Often, by this time, it is in a rather pathetic state. The leaves are drooping over the side of the pot, their edges have begun to curl and a few have given up the ghost. It reminds me of a sunburned man in tattered clothes crawling on his belly across the Sahara. It is only then that I realize that I haven't watered it since. . .well, I can't remember.

It's not that I'm into plant torture. I just don't think about it very often. This plant is not high on my priority list. And

(Continued)

even though giving the plant a regular watering is a simple task, it just doesn't get done.

I wonder how many of us treat our spiritual life like I do my plant. Are there long periods of drought between the times of watering our soul with the Word of God? It's not that we don't want our relationship with God to thrive; we just don't give it the attention it needs until our spiritual leaves are drooping and curling.

Are you thirsty? Then go to the well of His Word and drink, and drink often.

Todd Lauderdale, Assistant Pastor
Calvary Chapel Murietta
Murietta, California

April 18

LYDIA: A WOMAN WITH AN OPEN HEART

*"And a certain woman named Lydia, a seller of purple, of the
city of Thyatira, which worshipped God, heard us; whose heart
the Lord opened, that she attended unto the things which were
spoken of Paul. And when she was baptized, and her household,
she besought us, saying 'If ye have judged me to be faithful to
the Lord, come into my house, and abide there.'
And she constrained us."*
Acts 16:14,15

Is your heart open before the Lord? If He speaks to you, do
you hear His voice? And then, do you follow His commands? The apostle Paul had such a heart and, because of
his openness, he was given a vision while he was in Troas.

In the dream, a man from Macedonia urgently requested
that Paul *". . . come and help us."* So, following the Lord's
direction, he went to Europe certain that God would do great
things. But when Paul got there, he found that *no one* was
waiting for his help, and that no synagogue even existed.
Surely, this deflated Paul's expectations, but he went ahead
and held church at the riverbank in Philippi anyway. And
that's where God's miracles began.

At this small, insignificant place, God did a mighty work.
He opened a woman's heart. Her name was Lydia and she
came from Thyatira, a city in Asia Minor. She was an entre-
preneur, a seller of purple, engaged in merchandising the
dye for which Thyatira was famous. Lydia was the professional working woman of her time. She was a Gentile, yet

(Continued)

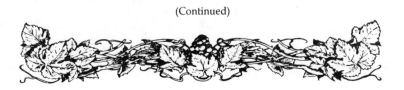

she worshipped God. She was a wealthy woman possessing houses both in Europe and Asia Minor. And yet, she was attentive to those things spoken by Paul *(Acts 16:14)* and, as a result, her heart was convicted and made open before the Lord. Lydia believed the truth, committed her life to Christ, and trusted the promises of God for salvation.

The story of Lydia tells us that there are several things necessary to having an open heart. The *first* is the preaching of the gospel — the hearing of God's Word. The *second* is the grace of God. The Holy Spirit, by the grace of God, softens and convicts us just as He did Lydia. The *third* is to be receptive and attentive. Lydia listened and sought the face of God. And God did not disappoint her.

There are changes in our life after having our hearts opened. In Lydia's life, friendliness was manifested. She opened her heart. She opened her home. She offered hospitality to the disciples. When Paul and Silas were imprisoned, it was Lydia who came and brought them food. And, most importantly, Lydia's whole family was baptized *(Acts 16:31)*. What incredible miracles Lydia experienced, simply because her heart was open before the Lord!

Ask yourself these questions to see how open your own heart is before the Lord:
1. Am I hearing what God is saying to me through His Word? *Am I listening?*
2. When I do hear His words, is the Holy Spirit able to work in my heart? *Am I softening?*
3. With the Lord's words and a softened heart, am I able to minister to others? *Am I available?*

Steve Mays, Senior Pastor
Calvary Chapel of South Bay
Torrance, California

April 19

PERSISTENT PRAYER

"And I say unto you, ask, and it shall be given you; seek, and ye shall find; knock, and it shall be opened unto you."
Luke 11:9

Jesus had been invited to dinner. As the people gathered around the table to eat, a weeping woman came up to Jesus, broke open an incredibly expensive bottle of perfume, and began anointing Jesus with the costly fragrance. Some of the guests at the dinner become indignant when they realized what she was doing. Why, she was throwing away at least $300 worth of perfume on Jesus! We read, when Jesus understood it, he said unto them, *"Why trouble ye the woman? For she hath wrought a good work upon me,"* *(Matthew 26:10).* You see, her act of sacrifice and worship to her Lord was more valuable and precious than they could ever realize.

In 1858, a scientific expedition passed through the Grand Canyon. A young lieutenant made the following entry in his report: "This region we last explored, the Grand Canyon, is, of course, altogether valueless. Ours has been the first, and doubtless will be the last, party of whites to visit this profitless locality. It seems intended that the Colorado River, along the greater portion of its lonely and majestic way, shall be forever unvisited and undisturbed."

Some people just don't understand what's truly beautiful or valuable. Just as many didn't understand the beauty or the value of the woman anointing Jesus with perfume. But don't worry, your Saviour does. Go ahead, pour out your heart and worship Him just as the woman did . . . even when others do not understand.

(Continued)

Jesus had been teaching His disciples how to pray when He told this story: *"Suppose one of you has a friend, and he goes to him at midnight and says, 'Friend, lend me three loaves of bread, because a friend of mine on a journey has come to me, and I have nothing to set before him.' Then the one inside answers, 'Don't bother me. The door is already locked, and my children are with me in bed. I can't get up and give you anything.' I tell you, though he will not get up and give him the bread because he is his friend, yet because of the man's boldness he will get up and give him as much as he needs,"* (Luke 11:5-8).

The word *"boldness"* translated literally means "shameless-ness." The friend was not ashamed to stand, at midnight, pounding on the door, to ask his friend for help. He simply kept at it. That's the point that Jesus was trying to make about prayer. In fact, the following verse could very well be translated *"Keep on asking and it shall be given to you, keep on seeking and you shall find, keep on knocking and it shall be opened unto you,"* (Luke 11:9).

Some would try to tell us that it lacks faith if we ask for something more than once. But it would be worthwhile to notice that even Jesus in the garden of Gethsemane prayed the same thing three times! R.A.Torrey wrote, "God does not always let us get things at our first effort. He would train us and make us strong men by compelling us to work hard for the best things."

The best things may still be ahead, beloved. Keep on ask-ing. Keep on seeking. Keep on knocking.

Rich Cathers, Senior Pastor
Calvary Chapel of Fullerton
Fullerton, California

April 20

READ ANY GOOD CHRISTIANS LATELY?

"You are our epistle written in our hearts,
known and read by all men."
2 Corinthians 3:2

Paul tells the Corinthian believers that they will first need to be "known" then "read." People will watch us before they ask us, "What's different about you?"

You've heard it said concerning your witness, "You may be the only Bible someone may ever read!" But I wonder <u>what part</u> of the Bible people are reading from your life?

Are they reading the <u>index</u> as you point them to the Word, but not live it out yourself? Are you a <u>concordance</u> to them, one who can quote scriptures, but really don't apply what they mean? Maybe they just see <u>maps</u> when they look at your life; you're great at giving others direction?

What we need to be is living epistles, or the love letters themselves, living out daily the precious, action-packed, Word of God.

Brian Bell, Senior Pastor
Calvary Chapel Murrieta
Murrieta, California

April 21

GOING, GOING, GONE

*"For I am the least of the apostles, who am not fit to be called
an apostle, because I persecuted the church of God. But by the
grace of God I am what I am and His grace toward me did not
prove vain; but I labored even more than all of them,
yet not I, but the grace of God with me."*
I Corinthians 15:9,10

It is interesting to note the progression of Paul's view toward his own self-worth. John the Baptist, speaking of Jesus after His baptism, said that Jesus would have to increase, as John would have to decrease. This seems to be the pattern in Christians as they mature in their faith.

Paul places himself at the back of the line of apostles. He acknowledges his persecution of the church, and also sees the grace of God working within himself. His heritage as a Pharisee would work both for and against Paul as he grew in this grace. His deep knowledge of the scriptures, would enable him to win debates and encourage the church. But his debates with the Jews, who Paul desperately wanted to reach, rarely produced new believers. Anyone willing to debate at Paul's level was already pretty convinced of where they stood.

*"To me, the very least of all saints, this grace was given, to
preach to the Gentiles the unfathomable riches of Christ."*
Ephesians 3:8

At this later point in Paul's life, he moves to the back of the line of the Christian church. Grace is still there and perceived more deeply. Paul's mission to the Gentile world —

(Continued)

~ 128 ~

the honor the Lord gave him in pursuit of that mission — is a part of that grace. He refused to place a value upon the grace and mercy that had been given to him by Jesus Christ. As Christ increases, Paul decreases.

"It is a trustworthy statement, deserving full acceptance, that
Christ Jesus came into the world to save sinners,
among whom I am foremost of all."
I Timothy 1:15

Paul now will allow no one at all to be in line for heaven behind himself. He sees his own depravity and utter need of the Savior in every aspect of his life. Still, the grace that Jesus provides saves him. Since he has moved to the back of the line, that grace is afforded to anyone, rich and free.

In a world where performance and position are considered very important, especially in our western society, we clamber to be at the front of the line. While there is nothing wrong with doing your best, the temporal position we grapple for is at odds with the eternal position Paul saw himself in as he grew up in his vocation with Jesus Christ. Never lose sight of who and Whose you are.

"I have been crucified with Christ; and it is no longer I who
live, but Christ who lives in me; and the life which I now live
in the flesh I live by faith in the Son of God, who loved me,
and delivered Himself up for me."
Galatians 2:20

Harry Pressley, Senior Pastor
Calvary Chapel of South New Jersey
Clarksboro, New Jersey

April 22

WHERE ARE WE BUILDING

In Matthew 7:24-27, Jesus describes the wise and the foolish man as to the foundations upon which they built their lives. The storm illustrates life's trials which reveals the foundation upon which we have built our lives. Storms are never fun, but they do give us opportunity to re-assess the foundation of our lives. Each re-assessment is an opportunity to replace sand with rock. We call this process, "experiencing the grace of God."

May we find the grace to rebuild wisely where the storm reveals we have built foolishly.

Dave Sweet, Senior Pastor
Calvary Chapel Paradise
Paradise, California

April 23

GOD'S GOT AN 800 NUMBER

Oh, if there were only someone I could talk to right now. Frantically I go through my phone book and find the number and dial. Instead of a person, I get, *"We're not here right now, please leave your name and number at the tone and we'll get back to you as soon as possible . . . beep . . ."*

Phone machines are a blessing and a curse. Sure, it's great to be able to leave someone a message when they're not home, but it sure would be nice to get in touch when you need to. Don't get me wrong, as a person who receives my share of phone calls, I know that it's nice to not always have to answer the phone. But, with that machine, you're still obligated to call them back. I once knew someone who didn't have a phone machine just so they wouldn't have to call people back. The Psalmist writes, *"I loveth the LORD, because He hath heard my voice and my supplications," (Psalm 116:1).*

Does God have an answer machine? I don't think so. He's always home, and He never gets burned out on too many phone calls. In fact, He enjoys receiving our calls. You don't have to worry about busy signals either when you call Him. He's never too busy for you. And when you call, you can be sure He'll answer because He's always home. It may not be exactly how you expect Him to, but He'll answer.

Billy Graham once said, "Heaven is full of answers to prayers for which no one ever bothered to ask." Phone home, precious one.

Steve Edmondson, Assistant Pastor
Calvary Chapel of Fullerton
Fullerton, California.

April 24

SHAKE THE HAND OF GOD

King Artaxerxes reigned over Persia from 465-425 B.C. In his seventh rule of reign, he commissioned Ezra the priest to return to Jerusalem, granting large privileges to him. This was the same king who, thirteen years later, allowed Nehemiah to rebuild the walls and govern Jerusalem.

Why did the king send this practicular priest? Why not send one of his own men who were politicians in Jerusalem? Well, first of all in *Ezra 7:6* we read, *"... that Ezra was skilled in the law of Moses, ... and the hand of the Lord was upon him."* Apparently he didn't have to be a yes man to the king to be appointed, only a yes man to God. *Ezra 7:10* explains best why he was chosen. *"For Ezra had set his heart to study the law of the Lord, and to practice it, and to each His statutes and ordinances in Israel."*

So what came out of him studying about the things of God, doing the things of God, and teaching the things of God? Besides the king giving Ezra and his men gobs of gold and silver to spend, the king also allowed Ezra to appoint his own government people over the land *(vs. 18, 25)*.

Immediately, Ezra thanked God, who put such a thing upon the king's heart, and for the hand of God upon his life. We need to recognize the hand of God upon our own lives. We need to study His Word, be obedient to His Word, and teach others about God's lovingkindness, and the truth of His coming judgment.

Ken Shaffer, Assistant Pastor
Calvary Chapel of Fullerton
Fullerton, California.

April 25

AGAPE

"Love suffers long and is kind, love does not envy;
love does not parade itself, is not puffed up;
does not behave rudely, does not seek its own,
is not provoked, thinks no evil; does not rejoice in iniquity,
but rejoices in the truth; bears all things,
believes all things, hopes all things,
endures all things. Love never fails."
I Corinthians 13:4-8

Do you really appreciate how much Jesus loves you? In the gospel of John, Jesus says, *"I am the good shepherd. The good shepherd gives His life for the sheep; and I know my sheep, and am known by my own."* We are His sheep, the ones He laid His life down for. Again in John He says, *"Greater love has no one than this, than to lay down his life for his friend."*

Phil O'Malley, Assistant Pastor
Calvary Chapel of Downey
Downey, California

April 26

"WHY SETTLE FOR SECONDS?"

Colossians 2:8

"Beware lest any man spoil (enslave) *you through philosophy* (human wisdom) *and vain deceit* (evolution), *after the tradition of men* (laws and words), *after the rudiments of the world* (fundamental principles, i.e., science), *and not after Christ. For in Him* (Jesus) *dwelleth* <u>*all the fullness*</u> *of the Godhead bodily."*

2 Peter 1:3:

"His divine power hath <u>*given unto us all things*</u> *that* (pertain) *unto life and godliness, through the knowledge of him that hath called us to glory and virtue."*

Jesus wants to be our all in all! Insist on the real thing! No substitutes, please!

Ed Cornwell, Senior Pastor
Calvary Chapel Costa Mesa
Santa Ana, California

April 27

IT'S ALL ABOUT LOVE

*"Teacher, which is the great commandment in the law? Jesus
said to him, 'You shall love the Lord your God with all your
heart, with all your soul, and with all your mind. This is the
first and great commandment. And the second is like it;
You shall love your neighbor as yourself. On these two
commandments hang all the Law and the prophets.'"*
Matthew 22:36-40

It's amazing the things we think Christianity is all about.
What we know, how we pray, what we give, what church
we attend, what others think of us, and on and on.

But, Jesus says it's all about loving God and loving people.
These are the two inseparable measurements of Christ-like-
ness in our daily lives.

So let's remember these words of Jesus today, and measure
ourselves not by outward things, but by our love for God
and others.

Jeff Stewart, Senior Pastor
Calvary Chapel Pomona Valley
Pomona, California

April 28

HOW MANY JORDANS HAVE YOU CROSSED?

*"Now it came about when all the nations had finished crossing
the Jordan, that the Lord spoke to Joshua, saying, 'Take for
yourselves twelve men from the people, one man from each tribe,
and command them, saying, ''Take up for yourselves twelve
stones from here out of the middle of the Jordan, from the place
where the priests' feet are standing firm, and carry them over
with you, and lay them down in the lodging place where you
will lodge tonight.'' So Joshua called the twelve men whom he
had appointed from the sons of Israel, one man from each tribe;
and Joshua said to them, 'Cross again to the ark of the Lord your
God into the middle of the Jordan, and each of you take up a
stone on his shoulder, according to the number of the tribes of
the sons of Israel. Let this be a sign among you, so that when
your children ask later, saying, ''What do these stones mean to
you?'' 'then you shall say to them, ''Because the waters of the
Jordan were cut off before the ark of the covenant of the Lord;
when it crossed the Jordan, the waters of the Jordan were cut
off.'' So these stones shall become a memorial
to the sons of Israel forever.'"*
Joshua 4:1-7

Memorial stones. When I was younger, I thought memorial
stones were grave markers. Now I have them all over my
office. I have a stone that my wife and I found that reminds
us of the time the doctors told us we would never have children. We have four children now! I have another stone that
signifies my salvation. What memorial stones do you have
for the Jordans you've crossed?

Bill Richard, Senior Pastor
Calvary Chapel Encinitas
Encinitas, California

April 29

CALL UPON ME

"Then you will call upon me and go and pray to me, and I will listen to you. And you will seek me, and find me, when you search for me with all your heart. I will be found by you, says the Lord, and I will bring you back from your captivity."
Jeremiah 29:12-14

How many days have I been taken captive? How many times, have I have listened to the lies of the enemy? I have wanted to do as Jonah, flee from God, hide in my sin, to return never more. I have cried out and said, "But who will listen to me?" And that still small voice reminds me, "Rick, I will. Call upon me, pray to me, I will listen to you. Don't worry, in your times of seeking I can be found as long as your heart is really turned towards me. You will find me - - and the captivity you ran to, I will release you from."

Rick Phelps, Senior Pastor
Calvary Chapel Lakewood
Lakewood, California

April 30

A TIME TO REFLECT

*"So I was great, and increased more than all that were before
me in Jerusalem: also my wisdom remained with me. And
whatsoever mine eyes desired, I kept not from them, I withheld
not my heart from any joy; for my heart rejoiced in all my
labour: and this was my portion of all my labour. Then I looked
on all the works that my hands had wrought, and on the labour
that I had laboured to do: and, behold, all [was] vanity and
vexation of spirit, and [there was] no profit under the sun."*
Ecclesiastes 2:9-11

How many of us reflect on our lives, and make New Years
resolutions and promises that have already been broken by
now? We can learn from Solomon what conclusion he came
to after reflecting upon his own life. Solomon covered his
entire life in three verses.

When Solomon was young, he fulfilled his desires. As he
matured he wrote Proverbs, and then finally, he evaluates
his life and sees what he accomplished with his own hands,
and realizes that there really is no profit under the sun.

How many of us start out fulfilling all of our youthful desires, then as maturing comes about, we grow up and re-
evaluate our lives? The same is true of our spiritual lives.
It's time to quit evaluating our youthful desires, and evaluate what we have done for the Lord. And then we need to
ask ourselves, "Has it been profitable?"

Mark Maciel, Assistant Pastor
Calvary Chapel of Downey
Downey, California

May 1

CONSEQUENCES

A little five-year-old was watching his father discipline his older brother. After a thorough lecture, the dad reminded his older son that he would now have to live with the consequences of his actions. A few minutes later, little Larry spoke with his dad and made a special request. "Dad, if David has to go live with the consequences, can I have his room?"

Too often today we hear that people are not responsible, nor should they face the consequences of their actions. But God's justice requires judgment for sin!

The consequence of our actions sent Jesus to the Cross in our place.

"For He hath made Him to be sin for us, who knew no sin; that we might be made the righteousness of God in Him."
2 Corinthians 5:21

What are the consequences of His action?

"The righteousness of God which is by faith of Jesus Christ unto all and upon all them that believe."
Romans 3:22

Neil Matranga, Assistant Pastor
Calvary Chapel of Downey
Downey, California

May 2

NOT BY SELF RIGHTEOUSNESS

*"Do not think in your heart, after the LORD your God has cast
them out before you, saying, 'Because of my righteousness the
LORD has brought me in to possess this land;' but it is because
of the wickedness of these nations that the LORD is driving
them out from before you. It is not because of your righteousness or the uprightness of your heart that you go in to possess
their land, but because of the wickedness of these nations that
the LORD swore to your fathers, to Abraham, Isaac, and Jacob.
Therefore understand that the LORD your God is not giving
you this good land to possess because of your righteousness, for
you are a stiff-necked people."*
Deuteronomy 9:4-9

For Israel, about to go into the Promised Land, there was a
looming spiritual danger ahead. After they were inside the
land and living a blessed life they come into the danger of
feeling morally better than the other nations. They began
to think they deserved every good thing they had from God
because of their own righteousness. So Moses warned them
of the temptation toward spiritual pride in advance, and
reminded them that they were really kept by God's grace
alone. How important it is for us Christians, to remember
our own lack of self-righteousness.

Remember, pride was the underlying sin in the garden, and
in Satan's fall. It seems the closer we are to God, the easier
it is to fall into this sin. These stories remind us that we
lack any personal righteousness apart from Jesus.

Ed Rea, Senior Pastor
Calvary Chapel Redlands
Redlands, California

May 3

THE FOUNTAIN THAT NEVER RUNS DRY

*"For my people have committed two evils; they have forsaken
me the fountain of living waters, [and] hewed them out
cisterns, broken cisterns, that can hold no water."*
Jeremiah 2:13

So often we are guilty of factoring Christ as <u>part</u> of our life
when, in reality, He <u>is</u> our life. In *John 15:5*, our Lord told
us, *". . . for without Me ye can do nothing."* It is imperative
that we as Christians keep our eyes on the Lord. *"I will guide
them with mine eye," (Psalm 32:8b).* We have a natural incli-
nation to cling to the illusion of control. We desire to be
recognized and appreciated on our own merit. When we
insist on calling the shots, we are not allowing the Lord, to
be <u>our</u> Lord. Often we will find ourselves laboring in vain.

A cistern represents a lot of work. They would have to hew
out basins in the rock and carve channels to direct the water. Often the cisterns would leak, or the water that remained
became stagnant. That is the nature of religion, they neither sustain true life, nor hold water.

God's fountain of living water is still available to us today.
He offers us His Spirit to enable us, equip us, lead us, and
refresh us. It is His very presence with which He inhabits
His people. In Him we can draw from the wellspring of
life-purpose and fulfillment as He receives the glory. Don't
let this day go by you without taking the time to be filled by
His life-giving Spirit.

Don Roach, Senior Pastor
Calvary Chapel of Western
Western, Massachusetts

May 4

COINCIDENCE OR GOD INCIDENCE?

Esther 6:1-10

I hate it when I can't sleep. But maybe, just maybe, God wakes us up for a reason. The same thing happened to King Maseuerus. *"During that night,"* the 11th hour, God steps in. So what does a king do when he can't sleep? He had plenty of choices, but he chooses a book to read. Not just any book, but the Chronicles. No doubt he was hoping to fall back to sleep, but God directed the servant to select the right book, at the right time, and read from the exact page God wanted him to -- the records from five years prior -- to accomplish His will.

Haman was up early the next morning to get permission to hang Mordecai. He thinks his plan is perfect *(Psalm 64:6)*. But before he can say anything, the king asks, *"What is to be done for the man whom the king desires to honor?"* Haman, in his pride, assumes it must be him. Who else?

But when the king orders <u>Mordecai</u> honored (vs. 10), it hits Haman like a ton of bricks. Was it a twist of fate, or a set-up by the King of Kings? Although God's name is no where to be found in the book of Esther, His hand is plainly seen. He is behind the scenes, but he moves the scenes He is behind. There are no accidents or coincidences. So the next time you have a flat tire, get locked out, your rent goes up, something breaks, or you get laid off, remember -- God is there, and He is working perfectly in every situation.

Jeff Johnson, Senior Pastor
Calvary Chapel Mountain Shores
Carpinteria, California

May 5

KEEP IT SIMPLE

*"And they continued steadfastly in the apostle's doctrine and
fellowship, in the breaking of bread, and in prayers."*
Acts 2:42

The Christian life is not complicated, although it is chal-
lenging! I believe God wants it to be simple, not complex
and difficult. In fact, in *2 Corinthians 11:3*, He warned us to
be careful not to be led astray from the simplicity in Christ.
I believe that here in *Acts 2:42*, He gives us a very simple
outline of what practical things we as Christians are to be
continually and consistently doing.

The Bible: "The Apostles Doctrine"
In the Bible God has given us "... *everything we need for life
and godliness," (2 Peter 1:3)*, so that we can be complete and
equipped for serving Him *(2 Timothy 3:16)*. God's Word
should play a major role in personal study and meditation,
as well as in group studies.

Fellowship:
God so designed us as believers that we are a part of one
another *(1 Corinthians 12)*. We need each other in order to
really live and serve God. None of us can make it alone, we
need other believers. This is more than just sitting in church
though, it means we need to develop these relationships.

Dependence: "Breaking of Bread"
This refers to communion, which we should actively par-
ticipate in as often as possible, but in many ways, you can
make every meal communion. Taking the Lord's supper
means that we recognize that Jesus died for us, and with-

(Continued)

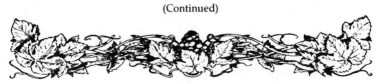

out that, we would have no hope. This should be an attitude of our heart every day, and meal time is a great time to remember it.

<u>Prayers:</u>
Prayer is our communication to God. I like that this scripture reads "prayers" and not "prayer." For prayer is not a duty that you do once a day and get it over with, it is to be a continual relationship. It is to realize that God is your best friend, and you can talk to Him all the time. Trusting details into His hands, and enjoying His fellowship.

Hold to these simple, uncomplicated, truths, and as you make them regular habits as a part of your life, you will soar as a Christian!

Jim Suttle, Senior Pastor
Calvary Chapel of Roswell
Roswell, New Mexico

May 6

SEE-THROUGH WINDOW

"Follow my example, as I follow the example of Christ."
I Corinthians 11:1

Wow! What an awesome responsibility to tell someone who might not know alot about Christ, to follow you until they can follow Christ on their own. We would have to be pretty sure of our own relationship with Him, first.

To disciple someone like this, our lives must first be like windows. You know, something someone can look right through. That way, whoever we ask to follow us as we follow Christ, will be able to look right through us and just see Jesus Christ, not us.

However, we sometimes pull the shades down when its not convenient or too hard to walk the walk. To truly be a discipler, our windows shouldn't have any fancy shades or trappings that would distract or prevent others from looking through. We have to live like display windows. The kind that only show Jesus, what He has done and is continuing to do in our lives. A display window has only one purpose: To display what's inside, not to bring attention to the glass.

Chick Chikeles, Senior Pastor
Calvary Chapel Saint Paul
Saint Paul, Minnesota

May 7

THE GREATER THING

"For I determined not to know anything among you except Jesus Christ and Him crucified."
I Corinthians 2:2

Paul could never write or speak without somehow turning back to the Cross. Paul was a man who defined himself by the Cross. *"I have been crucified with Christ, it is no longer I who live, but Christ lives in me," (Galatians 2:20).* In Charles Dickens' classic work "Tale of Two Cities," he tells of a man who gives his life for another by trading places with a prisoner and stepping up to the guillotine for him. On the platform awaiting death, the man says, "It is a far greater thing I do now, than I have ever done." This is what our Lord did for us by substituting Himself for us on the Cross.

Christ could say the same thing as the character in the book. Of all of the things that Christ has done, we believe that the Cross was the greatest work of God in all eternity; the greatest thing He ever did. Paul seemed to think so. He could have spent so much time speaking of the wonders of creation, or the miracles and acts of kindness and compassion that our Lord performed. And yet, Paul spoke of the Cross more highly and more often than anything else. It was his "best thought." May it be ours also. May nothing so enamor us as what our Savior did for us that day.

Peyton Jones, Assistant Pastor
Calvary Chapel of Huntington Beach
Huntington Beach, California

May 8

A BRIDE IN ARMOR

We, as Christians, are married to Jesus Christ and, as His bride, we are to live as chaste virgins.

As we study the armor of God, it's evident that there is a battle that we are engaged in. Our adversary, the devil, is actively at work trying to get us to break our vows of marriage to Christ, and revert back to living after the world and its values. Thank God that He has provided protection for us. The armor of the past is replaced by the armor of light, which is also the armor of righteousness.

For us to effectively stand for the Lord, we must be clothed with the complete armor of God. Saints, we are more than adequately equipped for both the defensive and offensive aspects of spiritual warfare. We can always be victorious in Christ.

Oh, how wonderful it is to know that Jesus, like any good husband, is watching out for his bride with holy jealousy. As we flee and fight, keeping our wedding garments clean, the hurting world around us will "see the light" and glorify Our Master Husband, Jesus.

Ray Viola, Senior Pastor
Koinonia Fellowship
East Rochester, New York

May 9

MASTER OF BREAKTHROUGHS

*"So they went up to Baal Perazim, and David defeated them
there. Then David said, 'God has broken through my enemies
by my hand like a breakthrough of water.' Therefore they
called the name of that place Baal Perazim."*
I Chronicles 14:11

David was met with a difficult situation. The Philistines
decided to go against him in battle when David became
king over Israel. Rather than taking matters into his own
hands, David sought the Lord's counsel. The Lord gave
David the victory over his enemy, and David called the place
of that victory, *"Baal Perazim,"* which means, "Master of
Breaks."

Throughout scripture, God is constantly proving Himself
to be the master of breakthroughs as He breaks through
impossible situations on behalf of His people. At the Red
Sea, at Jericho, in the fiery furnace, in the lion's den, and
elsewhere, God makes impossible situations possible.

Our God is a God of the impossible and there is nothing
too difficult for Him. When difficult situations arise in our
lives, we must seek and obey Him so that He may accomplish the breakthroughs He desires to do in the circumstances we face.

Ernest Finklea, Senior Pastor
Calvary Chapel of Durango
Durango, Colorado

May 10

HIS PROMISE STILL STANDS

"We know that God causes all things to work together for good to those who love God, to those who are called according to His purpose."
Romans 8:28

When the call came at 4:00 a.m., my wife and I instinctively knew the news wasn't good. All the nurse said was to hurry. Twenty minutes later we were at the bedside of our second son Jacob as the doctors and nurses worked to try to resuscitate his heart. After giving their best effort, the doctor gently told us that our son would die. There is no way to describe the pain and grief. I had felt as though someone had taken a shotgun and blown a large hole in my chest.

Over the next several months, as I reflected on why God allowed the death of our son, the Lord's gentle voice would interrupt my thoughts asking, "Wes, do you trust Me?" My answer was always, "Of course Lord, I trust you. But why?" Then I began to understand what the Lord was trying to teach me. Because we live in a fallen world, we will see and experience things we may not understand. But, God's promise that "*. . . all things work together for good,*" still stands. He has used this experience not only to truly deepen our faith, and trust in Him, but He also has given us the ability to minister to the brokenhearted more effectively.

What do you face today that may seem troubling? Look to how God will work all things in your life for your greater good and for His purpose.

Wes Denham, Senior Pastor
Calvary Chapel of Troy
Troy, Missouri

May 11

HAPPY MOTHER'S DAY!

The Lord knew exactly what He was doing when He created mothers. There's nothing like a mother's love. It's warm, peaceful, loving, caring, grateful, and unconditional.

I remember as I was growing up, that a kiss from mom always assured me of her love, and a hug always meant that things would be all right.

"She looketh well to the ways of her household, and eateth not the bread of idleness. Her children arise up, and call her blessed; her husband also, and he praiseth her. Many daughters have done virtuously, but thou excellest them all."
Proverbs 31:27-29

Moms, God bless you!

Mark Maciel, Assistant Pastor
Calvary Chapel of Downey
Downey, California

May 12

A MOTHER'S OVERWHELMING JOB

*"See, I have set before thee this day life and good, and death
and evil. . .I call heaven and earth to record this day against
you, that I have set before you life and death, blessing
and cursing; therefore choose life, that both
thou and thy seed may live."*
Deuteronomy 30:15,19

As we raise our children in the ways of the Lord, we do our
best to teach them to be "good." We teach them principles
from God's Word, we draw boundaries, we make rules, and
we shelter them from as much evil as we can. Yet, a child is
not truly good until he has the opportunity to do evil and
resists it. It was the same for Adam and Eve. They were
merely neutral until God gave them the opportunity to be
good by resisting temptation and obeying God. They failed
miserably! God continues to give us these opportunities
every day -- the opportunity to be good. Many times we
fail. But oh, how blessed it is when we learn the lessons of
obedience and reap the rewards of resisting temptation.

It is a wise parent who knows where to draw the line between sheltering their children and letting them loose to
choose. They will never truly be good until they have the
opportunity to sin and refuse it. "Lord, give us wisdom in
setting limits and allowing freedoms in raising our children
to be good! Father, teach us to appropriately change the
boundaries as our children grow into each stage and age.

Mike Sasso, Assistant Pastor
Calvary Chapel of Downey
Downey, California

May 13

HOW DOES A WISE MAN WALK?

"Therefore be careful how you walk, not as unwise men, but as wise, making the most of your time, because the days are evil. So then do not be foolish, but understand what the will of the Lord is. And do not get drunk with wine, for that is dissipation, but be filled with the Spirit, speaking to one another in psalms and hymns and spiritual songs, singing and making melody with your heart to the Lord; always giving thanks for all things in the name of our Lord Jesus Christ to God, even the Father; and be subject to one another in the fear of Christ."
Ephesians 5:15-21

Am I careful how I am walking? In other words, do I care what others see? Do I walk the talk, or just talk the walk? If you're like me, you know you're not comfortable with your answer. Today can be different. First, you have to know that every moment has the potential for good or evil to be done. If you want to be foolish, don't realize this truth. Do your will instead of God's. Paul goes on and talks about being controlled by alcohol. Is that the main focus of his message? No! He is saying that if we are wise, we should be controlled by the Holy Spirit. When we are, we find that our heart is filled with a song and we are thankful for all things, even the things that are not good. We will also be subject to, or submitted to, one another knowing God is watching how we get along with others. Being controlled by the Spirit means we have chosen not to be controlled by the flesh -- read Galatians, chapter 5. Today you can have a great day. It's your call!

Bill Richard, Senior Pastor
Calvary Chapel Encinitas
Encinitas, California

May 14

ALTARS IN OUR HEARTS

"And the Lord appeared to Abram and said, 'To your descen-
dants I will give this land.' So he built an altar there to the
Lord who had appeared to him. Then he proceeded from there to
the mountain on the east of Bethel, and pitched his tent, with
Bethel on the west and Ai on the east; and there he built an altar
to the Lord and called upon the name of the Lord."
Genesis 12:7,8

We desire to try to forget the mistakes that we have made.
We don't want to allow the enemy to use our past to cause
us to suffer condemnation. That is not what any of us need,
nor is it what the Lord wants for our lives.

Past mistakes can teach us many things if we let them. Until
the prophet Nathan confronts David about his sin of adultery with Uriah's wife, Bathsheba, David was continuing to
act and live as if nothing had happened, even though his
relationship with the Lord had faded. In Psalm 31, David
had become a reproach to even his friends. He was certainly broken before the Lord on that day. Fortunately, that
was not the end of King David because he repented and
gave his heart back to God. *Psalm 32:5* says that David confessed his sin to God, and the Lord forgave him.

The Lord used David's own weaknesses and failures to teach
this king how to depend on God, and not on his own
strengths and abilities. He would never forget the mercies
of God in his life. In *Acts 13:22* it is recorded that David had
". . . a heart after God." Isn't that incredible?

God is so faithful to work in us even when we have drifted

(Continued)

far from Him. David built an altar in his heart to worship God for His faithfulness to him even when he was not faithful to God.

Why don't you take a look back at how faithful God has been to you. Remember how He has carried you through those difficult times, and brought you back into fellowship with Him. The Lord has used those times to teach you valuable lessons that you probably would have never learned any other way. Let these lessons be as altars in your heart that you can return to and remember God's faithfulness.

"And such confidence we have through Christ toward God. Not that we are adequate in ourselves to consider anything as coming from ourselves, but our adequacy is from God."
II Corinthians 3:4,5

Mike Morris, Senior Pastor
Calvary Chapel of the High Desert
Hesperia, California

May 15

A TRUE HERO

"Are they ministers of Christ! I speak as a fool -- I am more: in labors more abundant, in stripes above measure, in prisons more frequently, in deaths often. From the Jews five times I received forty stripes minus one. Three times I was beaten with rods; once I was stoned; three times I was shipwrecked; a night and a day I have been in the deep; in journeys often, in perils of waters, in perils of robbers, in perils of my own countrymen, in perils of the Gentiles, in perils in the city, in perils in the wilderness, in perils in the sea, in perils among false brethren; in weariness and toil, in sleeplessness often, in hunger and thirst, in fastings often, in cold and nakedness."
2 Corinthians 11:23-27

All through our life, we look up to various heroes. The Presidents, Vietnam Veterans, Policemen . . . the list goes on. But one of the truest heroes we will ever find is in the Word of God. He was the Apostle Paul. Paul went through all this for the name *of* Christ. Paul was a "True Hero."

Louie Cruzado, Assistant Pastor
Calvary Chapel of Downey
Downey, California

May 16

THE CALL TO RUN AND FINISH WELL

*"But none of these things move me, neither count I my life dear
unto myself, so that I might finish my course with joy, and
the ministry, which I have received of the Lord Jesus, to
testify the gospel of the grace of God."*
Acts 20:24

It seems all of us are participating in the race. We run from
one thing to another. Everything becomes of vital importance to us. Are we ready for the finish to come? We need
a strong finish.

What moves you? What makes you change your course?
Is there anything you place before God? Do you believe
there is anything too hard for God to do?

*"I will cry to God most high; unto God that
performeth all things for me."*
Psalm 57:2

*"Behold, I am the Lord, the God of all flesh:
is there any thing too difficult for Me?"*
Jeremiah 32:27

That answers my questions, how about yours?

Glenn Kravig, Assistant Pastor
Calvary Chapel of Downey
Downey, California

May 17

GOLDEN OPPORTUNITY

"Therefore, as the Holy Spirit says:
'Today, if you will hear His voice.'"
Hebrews 3:7

Many times we make the mistake of thinking that God's will for our life lies in our tomorrows. The absurdity of this assumption is exposed in God's eternal existence. God is not bound to yesterday, today, and tomorrow. Everyday we are preparing our eternal destiny by the choices we make. Our future is determined by our present.

Because God sees the whole picture from beginning to end, it is imperative that we listen to His voice TODAY. This, of course, takes relationship, communication, and time alone with God. It is for this very reason that God purposely did not give the Israelites more manna than one day's supply. As humans, our tendency is to become self-reliant. If God makes that impossible, He can guard us from losing perspective. Christ said that we could do nothing outside of Him. How sad that so many settle for a life of nothing, when we can take hold of a God-breathed, abundant life.

When our time here is over, we will view our lives through the eyes of God. For some of us, that is a terrifying prospect. No longer will our own agendas seem so demanding, but the bottom line then will be what was important to God.

Don't get caught in the trap of the "I'll wait until tomorrow" trip. Today is the day to hear God's voice.

Bob Coy, Senior Pastor
Calvary Chapel, Ft. Lauderdale
Ft. Lauderdale, Florida

May 18

TRUE WORSHIPPERS

"But the hour is coming, and now is, when the true worshippers will worship the Father in spirit and in truth; for the Father is seeking such to worship Him. God is Spirit, and those who worship Him must worship in spirit and truth."
John 4:23,24

"These people draw near to Me with their mouth, and honor Me with their lips, but their heart is far from Me."
Matthew 15:8

Jesus told us that the Father seeks those who will worship Him in spirit and in truth, for such people are the *"true worshippers"* of God.

If there is a true worshipper, then there must be a false one, a phony. Jesus does not mean being loud and emotional in worship versus being quiet and reserved. The phony worshipper draws near to God with his lips, but his heart is far away. The true worshipper has his heart, mind, and emotions continually submitted to God's scrutiny because his delight is in the Lord. When he worships God, it's not a duty, but a privilege. A day does not go by that he is not consciously communing with his beloved Lord by prayer, meditation, or song.

How about you? Are you a true worshipper?

Bill Stonebraker, Senior Pastor
Calvary Chapel of Honolulu
Honolulu, Hawaii

FELLOWSHIP WITH THE SAINTS

The Greek word Koinonia contains within it the meaning, "fellowship or sharing." One of the most vital elements of Christian development is when the saints meet together. Of course, we gather in our larger corporate settings for worship and study of scriptures, but it doesn't end there!

Scripture tells us that we are to be a people given to hospitality. The word means, "to receive as a guest." It is translated in the RSV, *"entertained"* there in *Acts 28:7*. These smaller settings are the times when we really get to know our brothers and sisters. We get encouraged to hear how they came to Christ. We get blessed to hear how He is working in their lives. And, yes, we also find that many of them are carrying a load that is just too much to bear. This often develops into a heart-to-heart time of sharing and praying.

As the Lord continues to add to the local church, it cannot be stressed enough how important it is for every one of us to "lock-in" to those home study/fellowship times. Relationships develop there. Prayer partners are birthed. And needs of the saints are often met as those needs are made known.

The Apostle Peter writes that we should all be part of this hospitality ministry. Don't let your shyness rob you of this blessed fellowship. Don't allow a bad experience in the past to deprive you of a blessing in the present. The church was created to have fellowship with God, and with one another. I've noticed that when a person reaches out for fellowship that it is there, but the recluse or "why doesn't anyone call me or invite me over" attitude often turns to

(Continued)

bitterness and hurt.

Face it, we are all very busy. Certainly we all cannot get to know each other as deeply as we would like; but each one of us can reach out. We can extend that invitation to dinner to a lonely saint. We can drop a line of encouragement. We can suggest brunch after service to that "stranger" that we've worshipped with for some time. Hey, we can even open up our home for another "meal in the Lord."

We are a body. We need each other. Get off the bench. Get involved. Communicate, don't amputate. Do it!

Ray Viola, Senior Pastor
Koinonia Fellowship
East Rochester, New York

May 20

GREATER WORKS THAN JESUS?

"Most assuredly, I say to you, he who believes in Me, the works
that I do he will do also; and greater works than these
he will do, because I go to My Father."
John 14:12

"That's funny, Lord! Let me get this straight -- are you saying that I'll do even greater things than You did?" Yeah, that's
what He *said*, but what did He *mean*? I don't know about
you, but I've yet to give sight to the blind, and hearing to
the deaf!

Hey, but wait a minute! It's certainly a miracle to open blind
eyes, but it's a *greater work* to open a blind soul -- and we
can do that *through* Christ by leading that person *to* Christ.
And it's certainly a miracle to raise someone from the dead,
but it's a *greater work* to bring *eternal* life to someone who is
dead in trespasses and sins.

Jesus has commissioned us to do the *greater work* of intro-
ducing people to eternal life. How about you today? Have
you done any "greater works" lately?

Mark Scott, Senior Pastor
Calvary Chapel of College Park
College Park, Maryland

May 21

THE OVERCOMERS

*"If your enemy is hungry, give him bread to eat; and if he is
thirsty, give him water to drink; <u>for so you will heap coals
of fire on his head, and the Lord will reward you.</u>"*
Proverbs 25:21,22

This is not suggesting that we burn those who burn us. It is
not at all telling us to go by our feelings when we have been
wronged by an enemy. It is promising us that we can be
blessed by God if we properly respond to the blasting of
man.

The Apostle Paul comments on this very Proverb in *Romans
12:17-21.* It refers to our attitude during those times we are
tested. We are to have a Christ-like character. We are not to
seek vengeance, but to seek an opportunity to minister to
the needs of even our enemies, in hopes that God would
use it to soften their hearts.

"Do not be overcome by evil, but overcome evil with good."
Romans 12:21

Mike Stangel, Senior Pastor
North Shore Christian Fellowship
Haleiwa, Hawaii

May 22

AIM FOR PERFECTION

"Finally brothers, good-bye. Aim for perfection."
2 Corinthians 13:11

"Aim for perfection." The last words of any man will stand to be his most important words.

The word perfection is "katartizo" in the Greek. This same verb is found in the gospels of Matthew and Mark where Jesus called James and John as they were at the Sea of Galilee mending their nets. Fisherman wouldn't cast their nets unless they had been mended, or perfected. They were aiming for perfection. I take note of that because a few times in scripture, Jesus had instructed His disciples to drop their nets, and they pulled in nets full of fish. Now, if any of those nets had not been mended, they would have missed out on what Jesus had purposed for them.

As Christians, we know we can't be perfect, we've already missed the mark. Christians are like nets -- we come unravelled, we tear, and we come unglued. Therefore, I know there is a need to "aim for pefection," despite my imperfection, because I don't know when the Lord may tell me to drop my net. Just as a wise fisherman is prepared and always has his nets mended, how much more should I, as a child of Christ, aim for perfection by making sure my own nets are in good repair? Don't we all want to be ready to haul in a full load of the Lord's blessings?

Kent Nottingham, Senior Pastor
Calvary Chapel Tallahassee
Tallahassee, Florida

May 23

OUR NEVER FAILING, NEVER CHANGING GOD

"For I am the LORD, I change not."
Malachi 3:6

It is estimated that children laugh an average of 400 times a day. Adults laugh an average of 15 times a day. What is the change in our lives that robs us of the joy we experienced as children? Perhaps it is change itself. Each change brings its own set of choices that must be sifted through; choices that lead to decisions both large and small. The increase in the number of choices and decisions further complicates our lives. We live in an ever-changing world with ever-increasing lists of things to choose from.

With all of the change in our lives, how can we relate to a God who never changes? Perhaps this is where seeing our lives through the eyes of a child might make all the difference. We are not called to relate to God on the basis of our ever-changing world, we are called to relate to the world from the standpoint of God's unchanging Word. A simple reliance upon God and the promises of His Word uncomplicates our lives as we discover the choices that need not be made -- choices which seem so important now, but which matter little in view of eternity. Align your decisions according to the authority of His Word even as a child obeys their earthly father. He will never fail you.

Jeff James, Assistant Pastor
Calvary Chapel Tallahassee
Tallahassee, Florida

May 24

WHICH WAY ARE YOU MOVING?

"And indeed you do so toward all the brethren who are in all
Macedonia. But we urge you, brethren,
that you increase more and more."
1 Thessalonians 4:10

Paul was admonishing the Thessalonians not to be complacent in their love for each other, although it was very commendable.

The Christian walk is dynamic. It is either moving forward or sliding backward. If you are not increasing in the things of Christ, you are losing. As with our human bodies, atrophy lessens the unused muscles. So, too, as in the body of Christ, unexpressed love fades.

Les Prock, Senior Pastor
Calvary Chapel North Hill
Milton Washington

May 25

THERE'S NO PLACE LIKE HOME

*"And they continued steadfastly in the apostle's doctrine
and fellowship, in the breaking of bread, and in prayers."*
Acts 2:42

The early church experienced phenomenal growth. In the
first outreach, organized by the Holy Spirit Himself, the
believers gathered for prayer in an upper room. Three thousand people came to the Lord! Now <u>that's</u> church growth!

The question arises, "How do you minister to that many
people?" They didn't have an infrastructure set up with
pastors and programs. They didn't have others to call and
ask for their input on how it was done previously. They
had to go to the Lord and seek Him for direction.

In the verse quoted above, we see what God had them doing to grow in the knowledge and grace of the Lord Jesus
Christ: (1) they were in the word of God (the apostles' doctrine); (2) they were in fellowship with the believers; (3) they
were participating in the breaking of bread another fellowship issue, but commonly appreciated with partaking in the
communion celebration); and (4) they were in prayer.

God is not interested in numerical growth alone. As the
Lord continues to bless our fellowship with more and more
people week after week. He does not want us to stay babes,
but for us to continue to greater maturity. The four items
mentioned above are necessary for us to continue to do in
order to allow us to minister more effectively to others.

One of the best ways for us to do this is by participating in

(Continued)

the home fellowships. The issue of ONE BODY highlights our home fellowships and what God is doing there.

Luke tells us later in Acts 2 that the believers met both publicly and privately in the large group setting and the small group setting: *"So continuing daily with one accord in the temple, and breaking bread from house to house. They ate their food with gladness and simplicity of heart, praising God and having favor with all the people. And the Lord added to the church daily those who were being saved,"* (Acts 2:46-57).

Paul emphasizes this as well: *". . . I kept back nothing that was helpful, but proclaimed it to you, and taught you publicly and from house to house,"* (Acts 20:20).

Home fellowships are a wonderful way to meet people and develop relationships in the Body of Christ. They facilitate time in the Word, prayer, communion, and fellowship. Some of my times of greatest personal growth and ministry have come in the home fellowship environment, and I strongly encourage your involvement with them.

Brian Michaels, Senior Pastor
Rocky Mountain Calvary Chapel
Colorado Springs, Colorado

May 26

ANXIOUS -- NOTHING'S HAPPENING

"Something has to happen soon," we say. "Nothing ever seems to change. The same routine every day!" It's like the man who had his ear pressed up against the wall. His friend came along and said, "What in the world are you doing?" The response was, "Shh, come here and listen." The friend leaned over, listened intently, then said, "I don't hear anything, it's dead silent!" "I know," said the man, "It's been like that for a long time."

And so seems our relationship with the Lord sometimes -- dead silent. But we aren't alone. We read that Job, too, experienced God's silence:

"If I go to the east, He is not there; if I go to the west, I do not find Him. When He is at work in the north, I do not see Him; when He turns to the south, I catch no glimpse of Him."
Job 23:8,9

Does it seem as if God is listening and speaking to the whole world except you? Do you ask yourself, "Why would He do this to me? Is He angry at me?" Do you begin to wonder whether God really loves you or not?

We need to understand and trust our God as Job did. Job was a man who was tested like many of us will never experience. Yet, despite all his trials, read what he says in these next few verses:

"He knows the way that I take; when He has tested me, I will come forth as gold."
Job 23:10

(Continued)

"Though He slay me, yet will I hope in Him."
Job 13:15

When you don't sense His presence, feel His power or see any miracles, **TRUST HIS LOVE!** He hasn't forgotten you, He's working out *". . .all things for your good," (Romans 8:28).* He's not done yet -- there's much to do in your life. Remember the promise that:

". . .He who began a good work in you will carry it on to
completion until the day of Christ Jesus."
Philippians 1:6

Okay, so you don't sense His presence. Does that mean He's not there? Of course not! Whether you feel Him or not He is still near. The Apostle Peter says:

"Though you have not seen Him, you love Him; and even
though you do not see Him now, you believe in Him and
are filled with an inexpressible and glorious joy."
1 Peter 1:8

Remember that He has an objective for your life. Your life is not run by chance, luck or coincidence, but by His loving hand. Don't think He's being cruel because He's not showing you His plan all at one time. He knows what's best. You would probably freak right out if He showed you what was coming up in the next few weeks or months. So, hang loose, stay close to Him, remain flexible and enjoy Him loving and caring for you.

Fidel Gomez, Senior Pastor
Calvary Chapel Tamarac
Tamarac, Florida

May 27

STANDING IN THE GAP

"And I sought for a man among them, that should make up the hedge, and stand in the gap before me for the land, that I should not destroy it, but I found none."
Ezekiel 22:30

As Jerusalem was in the process of falling to Babylon, God speaks again to the nation about how often He had called them back to Himself, but they would not come. This remarkable verse above then follows. God was looking for anyone who would have stood in the gap for the land. <u>Anyone</u> praying. He had found no one! How awful when men turn from the Lord and not one is left to bring the nation back. Yet, how glorious to think that the prayers and stance in the gap of even one saint, could be used mightily by God to spare an entire nation. May we pray for our land and our leaders. . . may we stand in the gap.

Jack Abeelen, Senior Pastor
Morningstar Christian Chapel
Whittier, California

May 28

A RESTORATION OF LOVE

*"Remember therefore from where you have fallen, and repent
and do the deeds you did at first; or else I am coming to
you, and will remove your light stand out of its place
— unless you repent."*
Revelation 2:5

First love is a simple and joyful love, uncomplicated, and trusting. However, the wear and tear of everyday life can cool love, both for the Lord and one's mate. Whatever makes a heart grow cold to the Lord can also make the heart grow cold to the person's mate. When the flame dims, something else comes in that can threaten your love for God or your mate. Here is Jesus' cure for a lost or waning first love:

Remember: Recall the freshness, joy, contentment, need, attraction, and happiness that brought you together.

Repent: This word means more than sorrow. It means walking in the opposite direction. Purposely turn back towards God and your spouse.

Repeat: Demonstrate the early deeds of love. Go back to the things that made that love strong "in word and deed." As water is to a plant, so is conversation to a couple's relationship, and the Word and prayer to our relationship with God. Communication is the common thread in a courtship that becomes a cord of love.

Christ must be the foundation of our lives. Today, as our society struggles in many areas, the main problem is selfishness within ourselves. We have an answer, and it is quite

(Continued)

simple. It comes from God. Let's not complicate it. Let's keep it simple. *"Love your neighbor as yourself."* Living out this instruction won't cure all society's problems, but it will deal with the source of sin in your own heart. It won't cure poverty, but it will cure the poverty of your own spirit as you are enriched through loving others.

Some people ask how can a person show love to God in a practical way. The scripture answers that question with a single answer through a variety of voices. To the rich young ruler, Jesus said, *"Sell all you have and give to the poor."* To the Pharisees, Jesus said, *"Go study mercy."* Through Micah, we hear, *"Do justly, love mercy and walk humbly with thy God."* Through the pen of Moses, God said, *"Give generously to him and do so without a grudging heart; then because of this the LORD your God will bless you in all your work and in everything you put your hand to."* Through Paul we hear, *". . . serve one another in love."* Peter preached, *"Love one another deeply from the heart."* John spoke, *"Love one another as He has commanded us."*

So how can you love our neighbor? It is not always a warm, personal feeling. Love begins by praying for your neighbor as you pray for yourself. *"Carry one another's burdens and so fulfill the law of Christ."* God will open the opportunity for you to put your hand to fulfilling that kind of prayer.

Robert Fromm, Senior Pastor
North Valley Calvary Chapel
Yuba City, California

May 29

HEART VS. MIND

*"Then when he had come and witnessed the grace of God,
he rejoiced and began to encourage them all with resolute
heart to remain true to the Lord."*
Acts 11:23

Our society often places a good deal of emphasis on the
intellect of mankind as a whole, or on an individual person.
With the power of the mind, calculating and perceptive,
great things are accomplished. The idea is that the mind is
the driving force, the source of the will behind things.

Luke seems to take up opposition to that concept. The driving force in encouraging these brand new believers in Jesus
Christ was from the heart, the *cardia* (Greek). The bowels
were considered the seat of the emotions while the heart is
the seat of the will. Salvation is often referred to as a *change
of heart* when someone turns from their past and to Jesus. it
is a surrendering of the will, the cardia, to Jesus.

*"For with the heart man believes, resulting in righteousness,
and with the mouth he confesses, resulting in salvation."*
Romans 10:10

It is the heart that is regenerated at salvation.

Why the heart and not the mind? The mind is more changeable than the heart. During the process of making a decision between two or more things, the mind will go back
and forth. The heart, or will, is the source that drives the
direction of our lives. Our considerations and pronounce-
ments will be colored by our beliefs — the things that our

(Continued)

will holds firmly to — things that have taken a good deal of
time to determine, things that are very settled.

*"But let him ask in faith without doubting, for the one who
doubts is like the surf of the sea driven and tossed by the wind.
For let not that man expect that he will receive anything from
the Lord, being a double-minded man, unstable in all his ways."*
James 1:6-8

I have heard the phrase double-minded, or of two minds,
but never double-hearted or willed. If your basic, driving
beliefs and principles — your faith — were uncertain you
would be a basket case. This is not just true for a Christian
either. But with those fundamental ideals settled in the heart,
the only thing that can be doubled is the mind. If your faith
is firm, your mind will soon be cleared and rarely doubled
for any period of time.

Harry Pressley, Senior Pastor
Calvary Chapel of South New Jersey
Clarksboro, New Jersey

May 30

FALL UPON THE ROCK

*"My soul, wait silently for God alone, for my expectation is
from Him. He only is my rock and my salvation;
He is my defense; I shall not be moved. In God is my
salvation and my glory; the rock of my strength,
and my refuge, is in God.
Trust in Him at all times, you people; pour out your
heart before Him; God is a refuge for us."*
Psalm 62:5-8

Like a giant, tightly clenched fist, gripping and squeezing
the substance from an orange, so discouragement and disappointment drain the heart of its joy, the very substance
the Christian exists on, *". . . the joy of the Lord is my strength."*
But remember, Jesus has overcome the world. Your trial
will pass. You will be brought through; you will overcome
it in time.

Look for Jesus in the midst of your circumstances. Draw
your strength and hope from Him. He will never leave you
nor forsake you. He knows every pain and hurt. Fall upon
the rock of your salvation and be comforted.

Bill Stonebraker, Senior Pastor
Calvary Chapel of Honolulu
Honolulu, Hawaii

May 31

OUR SHIELD

It sure seems at times as if everything's going to fall apart. Like Job, some folks are going through major personal tragedies, and the hard times just keep piling up one on top of another. When you open up the newspaper, you see all kinds of disasters, let alone the crisis being played out in Washington. If this is all that life is about, enduring one discouragement after another, I can see why people get depressed.

But there's more. Much, much, more. The Psalmist writes, *"Behold, O God our shield, and look upon the face of thine anointed. For a day in thy courts is better than a thousand. I had rather be a doorkeeper in the house of my God, than to dwell in the tents of wickedness. For the LORD God is a sun and shield: the LORD will give grace and glory: no good thing will he withhold from them that walk uprightly. O LORD of hosts, blessed is the man that trusteth in thee,"* (Psalm 4:9-12).

You know, this is at the heart of what coming to church is all about. It's important that we fellowship with other believers, but the most important thing is being with Him. It's sitting at His feet, adoring Him, and receiving from Him. Yes, sometimes He's silent and sometimes we don't understand what He's doing. He's our shield, and when we take the time to enter into His presence and taste the grace and glory He has for us we realize that this is where we need to be. This is exactly where we need to be. With our God. I can hardly wait.

Steve Edmondson, Assistant Pastor
Calvary Chapel of Fullerton
Fullerton, California

June 1

TRIED AND CONVICTED

". . .having wiped out the handwriting of requirements that
was against us, which was contrary to us. And He has
taken it out of the way, having nailed it to the Cross."
Colossians 2:14

We are all in this world as condemned sinners. Every man
and woman has a warrant out on them from heaven for
their trial and conviction. Our only hope to escape judgment is for someone with no warrants or convictions to take
our identity, and receive our judgment and for us to take
their identity and be free. Jesus is that someone.

Les Prock, Senior Pastor
Calvary Chapel North Hill
Milton, Washington

June 2

WHAT IS OUR WORLD COMING TO?

"And ye shall hear of wars and rumours of wars: see that ye be not troubled: for all [these things] must come to pass, but the end is not yet. For nation shall rise against nation, and kingdom against kingdom: and there shall be famines, and pestilences, and earthquakes, in diverse places. All these [are] the beginning of sorrows. Then shall they deliver you up to be afflicted, and shall kill you: and ye shall be hated of all nations for my name's sake. And then shall many be offended, and shall betray one another, and shall hate one another. And because iniquity shall abound, the love of many shall wax cold. But he that shall endure unto the end, the same shall be saved."
Matthew 24:6-10,12,13

The violence in our streets and the hatred in our culture is just a sign that the Lord is coming soon. We are living in a society that is *"waxed cold"* to the things of God. We should not, as Christians, be frightened by the things we hear or see, but know these things are a sign that HE is coming soon.

Mark Maciel, Assistant Pastor
Calvary Chapel of Downey
Downey, California

June 3

THE REVEALED GLORY IN THE VESSEL

"But we have this treasure in earthen vessels, that the
excellence of the power may be of God and not of us."
2 Corinthians 4:7

The treasure Paul speaks of here is not one to be hoarded.
He refers to the treasure of the glory of God. The covenant
that God has made to give us mercy based on what Jesus
has done for us. And Paul is telling the Corinthian church
that they are the bearers of that covenant to the world.

In the book of Judges, the Lord calls Gideon to deliver the
nation of Israel from the Midianites. The Lord's plan included trimming Gideon's army from 32,000 to 300. The
Israelites were to take torches and place them in pitchers.
At the signal, all were to break the clay vessels, revealing
the light, and cry out, *". . .the sword of the Lord and of Gideon."*
The picture we see is the enemy surrounded by light coming out of darkness.

We, too, have the light of the gospel in our earthen vessels.
It is revealed to the world only when we allow the Lord to
break the earthen vessel of our flesh, with all its desires.
General Booth, founder of the Salvation Army, when asked
why God had used him in such a mighty way, replied,
"When I was a lad of seventeen, I determined that God
should have all there was of William Booth." We, too, need
to let God break the earthen vessel of our will, and give
God all of who we are.

Dave Fitzgerald, Senior Pastor
Hosanna Calvary Chapel
Maryland Heights, Missouri

June 4

VICTIMS OR VICTORS?

"These things I have spoken to you, that in Me you may have
peace. In the world you will have tribulation; but be of
good cheer, I have overcome the world."
John 16:33

Satan uses many weapons against the Christian, seeking to stumble him and halt his progress in the Lord. One of his favorites is discouragement. The avenues he uses to deliver this blow are the circumstances of life. It can happen any time, without warning. One minute we've got the joy of the Lord, and the next thing we know, some situation has thrown us into a fit of discouragement.

Don't be a victim of circumstances. Jesus has made us victors. He said, "I have overcome the world." The one thing that will determine whether we are victims or victors is our faith. You can either stand on the faith side of God's promises or stand in doubt. *"For whatever is born of God overcomes the world; and this is the victory that has overcome the world - our faith,"* (1 John 5:4)

Bill Stonebraker, Senior Pastor
Calvary Chapel of Honolulu
Honolulu, Hawaii

June 5

CLOUD COVERING

"So it was always: the cloud covered it by day, and the appearance of fire by night. Whenever the cloud was taken up from above the tabernacle, after that the children of Israel would journey; and in the place where the cloud settled, there the children of Israel would pitch their tents."
Numbers 9:16,17

"Why not just settle in one place? Why do we need to keep moving?" I'm sure there were at least thoughts along these lines, if not outright murmuring, to that effect. The Lord kept the children of Israel moving for the same reason He keeps us ready to move on a moment's notice.

There are two reasons, actually. The first is that it is very hard to steer a parked car. Often in scripture, we see Him asking the people of God to make the first move, and then He will direct their steps. He wants us ready to respond to Him at any time. Once we move, He can whisper in our ear "turn right" or "turn left."

The second reason is that when we are on the move, the enemy is confused and scattered. We see that in *Numbers 10:35*. As long as we sit comfortably in our designated pews, Satan really doesn't need to concern himself with us. But once the children of God start "movin' and shakin'," the enemy is scattered. So, let's keep moving, follow the cloud, and enjoy the lead of Jesus.

Phil Evans, Senior Pastor
Roseburg Christian Fellowship
Roseburg, Oregon

June 6

CHRISTIAN MARRIAGE: GOD'S DESIGN

Someone once said that marriage is like a violin: It doesn't work without strings, and when the music stops, the strings are still attached!

Often many find themselves looking at marriage in this fashion. We have a tendency to think of the relationship in unfavorable terms. The media, and many people around us, seem to solidify this concept by telling us, "Marriage is a three-ring circus: engagement ring, wedding ring, suffering!"

It would seem that a Christian's marriage especially is a prime target of Satan's attacks. I would think that Satan's opposition to marriage should alert us to its potential to be used by God. Marriage is an institution that was originated by God, not by man. *Genesis 2:24* says, *"Therefore a man shall leave his father and mother and be joined to his wife, and they shall become one flesh."* Thus, God must have a purpose for this most intimate of human relationships.

We must also realize that if God ordained marriage, then it is He who must be at the center of any marriage, and that it will work best when we live out this relationship in accordance with His directive. No one would think for a moment that an automobile would function best if we first discarded the owner's manual! The designer of the vehicle knows best how to maintain the vehicle to its optimal working order. It is the same with marriage; God designed and ordered it, and it functions best when His instructions are followed.

(Continued)

The Bible tells us that the union between a man and a woman, as husband and wife, is a picture of Jesus' relationship with every believer. He is the bridegroom, and we (collectively) are the bride. Therefore when a marriage works the way that God intended, it will be a picture to others around us of the beauty of Christ's love for the church. They will be able to see that Jesus wants an intimate relationship with us, the way we desire intimacy with our own spouses here on earth.

A Christian marriage, exemplifying Christ's love, will not only bless us as individuals and families, but will also speak volumes to the world in which we live.

Brian Michaels, Senior Pastor
Rocky Mountain Calvary Chapel
Colorado Springs, Colorado

June 7

MY SOUL WAITS

*"I wait for the LORD, my soul waits, and in His word I put my
hope. My soul waits for the Lord more than watchmen wait for
the morning, more than watchmen wait for the morning. O'
Israel, put your hope in the LORD, for with the LORD is
unfailing love and with Him is full redemption."*
Psalm 130:5-7

When I was in my twenties, I worked in a hospital in San
Diego. The department where I worked had floor to ceiling
windows that faced the sunrise. I worked the night shift,
so every morning I had a spectacular view of the sunrise.
This Psalm brings to my mind a picture of waiting for God
to intervene, like waiting for the sunrise to come. Each
morning, when the sky started to show a little light, I knew
that my work would soon be over and I could go to the
beach. As the sun rose, the room would suddenly fill with
sunlight and everything would seem to start over for me.
A new day had dawned -- everything was fresh and new.

In the same way that any of us would long for the daybreak
after a long night of toil, we need to recognize that as surely
as the sun rises every morning, God will complete what He
has started. As surely as the watchman will see the morning, we will see God's purpose in our lives achieved. Our
task is to be faithful and watchful as each day begins to
dawn. Look up, for your redemption is drawing near.

Greg Cull, Senior Pastor
Calvary Chapel Shingle Springs
Shingle Springs, California

June 8

ATTITUDE ADJUSTMENT

*"And Enoch walked with God after he begat Methuselah three
hundred years, and begat sons and daughters; and all the days
of Enoch were three hundred sixty and five years; and Enoch
walked with God; and he was not; for God took him."*
Genesis 5:22-24

That's all it tells us about Enoch; he walked with God. While
everyone else was living over 900 years, Enoch only lived
365 years. I guess a long life isn't always a sign of God's
favor.

The Hebrew meaning of walking with someone meant that
you <u>pleased</u> that person. In other words, Enoch's walk
<u>pleased</u> God, and <u>then</u> he was no more, for God took him.
We need to have Enoch's attitude in life. Instead of, "Can I
do this and still go to heaven," we should gauge our actions
by, "Will this please my Father?"

*". . . for you were formerly darkness, but now you are light in
the Lord; walk as children of light for the fruit of the light
consists in all goodness and righteousness and truth, trying to
learn what is pleasing to the Lord. "*
Ephesians 5:8-10

Blessed is the man who does not live to please the world, or
himself. And the irony is that the person who lives to please
God gets more satisfaction from life than the person who
lives to please self.

Chuck Trett, Senior Pastor
Calvary Chapel of Henderson
Henderson, Nevada

June 9

A SERVANT'S FIX

"Let all your things be done with charity. I beseech you,
brethren, (ye know the house of Stephanas, that it is the first
fruits of Achaia, and that they have addicted themselves to the
ministry of the saints). That ye submit yourselves unto such,
and to everyone that helpeth with us, and laboureth. I am glad
of the coming of Stephanas and Fortunatus and Achaicus: for
that which was lacking on your part they have supplied.
For they have refreshed my spirit and yours:
therefore acknowledge ye them that are such."
I Corinthians 16:14-18

Addiction is a horrible word in our culture, and most of the time that is appropriate. However, there were those in the Body of Christ in the days of Paul that were addicted to serving others in the name of Jesus! They brought what others lacked, made up for what others neglected, and restored men like Paul when they needed to be picked up and helped along! What are you addicted to? Self gain, influence, pleasure, comfort? Or to serving Jesus with everything you have, and leaving permanent fruit in your wake?

Jack Abeelen, Senior Pastor
Morningstar Christian Chapel
Whittier, California

June 10

HEAD OF THE HOUSE

*"And He shall turn the heart of the fathers to the children, and
the heart of the children to their fathers, lest I come and
smite thee earth with a curse."*
Malachi 4:6

This is my prayer for all you dads this day, that the Lord
will turn your heart to your children, and to your home.

But before you can do this, my second prayer is for Nehemiah 8:13 to become a reality in your life:

*"And on the second day were gathered together the chief of the
fathers of all the people, the priests, and the Levites, unto Ezra
the scribe, even to understand the words of the law."*
Nehemiah 8:13

Here we see the fathers continuing in the Bible study to
understand the Word of God! So dad's, dig in and continue to seek His direction and His Word. Then we will be
able to say as Nehemiah 4:14b says:

*". . . be not ye afraid of them: Remember the Lord, which is
great and terrible, and fight for your brethren, your sons, and
your daughters, your wives, and your houses."*
Nehemiah 4:14

Jeff Johnson, Senior Pastor
Calvary Chapel of Downey
Downey, California

June 11

HERO WORSHIP

*"Train up a child in the way he should go:
and when he is old, he will not depart from it."*
Proverbs 22:6

A mother recently told me of a conversation she had with her son when he was about four or five years of age. This mother was curious as to whom her son saw as a hero so she asked, "Who is your hero?" He sat there thinking with his little forehead wrinkled in thought. Then he said, "I know Mommy, Jesus is my hero." "Yes," thought the Mom. Then her son said wistfully, "He even has a red cape." He pointed to a picture on the wall of Jesus in the garden of Gethsemane. Jesus was wearing a red robe that looked like a cape to the boy. The important thing was that Jesus was this boy's hero, and still is. He has grown into a fine young person and is pursuing God's will for his life.

Whom do our children see as heroes? They want someone they can look up to. Someone they can imitate. Many times a child's first hero is a parent. I enjoy seeing a son who wants to dress and act like dad. It is a joy to see a little girl want to be like her mommy.

However, remaining as heros to their children depends on how the parents act and react with their children. Often our children imitate our actions, good and bad. Then, if we react in a negative way, the children who once wanted to be so much like mom or dad, end up wanting to be as opposite of their parents as they can.

Children also choose heros by what they are allowed to

(Continued)

read, watch on TV or in the movies, or listen to in the form of music, as well. Our children are so impressionable. They want to dress, talk, and act like their heroes. Why are parents so surprised when their kids end up in trouble when their children are allowed (and sometimes even encouraged) to emulate entertainment celebrities? Parents are so surprised when their children end up in gangs or on drugs. But the heroes they have been allowed to have, promote life-styles that are directly opposite to the teachings in the Word of God.

One more crucial thing will make a difference to children as far as having Jesus as a hero. When parents see Jesus as the Hero, their children will see Him that way too. If children do not see their parents love, devotion, and service to Jesus -- then their children will not have Jesus as a hero themselves.

Chuck Kelly, Senior Pastor
Calvary Chapel Bullhead City
Bullhead City, Arizona

June 12

WHO IS AT THE HELM?

"Moreover the Word of the Lord came unto Jeremiah the second time, while he was yet shut up in the court of the prison, saying, 'Thus saith the Lord the maker thereof, the Lord that formed it, to establish it; the Lord is His name; call unto me, and I will answer thee, and show thee great and mighty things, which thou knowest not.'"
Jeremiah 33:1-3

The Lord reminded Jeremiah that He was still in control and that everything was going right as planned. *"The Lord who made it, the Lord who formed it would establish it..."* Here, Jeremiah was tempted to think something terrible had gone wrong, and now his time was being wasted just sitting in a prison. But what a perfect place for the Lord to speak to one's heart; what a perfect time to pray. So, the Lord says, *"Call (pray) to Me, and I will answer you, and show you great and mighty things, which you do not know,"* (Jeremiah 33:3).

We, like Jeremiah, need to bear in mind that the Lord is in control and He wants us to call out to Him, to seek Him. How often I have sensed that the Lord had more to say to me, but I was not seeking. You have a problem? He has a promise -- *"Call to Me, and I will answer."*

Mike Stangel, Senior Pastor
North Shore Christian Fellowship
Haleiwa, Hawaii

June 13

ENTRUST IT TO THE ONE IN CHARGE

Have you ever wondered what it would be like to teach at Calvary Chapel? It is an awesome and frightening experience to stand behind the pulpit. There is an overwhelming sense of responsibility and privilege which would humble any man. The task of teaching taps every ounce of trust we can muster. You can then well imagine what a battle it is to step out into the sacred and scary arena of the altar call.

What if no one comes up? What if they do come up? Do I give a second call? How do I end it and pass it on? Because of God's grace in orchestrating so many salvations here, week after week, one might think this just comes with the territory and there is no personal turmoil involved. Wrong.

It occurred to me recently that this attitude of total inadequacy and complete dependency upon Christ should occur in every believer as they contemplate the awesome privilege we are given to be Ambassadors of Christ. It is probably the magnitude of standing before so many people that amplifies the charge we have been given, but it is, in fact, the same charge whether the crowd be one or many.

The reality is that it does not matter who is standing behind the pulpit. What matters is who is sitting on the throne, not where your pulpit is. Let your focus be to faithfully discharge the Good News. As you accept this challenge, you will know first hand the personal battle that happens with every altar call, and the joy of seeing salvation.

Mark Davis, Assistant Pastor
Calvary Chapel Ft. Lauderdale
Ft. Lauderdale, Florida

June 14

TRUSTING GOD

Have you considered how frail life is? How in an instant, in a twinkling of an eye, your whole life can change?

"Because all flesh is as grass, and all the glory of man as the flower of the grass. The grass withereth, and the flower falleth away."
1 Peter 1:24

While I was in the recovery room after my surgery, God spoke to me. He asked me if I trusted Him for my last breath. This had such an impact on me because, at that very moment, I was choking and gasping for breath.

"But the word of the Lord endureth for ever. And this is the word which by the gospel is preached unto you."
1 Peter 1:25

Glenn Kravig, Assistant Pastor
Calvary Chapel of Downey
Downey California

June 15

WONDERFUL COUNSELOR

*"Now after the death of Jehoiada the leaders of Judah came and
bowed down to the king. And the king listened to them.
Therefore, they left the house of the LORD God of their fathers,
and served wooden images and idols; and wrath came upon
Judah and Jerusalem because of their trespass."*
II Chronicles 24:17,18

What a sad turn of events. As soon as Jehoiada passed
away, some of the influential men of the nation came to
King Joash and convinced him the best course of action
was to return to the worship of idols.

Who are you taking counsel from? Who are you listening
to? The "experts?" The so-called "wise" whose counsel is
nothing more than the wisdom of this world? Only God's
Word provides the light we need to live successfully. Any
counsel we receive needs to be filtered through the Word
and counsel of God. In a world full of noise, who are you
listening to?

Lance Ralston, Senior Pastor
Calvary Chapel Coram Deo
Oxnard, California

June 16

REST STOP

"These things have I spoken to you, being yet present with you.
But the Comforter, which is the Holy Ghost, whom the
Father will send in my name, He shall teach you all things,
and bring all things to your remembrance,
whatsoever I have said unto you."
John 14:25,26

The Spirit of the Lord is the Comforter (advocate or intercessor), someone to whom you can rest upon to gain understanding and knowledge. We need to reside with the Comforter, to stop, slow down, and to rest in His everlasting arms -- and to know that He is God.

Rick Clarke, Assistant Pastor
Calvary Chapel of the Finger Lakes
Farmington, New York

June 17

TRUE LOVE

One of the hardest things in the world is to get along with another human being. Some are easier than others, but even the easy ones can be obnoxious every once in a while.

Judith Versed, in <u>Love and Guilt and the Meaning of Love</u>, said that: <u>Infatuation is</u> when you think that he's as gorgeous as Robert Redford, as pure as Solzhenitsyn, as funny as Woody Allen, as athletic as Jimmy Conners, and as smart as Albert Einstein. <u>Love is</u> when you realize that he's as gorgeous as Woody Allen, as smart as Jimmy Conners, as funny as Solzhenitsyn, as athletic as Albert Einstein, and nothing like Robert Redford in any category, but you'll take him anyway.

We want so much to be understood and accepted by others, we sometimes can be quite stingy when it comes to giving acceptance and understanding in return. Paul wrote:

"Since you have been chosen by God who has given you this new kind of life, and because of his deep love and concern for you, you should practice tenderhearted mercy and kindness to others. Don't worry about making a good impression on them, but be ready to suffer quietly and patiently. Be gentle and ready to forgive; never hold grudges. Remember, the Lord forgave you, so you must forgive others. Most of all let love guide your life, for then the whole church will stay together in perfect harmony."
Colossians 3:12-14

Rich Cathers, Senior Pastor
Calvary Chapel of Fullerton
Fullerton, California

June 18

READY AND ABLE

One very central theme in the Old and New Testaments is found in *Hebrews 9:22* and *Leviticus 17:11:*

> *". . .without the shedding of blood there can*
> *be no remission of sin."*

> *". . .the life of the flesh is in the blood, and I have given it to you*
> *on the altar to make atonement for your souls."*

Of course, it was the sacrificial Lamb of God, Jesus our Lord's death on Calvary, that made, *". . . atonement for our souls."* In *Hebrews 2:14,15,* the implied victorious death and resurrection of Jesus *". . . removed the power and fear of death that the devil . . ."* had over our lives. Blood sacrifice to cover our sins is even evident in the Garden of Eden, when God used animal skins to cover Adam and Eve. It's the power of Christ's shed blood sprinkled upon our lives that equips and protects us as vessels in His ministries *(Hebrews 9:21).*

In *2 Timothy 2:19-21,* we're told that we should *". . . abstain from wickedness."* And that we should *" . . . cleanse our vessels for honor, and be sanctified* (holy), *to be prepared and useful for the Master."*

Paul also writes to Timothy and to us, to be be ready at all times, in and out of season, to share our salvation through faith which is in Christ Jesus.

Ken Shaffer, Assistant Pastor
Calvary Chapel of Fullerton
Fullerton, California

June 19

IT MIGHT BE TODAY!

"Behold, what manner of love the Father hath bestowed upon us, that we should be called the sons of God: therefore the world knoweth us not, because it knew Him not. Beloved, now are we the sons of God, and it doth not yet appear what we shall be: but we know that, when He shall appear, we shall be like Him; for we shall see Him as He is. And every man that hath this hope in Him purifieth himself, even as He is pure."
I John 3:1-3

It might be today that Jesus returns for His bride, the church, and takes us home to heaven for eternity! Are we as prepared, as a bride is prepared for her wedding day? Are we anxiously awaiting and looking for His soon return? Are we busy about our Father's business? Does our everyday life-style reflect an urgency and desire to share God's love to the lost, as well as those in the faith?

It might be <u>today</u> that we see Jesus, our Savior and Lord, face to face! Maranatha!

Tim Hearron, Assistant Pastor
Calvary Chapel of Downey
Downey, California

June 20

GOD'S WORD

In Genesis 3:1-5, we read Satan's first recorded word with man. He asked Eve, *"Yea, has God said, you shall not eat of every tree of the garden?"* And Satan has been attacking God's Word ever since. He knows that the Bible is true because it is God's Word.

> *"He sent His word and healed them and*
> *delivered them from their destructions."*
> Psalm 107:20

> *"The Word of God is quick and powerful and*
> *sharper than any two edged sword."*
> Hebrews 4:12

Sadly, many have left out the Bible in their groups, clubs, and even some churches. When man begins to say their special group is Bible-based, but there are no Bibles allowed, I become suspicious. When churches no longer emphasize the teaching of God's Word, but rather offer specialty groups that have answers for social problems, this should alarm us.

The man or woman who stands today, is the one who trusts in God's Word and nothing else. Where are your priorities? Is the Bible first in your life? Or have you left off reading and trusting the Bible? Everything I'll ever need to know about life is in within the pages God's Word.

Steve Everett, Assistant Pastor
Calvary Chapel of Downey
Downey, California

June 21

OUR FATHER

It is vitally important to draw our image of God from scripture alone. No earthly father, good or bad, can be compared to our heavenly Father for obvious reasons. Even the best dad has limitations. Our Father in Heaven doesn't.

The scriptures emphasize the relationship between the "twice-born" child of God, and the God of the universe. In prayer, we address Him as, *"Our Father," (Luke 11:2).* As His children, He is, *"Abba Father," (Romans 8-15),* which is an Aramaic term of endearment. Truly, unto us who believe, *"He is precious," (1 Peter 2:7).* The Bible says that:

God is a God of patience and consolation *(Romans 15:5)*; He is the God of Hope *(Romans 15:13)*; the Everlasting God *(Romans 16:26).* How mighty! How Powerful! Indeed, our God is *". . . clothed with majesty," (Psalm 104:1).* God is faithful *(I Corinthians 1:9)* and He is the God of all comfort *(2 Corinthians 1:3).* The apostle John plainly states: *"God is Love," (1 John 4:8).* His *". . . name is as ointment poured forth," (Song of Solomon 1:3). "Jehovah is my strength and my song," (Isaiah 12:2)* who in His rich mercy *(Ephesians 2:4)* gave His only begotten Son *(John 3:16)* to redeem me from the Law's curse *(Galatians 3:10).* How wise is our God, *(1 Timothy 1:17).* Who can challenge His authority *(Job 38:41)*? My persuasion *(2 Timothy 1:12)* rests in His power to keep me *(1 Peter 1:5)* until that final day *(Philippians 1:6).*

May you know who He is, and glorify Him, today.

Ray Viola, Senior Pastor
Koinonia Fellowship
East Rochester, New York

June 22

FATHER ABRAHAM

"Hearken to me, ye that follow after righteousness, ye that
seek the LORD: look unto the rock whence ye are hewn,
and to the hole of the pit whence ye are digged.
Look unto Abraham your father."
Isaiah 51:1,2

Have you ever wondered how you're doing as a father? Or, if you're still single, how you <u>will</u> do some day? They don't give a test for fatherhood, do they? So how do you know whether you're passing or failing? Where do we learn fathering skills, anyway?

In *Isaiah 51:1,2*, the Lord tells the captive Israelites to look to Abraham their father as an example of righteousness and faith. Abraham, who was called "*. . . a father of many nations,"* (*Genesis 17:4*) by God Himself, was one of the most remarkable fathers in the Bible. But why? What made Abraham such a great father?

God tells the Israelites to "*hearken*" to His words — to listen carefully to what He has to say — and then directs them back to Abraham. When we read, in *Genesis 22:1-14*, of Abraham's willingness to sacrifice his only son — we discover what made Abraham such a great father. By his example, Abraham taught his son, Isaac, three very valuable lessons:

The Way of the Cross (Genesis 22:1-5)
- Abraham was sensitive to the voice of the Lord. When God spoke, Abraham responded immediately.
- Abraham had a tender love for his son.

(Continuued)

~ 200 ~

- Abraham had a willing and obedient heart. He went where God told him to go.
- Abraham was patient. It took three days to get to the place where God commanded him to go, and even then he did not complain.
- Abraham never lost his hope. He knew the covenant God had made with him and that such a promise would come through Isaac.
- Abraham provided the faith and reassurance his son needed. When Isaac asked him where the sacrifice was, he didn't avoid the issue, nor did he lie.

The Word of the Cross (Genesis 22:6-8)
- Abraham did not try to shelter Isaac from what was happening, but placed upon him the only burden a father should lay upon his son — the Cross of Christ.

The Work of the Cross (Genesis 22:9-14
- Abraham's loyalty and love were God's to command.
- Abraham gave his son to the Lord. He did not snatch him off that altar at the last moment unwilling to trust God's perfect will.
- Abraham taught his son what true faith was all about.

Now, more than ever, our sons need godly men like Abraham as examples to follow. They need true heroes of the Cross to pattern their lives after. May each one of us, as we read God's words and meditate on their meaning, "*hearken*" to the voice of the Lord just as Abraham did.

Steve Mays, Senior Pastor
Calvary Chapel of South Bay
Torrance, California

June 23

GREAT PEACE

*"Great peace have those who love Your law, and
nothing causes them to stumble."*
Psalm 119:165

Loving God's way makes a difference. Loving our way gets
us into trouble. We get all tripped up and life gets messy.
Not just "peace," but "great peace" comes from living life
God's way.

Carl Westerlund, Assistant Pastor
Calvary Chapel Costa Mesa
Santa Ana, California

(Continued)

June 24

HAVEN OF GRACE

*"God is our refuge and strength, a very present help in trouble.
Therefore will not we fear, though the earth be removed,
and though the mountains be carried into
the midst of the sea...there is a river..."*
Psalm 46:1,2,4.

When you're in trouble, it's important to get the right kind of help. Ann Landers tells this story: "A woman came into the beauty salon and asked one of their stylists, "Do you know how to stop hiccups?" The hair stylist said, "Sit in this chair, I'll be right back." She then went over to the shampoo bowl, soaked a towel in cold water, came back and smacked the lady in the face with it. The astonished woman jumped out of the chair and screamed at the stylist, "Why did you do that?" The stylist replied with a smile, "You don't have the hiccups now, do you?" "No," replied the baffled lady, "but I didn't have the hiccups when I came in here, either." She then added, "My mother is sitting outside in the car, and she has the hiccups. Would you care to go out there and smack her face with a wet towel?"

God is nothing like that hair stylist. He won't slap you around. He knows all about the real need and He has plenty of what is needed. When God says *"My grace is sufficient for you,"* He doesn't mean that He barely has enough to cover you. As your refuge He offers shelter. As your strength, He carries you. As your help, He offers hope. Don't just sip, drink deep from His river.

Steve Edmondson, Assistant Pastor
Calvary Chapel of Fullerton
Fullerton, California

June 25

BEFORE THE PARADE PASSES BY

As we grow older, we sometimes feel that life is passing us by. We feel useless and wonder where we can go to do something worth while. When we feel like that, all we need to do is read the Book of Titus in the New Testament. He gives us meaning and direction for our lives. He exhorts us to good works. He tells us to exhort the younger men and women to be good wives and husbands to be an example to those who are younger. We need to be examples to those who are following after us. Read Titus chapter 2 and be blessed!

Phil O'Malley, Assistant Pastor
Calvary Chapel of Downey
Downey, California

June 26

ASSURANCE FROM ABOVE

"For all have sinned, and come short of the glory of God;
For the wages of sin is death."
Romans 3:23, 6:23

"It is a fearful thing to fall into the hands of the living God."
Hebrews 10:31

Does the prospect of facing God scare you? Do you ever fear God's judgment? Listen to this amazing promise:

"To me this is like the days of Noah, when I swore that the
waters of Noah would never again cover the earth. So now I
have sworn not to be angry with you, never to rebuke you
again. Though the mountains be shaken and the hills be re-
moved, yet my unfailing love for you will not be shaken
nor my covenant of peace be removed,
says the LORD, who has compassion on you."
Isaiah 54:9,10

". . .For no matter how many promises God has made, they are
"Yes" in Christ. And so through Him the "Amen"
is spoken by us to the glory of God."
2 Corinthians 1:20

Mike Sasso, Assistant Pastor
Calvary Chapel of Downey
Downey, California

June 27

VALUES

"Wherefore seeing we also are compassed about with so great a cloud of witnesses, let us lay aside every weight, and the sin which doth so easily beset [us], and let us run with patience the race that is set before us."
Hebrews 12:1

As Christians, what values do we set? Not only before our children or friends, but what values do we set before the Lord in our own personal life! Whether it's movies, music, or social life, our conduct as Christians says a lot. What we do, what we watch, what we listen to, and where we socialize tells it all.

What direction do our thoughts and actions take when we are alone or away from church? There's a high standard we must follow, and it's the Lord we will answer to!

Mark Maciel, Assistant Pastor
Calvary Chapel of Downey
Downey, California

June 28

EXPRESS YOURSELF

What words do you use to convey to someone that you care for them greatly? We usually find ourselves saying, "I love you," or "You mean so much to me." You might even come up with something like, "You are very special to me." Yet, have you noticed that there are times that no matter how many catchy phrases you use, you find yourself feeling frustrated because words simply do not communicate the depth of your true feelings!

What about when it comes to expressing love for the Lord? How can we ever tell the Lord how much we love Him? What words can we use that will express to Him the depth of our love for Him? Oh, we seem to get so tongue-tied as we search for those elusive right words!

Have you ever found yourself trying to express to someone an important point, yet you became tongue-tied and frustrated? Then suddenly someone next to you says, "Do you mean . . . ?" And that other person gets your point across perfectly! You respond, "Yeah, yeah, that's it, that's what I was trying to say!"

I find this happens to me when I am reading through the Book of Psalms. The Psalmist helps us to express our feelings as he writes:

> *"Give thanks to the LORD, for He is good;*
> *His love endures forever."*
> *Psalm 118:1*

"He is good." The Hebrew word *"good"* means, "beautiful,

(Continued)

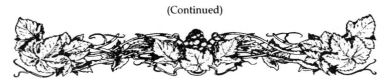

best, better, bountiful, cheerful, at ease, fair, fine, glad, gracious, joyful, kind, loving, merry, most pleasant, precious, sweet."

Did Jesus ever tell us how we could express our love for Him? Yes, in His Word He told us:

"If you love me, you will obey what I command."
John 14:15

Do you want to really express and clearly exhibit your love for Jesus? Then do what Jesus told us to do and, "... *obey what I command.*" Words are cheap. A life full of devotion, dedication, and deliberate obedience to His commands will be the best expression of our love for our God and Savior.

Today, do you want to truly, deeply, completely, and thoroughly express to your Savior how much you love Him? Obey Him! Don't be afraid of the results of your obedience. Leave the results to the One who is working out all things.

"I pray also that the eyes of your heart may be enlightened
in order that you may know the hope to which He has called
you, the riches of His glorious inheritance in the saints,
and His incomparably great power for us who believe."
Ephesians 1:18,19

Fidel Gomez, Senior Pastor
Calvary Chapel Tamarac
Tamarac, Florida

June 29

WORSHIP IN SPIRIT

"But the hour is coming, and now is when the true worshipers
will worship the Father in spirit and truth; for the
Father is seeking such to worship Him."
John 4:23

As we come to church, it's so easy to get caught up in traditions and rituals. We come to church week after week, hearing and singing the songs! How we need to remind ourselves what God expects. He desires us to worship Him from a heart of commitment, and to worship Him in SPIRIT! As we worship today, I encourage you to do so in the Spirit and not in the flesh! Let us break down any walls of rituals that will take away from what God truly deserves this morning.

"But the hour is coming, and now is. . ."

Louie Cruzado, Assistant Pastor
Calvary Chapel of Downey
Downey, California

June 30

HAVE YOU HIT THE WALL

*"In those days was Hezekiah sick unto death. And the prophet
Isaiah the son of Amoz came to him, and said unto him, thus
saith the Lord, set thine house in order; for thou shalt die, and
not live. Then he turned his face to the wall,
and prayed unto the LORD. . ."*
II Kings 20:1,2

Hezekiah had received bad news. This was in the middle
of his reign and he felt he had a lot of work ahead of him.
Now how would it be accomplished? He felt he was God's
chosen instrument, just as David and Solomon had been
chosen to guide the people into worship of the true and
living God.

Upon receiving the news of his impending demise, we don't
see him freaking out. He quietly dismisses Isaiah the
prophet, and then scripture says, *". . . he turned his face to the
wall."* I often think, what does it take for us to turn our face
to the wall and really seek God for answers? I hope not a
death sentence. But for some this is the case. God listened
to Hezekiah's prayer and answered in his favor -- fifteen
more years to complete God's work, not his own.

How long do each of us have? Will God grant us extra time?
I would encourage you to turn your face to the wall as often
as possible. The Lord is waiting and ready to grant you
what will glorify Him.

Rick Phelps, Senior Pastor
Calvary Chapel of Lakewood
Lakewood, California

July 1

THE HIGH COST OF WRITING PAPER

*"You are a letter of Christ, cared for by us, written not with
ink, but with the Spirit of the living God, not on tablets
of stone, but on tablets of human hearts."*
2 Corinthians 3:3

The human heart is the writing paper of God! The writing
implements are not ink and pen, but the Holy Spirit. Every
believer is a *"letter of Christ,"* known and read by all men.
But, have you ever considered the high cost of such writing
paper? It was the supreme price of the death of the Son of
God, Jesus Christ! Peter writes about this incredible cost
when he said,

*". . . knowing that you were not redeemed with perishable
things like silver or gold from your futile way of life inherited
from your forefathers, <u>but with precious blood</u>, as of a lamb
unblemished and spotless, the blood of Christ."*
1 Peter 1: 18,19

Every human heart is valuable to God -- a potentially high
priced piece of writing paper to write His story of redemption upon. But, the only way it can be used of God is that it
is first *"redeemed"* by the precious blood of Christ.

The message of redemption is to be *". . . known and read by
all men."* What do people read from the letter written on
your heart by the Holy Spirit? Is it about you, or Jesus?

Ron Finch, Senior Pastor
Calvary Chapel of Indio
Indio, California

July 2

RIGHT RELATIONSHIP WITH GOD

"So they answered Joshua, saying, "All that you command us we will do, and wherever you send us we will go. Just as we heeded Moses in all things, so we will heed you. Only the LORD your God be with you, as He was with Moses. Whoever rebels against your command and does not heed your words, in all that you command him, shall be put to death. Only be strong and of good courage."
Joshua 1:16-18

A first reading of Joshua 1:16 may sound rather radical in light of today's cultic activity. However, when taken in context, it is obvious that this blind devotion to Joshua was predicated completely upon the fact that Joshua was rightly related to God and hearing from Him. They were aware that their very lives depended upon staying in the protective shadow of their Deliverer.

In the same way, am I willing to put to death every act of disobedience to Christ's commands in my own life? If not, I will surely suffer the consequences of death -- although maybe not physically, quite possibly emotionally, intellectually, or spiritually. When I take seriously the commission to follow Christ, I will then be one that others can follow.

I pray that we become so sensitive to God that we obey everything He commands, putting to death any form of disobedience in our lives that would take us away from the protective hand, and perfect plan, of Christ.

Bob Coy, Senior Pastor
Calvary Chapel Ft. Lauderdale
Ft. Lauderdale, Florida

July 3

SUMMER TIME

Summer time, summer time, sum, sum, summer time! It's that time again. As we plan for vacations, BBQ's, and good fellowship, be sure to make the Lord the center of your summer events.

S . . . . Surrender To The Lord
U. . . . . . Utter The Word Of The Lord
M . . . . . Mind -- Put On the Mind Of Christ
M. . . . . . Memorize The Word
E . . . . . . Eager -- Having An Eagerness To Share Christ
R . . . . . . Respond To The Lord's Call

Let's remember these six applications, and apply them to our summer events. And don't forget to take your Bible on vacation with you!

Mark Maciel, Assistant Pastor
Calvary Chapel of Downey
Downey, California

July 4

DECLARATION OF DEPENDENCE

In the Book of Isaiah, God makes this declaration:

"...I am God, and there is none else; I am God, and there is none like me. Declaring the end from the beginning, and from ancient times the things that are not yet done, saying. 'My counsel shall stand, and I will do all my pleasure."'
Isaiah 46:9,10

It is God's good pleasure to reveal Himself to you as Wonderful, to be your Counselor, your Mighty God, your Everlasting Father, and your Prince of Peace.

Brian Phillips, Assistant Pastor
Calvary Chapel of the Finger Lakes
Farmington, New York

July 5

AIM HIGH!

"Be ye therefore perfect, even as your Father
which is in heaven is perfect."
Matthew 5:48

When looking at this verse, I notice that Jesus did not say
<u>please</u>! In fact, there is no request to that verse at all. How
often have we said something like this -- "nobody is perfect." One can accept that statement or reject it. The choice
is yours. Some choose responsibility, honesty, and integrity
-- the tough road -- some will back away and opt for an
easier, more passive route. The choice is yours.

Above all, remember that if you expect second best, you
will get it. If you expect third best, you will get it. If you
expect the worst, it will happen. On the other hand, if you
consistently expect the best, you will not always get it, but
you will achieve much more than any other alternative may
produce.

Rick Johnson, Assistant Pastor
Calvary Chapel of Downey
Downey, California

WELCOME! HOW MAY WE HELP YOU?

*"For you were called to <u>freedom</u> brethren, only do not
turn your freedom into an opportunity for the
flesh, but through love serve on another."*
Galatians 5:13

"Be hospitable to one another without complaint" (I Peter 4:9).
This verse should be modeled by each and every Christian.
*"By this all men will know that you are My disciples, if you have
love for one another,"* (John 12:35). These are Jesus' own words.
My prayer is that our fellowship will be known for our love
and concern for each other. May every visitor or new believer experience God's love in action.

Glenn Kravig, Assistant Pastor
Calvary Chapel of Downey
Downey, California

July 7

WORDS OF ETERNAL LIFE

"From that time many of His disciples went back and walked with Him no more. Then Jesus said to the twelve, "Do you also want to go away?" But Simon Peter answered Him, "Lord, to whom shall we go? You have the words of eternal life."
John 6:66-68

Peter recognized that there was no where else one could go and get, *"... the words to eternal life."* No other religion, no other person, only JESUS had these words. Even though some of the teachings of JESUS are not what people want to hear, they are still, *"... the words of eternal life."*

When you find yourself confronted with these *"words,"* always remember they carry eternal purposes and are not limited to the temporal.

"May HIS words always be a lamp unto my (our) feet, and a light unto my (our) path."
Psalm 119:105

Rick Coburn, Senior Pastor
Calvary Chapel of Dallas
Piano, Texas

July 8

WHERE ARE YOUR EYES?

"But we all, with open faith, beholding as in a glass, the glory of the Lord, are changed into the same image from glory to glory, even as by the Spirit of the Lord."
2 Corinthians 3:18

". . .for we have no might against this great army that comes against us, neither know we what to do, but our eyes are upon thee."
II Chronicles 20:12

Corrie Ten Boom said "Look around and you get distressed, look within, you get depressed, look at Jesus and you're at rest." Sometimes we get frustrated with ourselves and with our circumstances because we really can't change either one. The Holy Spirit changes us into the image of Jesus, but we need patience and it takes time. The Bible says from *glory to glory*. And we won't be satisfied until we awake in His likeness, when we see Him face to face. We are to look at the glory of God in the face of Jesus Christ.

As far as circumstances, Jehoshaphat faced an army far beyond his capacity to handle and he did not know what to do. Does this sound familiar? What was the answer? He said, *"Our eyes are upon thee."* It all seems too easy, and that's the problem. We want to work for it. But Jesus said, *"My yoke is easy and my burden is light!"*

Where are your eyes?

Mike Bucher, Senior Pastor
Calvary Chapel of Cleveland
Cleveland, Ohio

July 9

PERFECTLY MENDED IN CHRIST

"And after you have suffered for a little while, the God of all grace, who called you to His eternal glory in Christ, will Himself perfect, confirm, strengthen (and) establish you."
I Peter 5:10

I'd like to draw your attention to the word *"perfect"* in this most encouraging verse. What is so fascinating about this word is how we find it being used elsewhere in the scriptures, in particular, *Matthew 4:21*.

Here we have a picture of James and John sitting in their boat mending their nets. The same word that is translated as *"perfect"* in *I Peter 5:10* is translated as *"mend"* in *Matthew 4:21*. This provides a wonderful picture of what is taking place after our suffering -- our Father perfects us. Just picture those fishermen sitting in their boat holding the net and working with such detail, meticulously mending all of the broken places with careful precision. This is a picture of what takes place with us after our suffering. Our Father, the God of all grace Himself, holds us and meticulously mends all of our wounds with such tender precision. He works on every area where we have been broken and torn until we are totally mended and perfected from that experience of suffering. So those of you, today, who are broken, know that He, Himself, holds you and will mend all of your brokenness.

James Wenger, Assistant Pastor
Pacific Hills Church
Aliso Viejo, California

July 10

THE LONG HAUL

"We are hard pressed on every side, yet not crushed; we are perplexed, but not in despair; persecuted, but not forsaken; struck down, but not destroyed."
2 Corinthians 4:8,9

There is a great illustration about an old, missionary couple that had been on the missionary field for 47 years. They are coming home on a boat. It's the same boat that Teddy Roosevelt is on, and he is coming back from a hunting trip (a Safari). They pull into port and it is packed with people who had come to see Teddy Roosevelt. He gets off the boat, they interview him, they take pictures, the bands are playing, and there is a great celebration.

The missionaries had not a soul there to meet them. Nobody. They get off the boat and go to their modest little hotel room. The missionary looked at his wife and said, "Honey, it just isn't fair that a man could come home from one foolish hunting trip and receive such accolades, and we come home and nobody's here to meet us." And she looks at him and said, "I know dear, but we're not home yet!" When you walk with the Lord - you must be in it for the long haul.

Chuck Wooley, Senior Pastor
Calvary Chapel Palm Springs
Cathedral City, California

July 11

GOD IS MY REFUGE

*"He who dwells in the shelter of the Most High will rest in the
shadow of the Almighty. I will say of the LORD, 'He is my
refuge and my fortress, my God, in whom I trust.' Surely He
will save you from the fowler's snare and from the deadly
pestilence. He will cover you with His feathers, and under
His wings you will find refuge; His faithfulness
will be your shield and rampart."*
Psalms 91:1-4

I know that some of you have been in some pretty fearful
places. Oh, how we need the protection of the Lord, and the
peace that comes when we stay as close to Him as possible.

Perhaps that *". . . secret place of the most High,"* is in your car,
or on your bed, late at night. Perhaps it's in that quiet place
deep down in your heart. Wherever it is, wherever we are
able to draw near to God, that's where we need to get to.
And that's where we need to stay.

A believer was fleeing from his enemies during a persecution. Pursued with no place to hide, he fell exhausted into a
cave, expecting to be caught. Awaiting his death, he saw a
spider weaving a web. Within minutes, the spider had
woven a beautiful web across the mouth of the cave. The
man's pursuers arrived, but on seeing the unbroken web,
assumed it impossible for him to have entered the cave. That
believer exclaimed, "Where God is, a spider's web is like a
wall. Where God is not, a wall is like a spider's web."

Rich Cathers, Senior Pastor
Calvary Chapel of Fullerton
Fullerton, California

July 12

SAFETY NET

"Thus says the LORD: 'I will return to Zion, and dwell
in the midst of Jerusalem. Jerusalem shall be called
the city of Truth, The Mountain of the LORD
of Hosts, The Holy Mountain. Thus says the LORD of hosts:
'Old men and old women shall again sit in the streets of Jerusa-
lem, each one with his staff in his hand because of great age.
The streets of the city shall be full of boys and
girls playing in its streets.'"
Zechariah 8:3-5

Let's all take care of our children. I have heard people become so exasperated with their children that they say to
them, "Why don't you go play in the street?!" They were
joking, of course! But did you know that the Lord's desire
is for our children to one day be able to play in the streets?

When Jesus returns, ruling and reigning from Jerusalem,
there will be such righteousness that we will not have to
fear for the safety of our children anymore. We will be able
to send them out to play, and tell them to come back next
weekend! Sadly, that is not the situation today. As we PRAY
for our children, there are some who PREY upon them.

We all desire to minister to the children that God has blessed
us with in as safe an environment as possible. This includes
recognizing that, as children, they desire to play more than
anything else. We can easily lose sight of the important fact
that God endorses the idea of children playing.

For a child, play time often teaches necessary life skills. Children learn to communicate, share their belongings, solve

(Continued)

problems, get along with others, etc. It is important for us to provide an atmosphere where children may play and learn the Word of God at the same time. It's a challenge to provide a safe, effective and enjoyable time for the children.

"Behold, children are a heritage from the Lord."
Psalm 127:3a

May we never lose sight of their contribution to the body of Christ, and may we never cease to offer our service to the Lord by serving them.

Brian Michaels, Senior Pastor
Rocky Mountain Calvary Chapel
Colorado Springs, Colorado

July 13

COMFORT AND JOY

"Come to Me, all you who labor and are heavy laden, and I will give you rest. Take My yoke upon you and learn from Me, for I am gentle and lowly in heart, and you will find rest for your souls. For My yoke is easy and My burden is light."
Matthew 11:28-30

Serving God is a blast! Somehow I think Satan has deceived so many Christians today. He has convinced them that God's will in their life would be a bummer, that it would be a burden and that they would be miserable if they were serving God. But did you know that is exactly false! Look what Jesus says: To those who are laboring and burdened down in life - come to the Lord and try it His way. He is calling us out of a life that is heavy and stressed, not <u>to</u> that life!

It is here that you find rest! I love this! When we take on the yoke with the Lord - it is restful. There is a peace that settles over life. It is as if everything falls into place, you are where you are meant to be — and in your heart, you really have peace. Have you discovered this walk with the Lord? It is there if you will just take it.

Sadly, some who say they are serving God look very burdened, but we know from this scripture alone that they must not be carrying the Lord's burden. Don't get me wrong, this doesn't mean life will be easy. But with the Lord, we can handle it. It is not too much to bear, because His burden is not heavy . . . it's a blast!

Jim Suttle, Senior Pastor
Calvary Chapel of Roswell
Roswell, New Mexico

July 14

POSSIBILITIES

". . .But with God all things are possible."
Matthew 19:26b

We believe that all things are possible with God, and nothing is too difficult for God. Miracles are possible today because God is alive. And if God is alive, then every day is an opportunity to experience the miraculous power of God. The question is, are you looking to your own wisdom or ability to handle the situations in your life, or to the wisdom and ability of the Almighty?

Larry DiSimone, Senior Pastor
Calvary Chapel of the Canyons
Silverado, California

July 15

THE CALL TO ENDURE

*"By faith he forsook Egypt, not fearing the wrath of the king:
for he endured, as seeing Him Who is invisible."*
Hebrews 11:27

We read in Hebrews 11:27 that Moses endured because he "saw" Him who is invisible. Endurance is the God-given ability every child of God has to withstand hardship or stress. False possessors can only endure for a time, whereas Spirit-filled followers of Christ will endure unto the end.

The Thessalonian believers were commended for their enduring faith and patience in all of their tribulations. Paul told Timothy to endure hardness as a good soldier of Christ. Paul himself saw beyond his difficulties. He endured sufferings and trials for the elect's sake. His example encouraged the saints to trust God, no matter what the trial.

Face it, we will all have seasons when we will have to endure affliction. There are times when we are going to have to endure wrong treatment. God's correction is proof that we are His children. James writes about those who suffered affliction patiently. What was the net result? They are counted "happy" that endure.

Perhaps our problem with life's adversities is that we think that we are supposed to enjoy the difficulty. No, our joy is in the Lord, not the trial. Hold your ground, and endure the storm with the assurance that Jesus is in control!

Ray Viola, Senior Pastor
Koinonia Fellowship
East Rochester, New York

July 16

A BLESSING IN DISGUISE

*"Consider it all joy, my brethren, when you encounter various
trials, knowing that the testing of your
faith produces endurance."*
James 1:2,3

Even in difficult or discouraging circumstances, we know
that God is in control. We cannot allow ourselves to become depressed or lose faith in our purposes. We must trust
that each situation is a part of God's plan for our lives. As
we focus on gaining maturity and enduring through to the
end, we can gain a perspective of joy even in the midst of
trials. It is often in the most difficult situations that we grow
and learn the most.

Matt DeWitt, Assistant Pastor
Calvary Chapel Church Planting Mission
Vista, California

July 17

THE MEANING OF MINISTRY

"You know that the rulers of the Gentiles lord it over them, and those who are great exercise authority over them. Yet it shall not be so among you; but whoever desires to be great among you, let him be your servant. And whoever desires to be first among you, let him be your slave -- just as the Son of Man did not come to be served, but to serve, and to give His life a ransom for many."
Matthew 20:25-28

The word "minister" has had different meanings over the centuries. Today it means that if you want to minister, you are willing and eager to serve God in whatever capacity you are called to serve, and is often hidden where no one sees except your heavenly Father.

If there are any heroes of the faith, they began as ministers of God in small, trivial things. They did what no one else was willing to do, or didn't have the time to do, or were blind to the fact that it even needed to be done. God takes those faithful in small things, and puts them in charge of greater things, because they, like Jesus Christ, are ready to serve, not to be served.

Bill Stonebraker, Senior Pastor
Calvary Chapel of Honolulu
Honolulu, Hawaii

July 18

BEING A SERVANT

*"If thou wilt be a servant unto this people this day, and wilt
serve them, and answer them, and speak good words to
them, then they will be thy servants for ever."*
1 Kings 12:7

King Rehoboam rejected the counsel of the wise elders, who
counseled him to be a servant to the people, and he followed the counsel of his friends. Their counsel was not
servanthood, but prideful rulership and oppression of the
people. The result was the division of Israel and Judah.

Everyone who follows Jesus Christ is a leader! You may
not be a pastor, worship leader, Sunday school teacher, etc.
. . . but by your actions, you are leading others. Children
watch you and learn from your ways, new believers will
glean from your life, nonbelievers will look to you.

There are two types of leaders that we can be; either a Godly
leader, or a worldly leader. The world's version of a leader
is one who is proud, and makes demands from the people.
God's version of a leader is one who is humble. One who
gives of him or herself for the people.

The counsel of the wise elders to Rehoboam, was if you will
serve these people, answer them, and speak good words to
them . . . they will become servants! May we listen to the
counsel of the wise elders, and serve people.

Thomas McCartin, Assistant Pastor
Calvary Chapel North Edwards
North Edwards, California

July 19

MIND SET

"Set your mind on things above, not on things on the earth."
Colossians 3:2

Our thought life is the road map for our hearts to follow.
We always think of where we would rather be, and our
hearts are not far behind. Our heart can be lost in the things
of the world, and we need to guide it by setting our minds
on things above.

Les Prock, Senior Pastor
Calvary Chapel North Hill
Milton, Washington

July 20

ARE YOU BRINGING GLORY TO CHRIST?

How is it that you bring glory to Christ? Is it being a servant? Is it teaching a Bible study? The scriptures are clear and it's awesome to know that we can all bring glory to Jesus Christ.

"And whatsoever ye do in word or deed, do all in the name of the Lord Jesus, giving thanks to God and the Father by him."
Colossians 3:17

Whatever we do, we can bring glory to Christ. Whether it's surfing, biking, teaching, spending time with your kids, wife or husband, we can give God the glory. The question we must ask is, "How am I bringing glory to Jesus Christ today?"

Louie Cruzado, Assistant Pastor
Calvary Chapel of Downey
Downey, California

July 21

FRUIT IN ITS SEASONS

"How blessed is the man who does not walk in the counsel of the wicked, nor stand in the path of sinners, nor sit in the seat of scoffers! But his delight is in the law of the Lord. And in His law he meditates day and night. And he will be like a tree firmly planted by streams of water, which yields fruit in its season."
Psalm 1:1-3a

Even the "blessed" man of Psalm 1 has his seasons. Although he avoids all the choking weeds and poisons of the world, though He's perpetually nourished in the rich soil of God's Word, though he is rooted firmly beside the waters of the Holy Spirit, he still has his seasons.

It seems that one of the greatest challenges of growing up in the Lord is in recognizing and respecting the seasons which He has ordained. Mary was commended by the Lord when she poured out the entire vial of costly perfume upon His head. She took an opportunity that would never come again. There are seasons of total abandonment.

In the same way there are seasons of enforced retirement when we are bursting to "do" and all He says is, "Wait!" What did Paul accomplish in the years of imprisonment at Caesarea where he wrote no epistles? Like Mary, he obeyed, and like Mary, he was criticized by the brethren. Jesus, to each in their season, says, "Well done!"

Bruce Mumper, Senior Pastor
Calvary Chapel of Fresno
Fresno, California

July 22

OUR GOD REIGNS

"I will rejoice in Jerusalem, and joy in my people."
Isaiah 65:19

Believer, isn't your soul like Jerusalem? Often in perilous turmoil, surrounded by enemies, it still is the dwelling place of God's choice, soon to be rescued, glorified, and forever exalted since His delight is in you.

"This is my Father's world, and let me ne'er forget, that though the wrong seems oft so strong, God is the ruler yet."

John Van Scott, Assistant Pastor
Calvary Chapel of the Finger Lakes
Farmington, New York

July 23

REVIVAL

". . .My soul clings to the dust; revive me according to Your Word. . . My soul melts from heaviness; strengthen me according to Your Word. . . I cling to Your testimonies; O Lord, do not put me to shame! I will run the course of Your commandments, For you shall enlarge my heart. "
Psalm 119:25,28,31,32

There is a lot of talk about revival these days. Most revival meetings consist of emotional hoots and hollers with very little substance.

WHAT IS THE KEY TO REVIVAL?

Mike Sasso, Assistant Pastor
Calvary Chapel of Downey
Downey, California

July 24

THE EVERLASTING LIGHT

"Arise, shine; for your light has come! And the glory of the Lord is risen upon you. For behold, the darkness shall cover the earth, and deep darkness the people; but the Lord will arise over you, and His glory will be seen upon you."
Isaiah 60:1,2

As you go about your workday, do people see the glory of the Lord upon you? In your neighborhood, does God's glory shine out from you? In your family, do you so reflect His glory and grace that even they -- the ones that know you the best -- sit up and take notice?

In Isaiah 60, the prophet opens the chapter with a command from Jehovah. The Israelites were God's elect people, chosen to bring light into a spiritually dark world. They knew Him as the pillar of fire that led them out of Egypt, as the glory that shone around the tabernacle, and as the God who thundered before them at Mt. Sinai. Yet, over the years, they had lost the marvelous fellowship they had once shared with the Lord. Hard times had come upon them, times which the Lord promised (vs. 19-20) would not last forever.

We have much in common with the Israelites. Like them, we have been given the incredible privilege of fellowship with the light of the world, Jesus Christ. Like them, we have an extraordinary responsibility to display that light to the world. Like them, we often stumble and fall. As each day comes and goes, are you reflecting His glory? Or, like the Israelites, do you find yourself in hard times, struggling with some situation that seems overwhelming.

(Continued)

If so, take heart! Your responsibility is not to <u>produce</u> the light, but merely to fellowship with the One who <u>is</u> the light. As the moon reflects the light of the sun, you have only to reflect the Lord's glory. As the Israelites found, the key to success lies in your relationship with the Lord.

When you spend <u>quality</u> time with Jesus, you can't do anything except reflect His marvelous light. Time spent in real communion with your heavenly Father -- whether it's reading and meditating on His Word, in prayer and worship, or listening to His words of wisdom -- will not only richly satisfy your soul, but will also settle His glorious light firmly upon your face.

We live in a world filled with increasing darkness. As we watch such evil, we often despair, fearfully wondering what else could possibly go wrong. We don't see any answers and yet, like the Israelites, we who are called by His name already <u>have</u> the answers. He is the one the hearts of the unsaved continually search for.

Show the world the righteousness of Jesus Christ as you reflect His love and His goodness in your dealings with a lost and dying world. As you draw closer to the Lord, delighting yourself in sweet communion with Him, let His glory shine out of your life. Someday someone in heaven will thank you.

"Let your light so shine before men, that they may see your good works, and glorify your Father which is in heaven."
Matthew 5:16

Steve Mays, Senior Pastor
Calvary Chapel of South Bay
Torrance, California

July 25

MEET AT JESUS' FEET

I like to meet at "Jesus Feet" no matter what the need.
Whether sick or dead, or at home in bed,
or even if you bleed.
Blind men did come by two
and by one and found true compassion,
And a sole leper came and gave thanks to His name
Whilst the other nine were a dash'n.
Two demons whose pleas were "don't torment me."
'Even fell at the feet of Jesus.
With no bid of a show He spoke, "Demons go!
"They said,"Into the pigs would please us"
Then a woman named Mary crushed many a berry
To bottle a sweet perfume.
On His feet perfume rare then dried with her hair
As the fragrance did fill all the room.
Martha was one who never had fun
constantly slave 'n in the kitchen.
Whilst Mary thought it near just to sit as his feet
With her focus simply on listen'n.
Even Satan one day with fear and dismay
will see his foe not beat.
For Jesus will rule with a rod for His tool
and His enemies will be under His feet.

Brian Bell, Senior Pastor
Calvary Chapel Murrieta
Murrieta, California

July 26

A CHALLENGE

*"Then the Pharisees and Sadducees came, and testing Him
asked that He would show them a sign from heaven. He answered and said to them, 'When it is evening you say, "It will
be fair weather, for the sky is red"; and in the morning, "It will
be foul weather today, for the sky is red and threatening."
'Hypocrites! You know how to discern the face of the sky, but
you cannot discern the signs of the times. A wicked and
adulterous generation seeks after a sign, and no sign shall be
given to it except the sign of the prophet Jonah.' And He left
them and departed."*
Matthew 16:1-4

This sign is the sign of the death and resurrection of Jesus,
the Son of God. The message of Jonah is coming judgment.
I have spoken with many people wanting a sign from God.
A personal burning bush that would be enough to convince
the hardest of hearts. The truth is, we must take the first
step toward God by faith. This is the challenge.

*"Now faith is the substance of things hoped for, the
evidence of things not seen."*
Hebrews 11:1

"For we walk by faith, not by sight."
2 Corinthians 5:7

Rick Kiscadon, Senior Pastor
Calvary Chapel Alamogordo
Alamogordo, New Mexico

July 27

HOW WAS YOUR DAY?

David was definitely having a bad day. To start off, his old boss had this tendency to throw spears at David. Real spears. So David changed jobs. He started to work for a man named Achish, a nice Philistine king, but one whose colleagues didn't seem to care for David. When the Philistines planned their next big campaign against the Israelites, the other managers voted for David to resign.

Dejected, David arrived home to find that his town had been raided, and everything had been taken -- women, children, and possessions. That's one bad day. But to make things even worse, the rest of his support team then turns on him ". . . *and David was greatly distressed; for the people spake of stoning him, because the soul of all the people was grieved, every man for his sons and for his daughters: but David encouraged himself in the LORD his God,"* (I Samuel 30:6).

What do you do when it seems like everyone is against you, and life seems rotten? God's desire is that we follow David's example, and get our help directly from God. If you've been discouraged, take heart! God is there, ready to listen and encourage you.

If you're ready for His help, why not check out these further verses - Psalm 18:6; 27:1-3, 34:1-8; 40:1,2; 42:5; 56:3,4; 62:1,5,8; Proverbs 18:10; Isaiah 25:4; 37:14-20; John 16:19; Habakuk 3:17-18; Romans 8:31; 2 Corinthians 1:9,10.

Rich Cathers, Senior Pastor
Calvary Chapel of Fullerton
Fullerton, California

July 28

THIS IS A TEST OF THE ETERNITY BROADCASTING SYSTEM

Job had been through an incredibly difficult time. His friends only made things worse in accusing him of some hidden sin. Yet we were told in the beginning that the reason for Job's troubles was God's choice to allow Job to be tested. The concept of God allowing a difficult time to come for any other reason than for judgment was simply beyond Job's understanding of God. This made Job frustrated with God.

Finally, God steps in to clear things up. God begins to ask Job a series of questions *(Job 38-41)* to show Job just how inadequate his understanding of God was. Job had been upset because he had wanted God to start acting the way <u>he</u> thought God ought to act. But God's whole point was to show Job that He, God, was much bigger than Job's limited concept of Him.

Indeed, Job's breakthrough came when he admitted something like, *"Okay, You are God and You can do whatever you choose to do, and I submit to Your will,"* (*Job 42:2)*. When you completely surrender to God, admitting He can do whatever He wants with you, then you begin to truly know Him.

Have you been feeling frustrated with God lately? Could it be that you think God ought to be doing something a certain way? When you realize He loves you as much as He does, there's no need to be afraid of surrendering yourself Him.

Steve Edmondson, Assistant Pastor
Calvary Chapel of Fullerton
Fullerton, California

STANDING ON THE PROMISES

*"And the Lord visited Sarah as He had said, and the Lord
did unto Sarah as He had spoken."*
Genesis 21:1

The Lord keeps His word. He is faithful to His promises.
He may not do it as quickly as we would like it, or in the
way that we expect, but He will do it. So don't be weary in
your well doing this morning, for in due season you will
reap the harvest if you faint not. Keep standing on the promises of God.

John Corcoran, Assistant Pastor
Calvary Chapel Costa Mesa
Santa Ana, California

July 30

MUST I?

In the gospel of Luke we read the first words of Jesus spoken as a 12 year-old youth. *"And He said unto them, 'How is it that ye sought me? Know ye not that I <u>must</u> be about my Father's business?'"* When someone says *must*, that person is fully set in his mind to finish his assigned task! And this Jesus knew at the young age of 12!

How about the *musts* in your life? There are a lot of options facing us, but as Jesus said, there are some things that are *musts*. You *must* be born-again, and as a child of God, we too *must* be about our Father's business.

And as Jesus, the business is to preach the gospel taking His message to the world.

Neil Matranga, Assistant Pastor
Calvary Chapel of Downey
Downey, California

July 31

COUNT YOUR BLESSINGS!

"Bless the Lord, O my soul, and forget not all his benefits:"
Psalm 103:2

How many blessings (benefits) can you find
in the 103rd Psalm?

1. _____
2. _____
3. _____
4. _____

Ed Cornwell, Assistant Pastor
Calvary Chapel Costa Mesa
Santa Ana, California

August 1

PIECES OR POWDER

"And whosoever shall fall on this stone shall be broken: but on whomsoever it shall fall, it will grind him to powder."
Matthew 21:44

We have only two choices when it comes to our relationship with Jesus:

1. **<u>Lord & Savior</u>** - Jesus is our rock of salvation! Fall upon the rock in repentance. Come to Him humbly for salvation & forgiveness. If you fall upon Him, yes, you will be broken. But that is the only way to enter into the abundant life Jesus offers.

2. **<u>Judge</u>** - If you refuse to fall at His feet, your only other option is judgment. You can be sure that all who are found under His wrath will be ground to powder! Everything He does, He does well!

Mike Sasso, Assistant Pastor
Calvary Chapel of Downey
Downey, California

August 2

THE PITFALLS OF PRIDE

One of the saddest stories in the Bible is the life of Saul. From a humble beginning, to a hideous end, his life is a picture of the pitfalls of pride. Chosen by God to be king over Israel, Saul initially felt unworthy of the call. In that humble state, God accomplished mighty things through him. But in time, as God wrought victory after victory and prospered the nation, a subtle switch flipped in Saul's heart. He began to believe his own press and forgot to acknowledge the Almighty Hand of Jehovah as the resource of his success.

The insidious and inherent aspect of pride is that it is deceptive. Not only does it exaggerate our own value and worth, but it blocks out the truth. We become so large in our own eyes that God is no longer visible. It was at this point that the Lord had to send someone to rebuke Saul. In the authority and power of God, the prophet Samuel spoke these words to all who have fallen prey to the sin of pride.

"So Samuel said, "When you were little in your own eyes, were you not head of the tribes of Israel? And did not the LORD anoint you king over Israel?"
1 Samuel 15:17

When we remain little in our own eyes, God is able to do great and mighty things through us. When we keep a humble perspective of ourselves, God will always be magnified and glorified in and through us.

Bob Coy, Senior Pastor
Calvary Chapel Ft. Lauderdale
Ft. Lauderdale, Florida

August 3

MORE THAN WORDS

"If you love Me, keep My commandments."
John 14:15

My wife doesn't put a lot of stock in words. She sees actions. I can say, "I love you, honey," but actions are far more significant when I want to prove my love to her.

If I really want to tell her I love her, I'll take out the trash. Now to her, that's love! I know, it's twisted -- but to her it's important because I'm showing my love by doing the things that really matter to her.

I think a lot of us say, "I love you, Lord," but the Lord, like my wife, is far more impressed with <u>life</u> service than He is with <u>lip</u> service. Friend, do you really love God? Then show Him that you love Him by your actions and simply obey His commandments.

Mark Scott, Senior Pastor
Calvary Chapel of College Park
College Park, Maryland

August 4

NOT TO BE MOVED

"And see, now I go bound in the spirit to Jerusalem, not knowing the things that will happen to me there, except that the Holy Spirit testifies in every city, saying that chains and tribulations await me. But none of these things move me; nor do I count my life dear to myself, so that I may finish my race with joy, and the ministry which I received from the Lord Jesus, to testify to the gospel of the grace of God."
Acts 20:22-24

What is it that moves you today? What is it that moves you from the place of trusting in Jesus Christ? In our day and age, the smallest things can move us from our place of being still in His arms. What moves you?

Paul knew well that chains and tribulation were awaiting his life. Paul knew that pain and hardships were in his future and yet, Paul declared that none of these things moved him. How could a man say such a thing? How could he say that chains and tribulations don't move him when traffic jams and broken fingernails move me?

Paul said, *"I don't count my life dear to myself."* Dear brother or sister, may today be a day where you don't count your life dear to yourself. A selfless life is abundant life. He who loses his life shall not be moved.

Chris Rehers, Assistant Pastor
Calvary Chapel Big Bear
Big Bear, California

August 5

A MOUNTAIN MAN

*"For if anyone is a hearer of the word, and not a doer, he is like
a man who looks at his natural face in a mirror for once he has
looked at himself and gone away, he has immediately
forgotten what kind of person he was."*
James 1:23,24

During the formative years of our country, there were
mountain men. They would go to the mountains to escape. When they would come down, they would have no
effect on the people they would come in contact with. All
that was on their mind was when they could return to the
mountain! Maybe they were seeking some type of experience.

Our next example is Moses. He went up to the mountain
and there met God. When he came down, there was a no-
ticeable difference, and he had an effect on the people he
met.

*"When Aaron and all the sons of Israel saw Moses, behold the
skin of his face shown, and they were afraid to come near him.
Then Moses called to them and spoke to them, commanding
them to do everything that the Lord had spoken to him."*
Exodus 34:30-32

What kind of a mountain man are you? <u>Be a doer</u>!

Glenn Kravig, Assistant Pastor
Calvary Chapel of Downey
Downey, California

August 6

QUENCHING YOUR THIRST

". . .If any man is thirsty, let him come to Me and drink. He who believes in Me, as the scriptures said, 'From His innermost being shall flow rivers of living water.'"
John 7:37,38

In the next verse we see that this living water that Jesus spoke of was the Holy Spirit. He promises to give to us His Holy Spirit. Thirst is the strongest desire the human body has. We can live without many things in our lives, but we cannot live without water.

In addressing the spiritual needs of man it is also true that the spiritual man can survive without many things, but he cannot survive without the Holy Spirit in his life. We are given the invitation to come and drink our fill. We don't have to ration out this water as if it might run out if we take in too much.

In *Ephesians 5:18*, Paul instructed us to *". . . be filled with the Holy Spirit."* This is not a one-time trip to the well; we have the well available to us 24 hours a day, seven days a week.

The word *"filled"* in verse 18 is used in the Greek as a present tense verb. That means this filling of the Holy Spirit is an action that is supposed to happen every moment of every day. Are you thirsty for some living water in your life today?

Mike Morris, Senior Pastor
Calvary Chapel of the High Desert
Hesperia, California

August 7

A TIME TO DECIDE

*"But in a great house there are not only vessels of gold and
silver, but also of wood and clay, some for honor and some for
dishonor. Therefore if anyone cleanses himself from the latter, he
will be a vessel for honor, sanctified and useful for the Master,
prepared for every good work. Flee also youthful lusts; but
pursue righteousness, faith, love, peace with those who
call on the Lord out of a pure heart."*
2 Timothy 2:20-22

There is a prayer that goes like this: "Lord so far today I
haven't been jealous, I haven't been boastful or lusted. So
far today, I haven't been selfish or thought evil of anyone.
But Lord, I'm about to get out of bed and, from that point
on, I'm going to need your help."

Paul gives to Timothy, and to us, a list of the choices that we
have to make every day. We have to decide what type of
vessel we will be. We have to decide how we will respond
when (not if) those lustful selfish temptations meet us head
on. The problem is we struggle with making decisions. We
don't like to decide.

A waitress at a local restaurant told me one of the most interesting aspects of her job is watching people who are hungry struggle over deciding what to order. Some will finally
say to her, "Just bring me what everyone else is eating today." That way if they don't like it they have someone other
than themselves to blame. But Paul tells us we must decide. We can't let anyone do that for us. Joshua told the
Israelites, *"Choose this day whom you will serve."*

(Continued)

~ 250 ~

Decide right now. When the temptation to lust comes, you will run away from it and run toward worshipping God, for nothing loosens lust like a worship song. Decide right now. When the temptation for materialism comes you will stop and be thankful for all that you have, for nothing loosens the grip of materialism like a thankful heart. Decide right now. When pride comes knocking, you will find someone to serve, for nothing melts away our pride like extending ourselves to someone other than to "me."

Don't wait for the circumstances of the day to make the decisions for you. You decide right now how this day will go, and the Lord will give you the victory.

Bob Botsford, Senior Pastor
Horizon North County
Rancho Santa Fe, California

August 8

GOD: THE PROBLEM SOLVER

"And the LORD God said, 'It is not good that the man should
be alone; I will make him an help mate for him.'"
Genesis 2:18

God saw a problem; that man was alone and He said, "This is not good." So God became the solver of this relationship problem for man. God wants to be the problem solver for you and me in the area of relationships. Whether it's the lack of relationship, break up of a relationship, or the mending of a relationship, God wants to be the problem solver!

What is man's position in all this?

The answer is in Genesis 2:21. . . *"And the LORD God caused a deep sleep to fall upon Adam, and he slept: and he took one of his ribs, and closed up the flesh instead thereof."* Man's position is to be at rest. God doesn't need my help. God would rather work alone in solving relationship problems. If I choose to help out he will let me. But what I do is only on the surface. What God does is a radiation treatment to the core of our heart. The Lord can do true healing, restoring, and mending. . . all I can do is put a band-aid on it.

The Lord will solve the problem, if I just let Him. I know I can rest as He finishes the work.

Kent Nottingham, Senior Pastor
Calvary Chapel Tallahassee
Talahassee, Florida

August 9

A VOICE

"And there he went into a cave, and spent the night in that place; and behold, the word of the LORD came to him, and He said to him, 'What are you doing here, Elijah?' So he said, 'I have been very zealous for the LORD God of hosts; for the children of Israel have forsaken Your covenant, torn down Your altars, and killed Your prophets with the sword. I alone am left; and they seek to take my life.' Then He said, 'Go out, and stand on the mountain before the LORD.' And behold, the LORD passed by, and a great and strong wind tore into the mountains and broke the rocks in pieces before the LORD, but the LORD was not in the wind; and after the wind an earthquake, but the LORD was not in the earthquake; and after the earthquake a fire, but the LORD was not in the fire; and after the fire a still small voice. So it was, when Elijah heard it, that he wrapped his face in his mantle and went out and stood in the entrance of the cave. Suddenly a voice came to him, and said, 'What are you doing here, Elijah?'"
1 Kings 19:9-13

Elijah was the mighty Prophet of the Most High God. After greatly defeating and slaying the prophets of Baal, Elijah became intimidated by the threats of Jezebel and ran away. God demonstrated to Elijah His great displays of power in the wind, the earthquake, and the fire. However, it was the still small voice of God that Elijah knew and responded to.

<u>If you have heard that still small voice your call is clear:</u>

". . . and do this, knowing the time, that now it is high time to awake out of sleep; for now our salvation is nearer than when we first believed. The night is far spent, the day is at hand."

(Continued)

"Therefore, let us cast off the works of darkness, and let us put on the armor of light. Let us walk properly, as in the day, not in revelry and drunkenness, not in lewdness and lust, not in strife and envy. But put on the Lord Jesus Christ, and make no provision for the flesh, to fulfill its lusts."
Romans 13:11-13

<u>In the face of adversity remember the words of our Lord:</u>

"These things I have spoken to you, that in Me you may have peace. In the world you will have tribulation; but be of good cheer, I have overcome the world."
John 16:33

Rick Kiscadon, Senior Pastor
Calvary Chapel Alamogordo
Alamogordo, New Mexico

August 10

HEAT WAVE

"Set your affection on things above."
Colossians 3:2

During August we've always experienced HEAT with more to come! We've been running air conditioners, central air, fans, and looking for shade just trying to stay cool. In the midst of it all, we blame the current weather condition. It's amazing that we are a people who like to put the blame on someone or something else. We need to accept SUMMER for what it is . . . HOT!

Praise God, as Christians, the heat that we experience is nothing to be compared with the heat that those who reject Christ will experience. They will die in their sins, go to hell and be tormented with a consuming fire day and night, with no relief in sight.

> H - Have His desire be our desire
> E - Earnestly seeking the Lord
> A - Await His coming
> T - Tend to his Word

However, if we take a look at heat, we can turn a "hot" situation into something meaningful.

Mark Maciel, Assistant Pastor
Calvary Chapel of Downey
Downey, California

August 11

GOD OF ALL THE "IMPOSSIBLES"

*"Jesus said to him, "I am the way, the truth, and the life. No
one comes to the Father except through Me."*
John 14:6

Pride is a large cause of problems in our homes, marriages,
careers, and church. This problem begins in the heart. "I
want." One of the problems with pride is the loss of truth
as it pollutes hearts and perception. A person can become
indignant due to a misunderstanding. In trying to get their
point across, frustration often arises and pride enters into
the heart. It is here that truth is lost in the error of bad
attitude. God resists the proud. Truth is more than facts,
and it begins with a person: Jesus. To borrow a proverbial
phrasing, "Factual accuracy in the mouth of a prideful person is like a jewel in the snout of a pig." Hold truth in a
pure heart. This is true godliness, and one more way in
which the pure in heart will see God.

How can this be?

*"Then said Mary unto to the angel, "How shall this be, since I
know not a man?" And the angel answered and said unto her,
"The Holy Ghost shall come upon thee, and the power of the High-
est shall overshadow thee; therefore also that Holy One which
shall be born of thee shall be called the Son of God." (Luke 1:34,35).*
When the angel told Mary that God was going to use her to
send His Son into the world, she was astounded and confused. There seemed to be a slight problem with the Lord's
plan. Mary wasn't married yet, and therefore was not in a
position to have children. But God was going to do the
impossible.

(Continued)

There are times in our Christian walk when the Lord will ask us to do something that is beyond our ability and our comprehension. Like Mary, we ask the Lord, "How will this be?" How are You going to pull this one off?"

If God asks us to do only what is within the walls of our abilities, we will never grow and mature as children of God. We will stagnate and never move on into a deeper trust and relationship with Him. Moreover, when God uses us beyond our ability, He gives glory to Himself and shows Himself to be who He says He is. He reveals His power through us.

When the Lord asks us to do something beyond our comfort, understanding or ability and we ask, "How can this be?" The Lord responds, *"Not by might, nor by power, but by My Spirit says the Lord,"* (Zechariah 4:6). Let us respond to the Lord's call as Mary did. *"I am the Lord's servant, may it be to me as You have said,"* (Luke 1:38). In doing so, we will see the Lord do great things in us and through us.

> Ernest Finklea, Senior Pastor
> Calvary Chapel of Durango
> Durango, Colorado

August 12

THE OLD, OLD STORY

"For I am not ashamed of the gospel of Christ: for it is the power of God unto salvation to every one that believeth; to the Jew first, and also to the Greek. For therein is the righteousness of God revealed from faith to faith: as it is written, the just shall live by faith."
Romans 1:16,17

Have you ever noticed how often advertisers have to come out with a new and improved version of their product to keep interest and sales up? Then, after some time, the newness wears off and the process is repeated and repeated. Not so with the glorious gospel of the unchanging God we love and serve. The old, old story of the Cross is still the same today, and it is the power to bring <u>new</u> life to all who believe. It needs no improvements or a new version.

Tim Hearron, Assistant Pastor
Calvary Chapel of Downey
Downey, California

August 13

IT NEEDS SALT

"Salt is good, but if the salt loses its flavor, how will
you season it? Have salt in yourselves,
and have peace with one another."
Mark 9:50

Salt may sting or it may make something tastier, but its influence always purifies and preserves that which comes into contact with it. In this verse, Jesus is saying that I am to first have salt in myself -- for myself. My words of exhortation should apply to me first, and only then may be passed on to others. Also, I must be accountable of salt in my personal life. I am to discern when to speak up with boldness; not hope that someone bolder than myself would come along and be the salt, *"Have salt in yourselves."*

Too often, as we share with others, we prefer the stinging nature of salt, rather than how it can make our words more palatable. Salt should be applied in such a way that we end up having *"peace with one another."* Who's been salt in your life lately? Have you thanked them? Are you at peace with them? That's the way Jesus would have it.

Mike Stangel, Senior Pastor
North Shore Christian Fellowship
Haleiwa, Hawaii

August 14

PULL UP THE REAR

*"All they that were numbered in the camp of Dan were an
hundred thousand and fifty and seven thousand and six
hundred. They shall go hindmost with their standards."*
Numbers 2:31

In this day and age, everyone wants to be first; no one wants
to go last. The tribe of Dan held a very important position
by going last. They were to follow and pick up the strag-
glers, gather the lost articles, and protect the rear from at-
tack. In the church, everyone wants to have a visible position of importance and few wish to be the nursery workers
and Sunday school teachers. Yet, without these, who will
take care of the church of tomorrow? The enemy will at-
tack from behind, and without laborers to stand guard, the
church will suffer great loss. If it is crowded in the front,
maybe God has called you to the rear where there is plenty
of room and great honor.

"But many that are first shall be last; and the last shall be first."
Matthew 19:30

Cary Wacker, Assistant Pastor
Morningstar Christian Chapel
Whittier, California

August 15

THE POWER IS IN THE BLOOD

" . . without Me you can do nothing."
John 15:5

"I can do all things through Christ who strengthens me."
Philippians 4:13

Do we really believe the Bible? Oh, I know that most of us would say, "Yes" to that question, but when it comes down to brass tacks, do we believe it in our lives? I think this is an issue regarding just how much we can do in this life.

First of all, you can do nothing! The idea here is that you can do nothing of <u>eternal value</u> on your own -- it is impossible. This is tough to swallow, and very humbling, but any time you rely on yourself -- your ability and talents -- what you do is, again, of no eternal value. You can do nothing! But yet, you can do everything, <u>with the Lord</u>. Then nothing is impossible for you if God is in it. There is no work that is beyond you, no mission field too tough.

The problem is that most of us live somewhere in the middle of these two truths. We find it hard to believe that we can't do anything of spiritual value by ourselves, but we also find it hard to believe we can do all things through Him -- so we don't do anything at all.

Lord, help us to truly believe your Bible, and strengthen me in my belief that you indeed are a God of the impossible.

Jim Suttle, Senior Pastor
Calvary Chapel of Roswell
Roswell, New Mexico

August 16

THE WARNINGS OF SIN

The author of Hebrews gave a stern warning to the Jewish believers. He said this:

"Take heed, brethren, lest there be in any of you an evil heart of unbelief, in departing from the living God. But exhort one another daily, while it is called today; lest any of you be hardened through the deceitfulness of sin."
Hebrews 3:12,13

I pray that we would have the fear of the Lord and see the destruction of sin; how sin can destroy our lives, our families' lives, and all who allow sin to reign!

May we heed the warnings!

Louie Cruzado, Assistant Pastor
Calvary Chapel of Downey
Downey, California

August 17

HIS REST

"Come unto me, all ye that labour and are heavy laden, and I will give you rest. Take my yoke upon you, and learn of me; for I am meek and lowly in heart: and ye shall find rest unto your soul. For my yoke is easy, and my burden is light."
Matthew 11:28-30

I have been told that when you put two oxen together under a yoke, you usually put an older, stronger ox along with a younger, weaker one. The yoke is usually built in a way so that the majority of the burden falls on the older ox. Jesus is the one who should be carrying the burden , He is the one who pulls the load. Have we found ourselves a little tired lately? Perhaps we've hitched ourselves into the wrong side of the yoke!

Many years ago, in the deep jungles of Africa, a traveler was making a long trek. Coolies had been engaged from a tribe to carry the loads. The first day they marched rapidly and went far. The traveler had high hopes of a speedy journey. But the second morning these jungle tribesmen refused to move. For some strange reason they just sat and rested. On inquiry as to the reason for this strange behavior, the traveler was informed that they had gone too fast the first day, and that they were now waiting for their souls to catch up with their bodies.

Beloved, take time to let Jesus carry your load. Take time to receive rest for your soul.

Rich Cathers, Senior Pastor
Calvary Chapel of Fullerton
Fullerton, California

August 18

BE WORTHY OF YOUR CALLING

The word "called" in Isaiah 54:5 is "QARA." In the Hebrew it can mean, to be called to a specific purpose. As Jesus was called to an appointed purpose, so are each of us.

Today is a wonderful time to reflect on our lives and what God has called us to do. After all, Jesus Himself said that, *". . . apart from Him we can do nothing"* worthwhile *(John 15:5)*. So it would be good to pray that we would fulfill that specific purpose He has designed for our lives.

Jack Trent, Assistant Pastor
Calvary Chapel of the Finger Lakes
Farmington, New York

August 19

TRAVEL PLANS

"For whom He did foreknow, He also did predestinate to be
conformed to the image of His Son, that He might be the
firstborn among many brethren. Moreover whom He did
predestinate, them He also called; and whom He called,
them He also justified; and whom He
justified, them He also glorified."
Romans 8:29,30

When we make plans to travel, we first decide where we are going. Then we make arrangements how to get there, pay the price, and hope all goes well so we can arrive at our destination on time.

As Christians, God has already decided where we are going, made arrangements on how to get there, and paid the price for us. To Him, we have already arrived!

Dan Marks, Assistant Pastor
Calvary Chapel of Downey
Downey, California

August 20

THE ANSWER

Does being a Christian eliminate frustration, disappointment and difficulties in this life? In a sense, yes, because we see their temporal existence, and know that one day they will be done away with totally. But the fact is that until that time, these unwelcome events happen to all of us. None of us are "pain exempt" in this life.

These times in our life remind us of how mortal and changeable we are. We can be a hero one day, and a goat the next; rich one day and poor the next; healthy one day, and sick the next. Man comes and he goes. Does that make life meaningless or vain? Of course not.

King Solomon attempted to suppress these valleys of life with the things of this world *(Ecclesiastes 2:4-10)*. Jackpot! Solomon wins Jerusalem's lottery! No more poverty, no more depression, no more frustration . . . oh, really?!

You and I may think that if we had what Solomon had, our lives would change. And, do you know what? They would. Solomon's did, and he forsook the Lord. The result? Frustration, disappointment, and vanity. No, we cannot eliminate our problems, but only through a relationship with Jesus can we cope *(John 15: 1-7)*.

Don't be like Solomon. The answer lies not in your pocket, on your back, or in your head. The answer lies in your heart *(Proverbs 4:23)*.

Ray Viola, Senior Pastor
Koinonia Fellowship
East Rochester, New York

August 21

IN HIM

"In Him we have redemption through His blood, the forgiveness of sins, according with the riches of His grace."
Ephesians 1:7

Paul points out that it is through Jesus, and in Jesus, that we have forgiveness. It is not through our earnest pleas to God for mercy that we are forgiven time and time again. Forgiveness is not based upon our own labor, toil, or sorrow. It is all in Him. As the old hymn says:

> Could my tears forever flow,
> Could my zeal no respite know,
> All for sin could not atone.
> Thou must save me, Thou alone.

The Son of God became the sin bearer for us. Hanging on the Cross that day, He took the wrath of God for our sins. God punished His beloved Son. In punishing Him as if He were our sin, we now become the *"beloved."* He has made us accepted in the beloved (vs. 6). Now we hear Him say to us, *"Behold my beloved son in whom I am well pleased."* Let us continue to be well-pleasing to Him, knowing that we are already well pleasing to Him as being in Him; accepted in the beloved.

Peyton Jones, Assistant Pastor
Calvary Chapel of Huntington Beach
Huntington Beach, California

August 22

THE HEART OF ASA

Asa, the king of Judah was about to do battle against an army much larger than his. The Cushite army had come to do battle with Asa in the Valley of Zephathah. Asa, however, understood one principle that is vital to us today as twentieth century believers. Let's look at the scenario.

In 2 Chronicles 14:1-7, Asa is used mightily by the Lord. Verses 9-10 , show us that the enemy is also well aware of how God is using Asa. The Cushite army is greater in size than Asa's army, but does Asa respond to this threat from the enemy by panicking? No, instead we see in verse 11, that Asa doesn't panic, but prays. Asa does not come against the enemy in his own strength, but cries out: *"Help us O Lord our God for we rely on you!"*

Asa's enemy is stronger and more powerful than he, so he looks to a strength that is greater than the enemy he is facing. He knows he is about to have a difficult day. We've all had days that didn't turn out the way we had planned, haven't we? Do we pray or do we panic?

Samson chose to cry out to the Lord instead of panic as he faced the powerful Philistines:

> *"God, please strengthen me just once more, and let me with one blow get revenge on the Philistines."*
> *Judges 16:28*

Hannah, the woman who was barren for many years, in her distress also called upon the Lord in fervent prayer instead of panicking:

(Continued)

*"LORD . . . if you will . . . remember me, and not forget your
servant, but give her a son, then I will give him
to the Lord for all the days of his life."*
I Samuel 1:11

Asa, Samson, and Hannah all looked to a power greater than themselves to help them in their time of trouble. Do we?

Often, we find that we have a tendency to be overwhelmed by our circumstances, and not by God's greatness. But prayer brings our troubles and problems back into perspective. Prayer shifts the burden of responsibility from us to the Lord. Don't underestimate the power of prayer. When we pray, God listens.

*"The eyes of the LORD are on the righteous and
His ears are attentive to their cry."*
Psalm 34:15

Today, meditate on the prayer Asa prayed as he was about to be attacked by an enemy that wanted to overpower him.

*"Asa. . . called to the LORD. . .and said, "LORD, there is no
one like You to help the powerless against the mighty.
Help us. . .our God, for we rely on You, and in Your name we
have come against this vast army. LORD, You are
our God; do not let man prevail against You."*
2 Chronicles 14:11

Our Lord can make a way when there is no way. He can open doors no man can open. Trust Him.

Fidel Gomez, Senior Pastor
Calvary Chapel Tamarac
Tamarac, Florida

August 23

THE WILL OF GOD IN YOUR LIFE

*"Commit your works to the Lord, and your plans will be
established . . The mind of man plans his way,
but the Lord directs his steps."*
Proverbs 16:3,9

One of the most common problems that people face today
is trying to determine the "will" of God. As we struggle to
make plans for our future, we find ourselves simply throwing up our hands in frustration and saying something like,
"God just hasn't shown me His will!" I am learning that
many times I do know God's will. What I do not know is
the future. This is where faith and obedience come in.

You see, the question is not, "What do I do?," but rather,
"Will I do it?" Up to this point God hasn't made a habit of
revealing to me what He's going to do tomorrow! What He
has done, however, is given me His Word. By looking to
His Word, I come to understand His nature, and His purpose for creating me. Then I also begin to understand what
His will is for my life.

This is true for human relationships as well. The more inti-
mately we know a person, the more we know their thoughts,
tendencies, and desires. We then know what pleases them,
and what they would do in certain situations. Now I do
not purpose to bring the infinite God down to the finite level
of man. However, there is a principle here: To know the
will of God, I must first know God.

Sometimes He has a very specific task for us to do. Other
times, there may be several options available. The fact that

(Continued)

there is more than one option shouldn't frustrate us. It should cause us to thank Him for His goodness and grace. He has demonstrated His love by giving us both the capacity to choose, as well as options from which to choose.

What is most important, however, isn't necessarily what I choose. What is most important is that it fall within the parameters of His righteousness. In other words, I must ask myself, "Does what I am proposing to do violate God's standards in any way?" (i.e. deception, lying, stealing, manipulation, selfish ambition, etc.) The next question I ask myself is, "Does this ultimately bring glory to God?"

In his first letter to the Corinthians, Paul said, *"All things are lawful, but not all things edify,"* and *"...whatever you do, do all to the glory of God,"* *(1 Corinthians 10:23 & 31).* You see, it is very natural and easy to think in terms of, "What's best for me?" And yet scripture seems to always point out a different perspective. The issue is, what will most glorify God?

Therefore, we have to be very careful to look at our decisions in light of scripture. As we do, two things will happen. First of all, we will get to know God. (Interestingly, the natural result of that is that we will also discover His will for us.) Secondly, we demonstrate a heart of submission to God's authority in our lives. God has declared that His eyes, *"...move to and fro throughout the earth that He may strongly support those whose hearts are completely His,"* *(2 Chronicles 16:9).*

God wants to reveal Himself and His will to us and, yes, He wants to bless our works and plans! But our priority must first be to seek Him through His word and prayer. Jesus said *"But seek first His kingdom and His righteousness; and all these things shall be added to you,"* *(Matthew 6:33).* In other

(Continued)

words, our relationship with Him is more important than our daily agenda. As we seek Him, then He will take care of all the other details and needs that we have. He knows that if we follow our tendency to put our plans, aspirations, and even good works before Him, then we will be disappointed. Satan will rob us of the real joy, peace, and fruitfulness that comes from simply abiding in and serving Him *(John 15)*.

Our Lord Himself expressed this so clearly in the sermon on the mount when He said, *"Blessed are those who hunger and thirst for righteousness, for they shall be satisfied,"* *(Matthew 5:6)*. Tragically, few people today know what it means to be satisfied. I believe this is the case primarily because they don't really know God as He intends for them to know Him *(2 Peter 1:2)*.

Therefore, as we seek to know the will of God in our daily lives, we must first realize that our ability to live in, and accomplish, His will depends upon and flows from our relationship with Him. We can be thankful that scripture doesn't speak specifically to every situation in life. If it did, then faith would not be necessary. This would mean that our relationship with God would not be necessary either. The fact is, we do need God. We need to know Him, and we must walk by faith! He graciously allows us to make choices, often times with a great deal of freedom. And He patiently waits to see how we are going to approach each decision. His heart, however, is that we commit ourselves and our decisions to Him. As we do, He will respond faithfully. Indeed, our plans will be established.

Jon Sanne', Senior Pastor
Calvary Chapel of Olympia
Olympia, Washington

August 24

THE POTTER AND THE CLAY

"Then I went down to the potter's house; and behold, he wrought a work on the wheels. And the vessel that he made of clay was marred in the hand of the potter; so he made it again another vessel, as seemed good to the potter to make it."
Jeremiah 18:3,4

Have you ever watched a potter at work? Unless you're an arts and crafts kind of person, you probably haven't. But if you did watch, you'd find the potter behind his pottery wheel, with pieces of clay spattered on the floor, as well as a bucket of water near by. You'd notice right away that the potter's focus is on the clay -- he knows exactly what he wants to do with it.

What, though, do you imagine the clay is thinking? Would it say something like, "I want to be special -- refined, expensive! I want to be shipped to Italy, or maybe Greece! I want to be seen in only the best homes!" Is this, however, what the potter wants, or even why it was made?

In *Jeremiah 18:1-6*, the prophet gives us a beautiful illustration of the potter and the clay. Jeremiah watches the potter working at the wheel -- forming the clay into a vessel. But, just as the clay began to take shape, something contaminated the clay and when the potter touched it, the vessel was damaged. Pieces of clay splattered and Jeremiah watched as it crumbled in the potter's hands.

How about you? Have you ever felt crumbled under the Potter's hands? Have you ever felt like your life was falling apart? Did you know that Jesus is the Potter in your life?

(Continued)

He has a goal in mind for you, a purpose He works through your life with His own hands. So what does that make you? The clay.

When Jesus places his hand upon your life -- when He begins to mold and shape -- it can hurt! But He wants you to be a beautiful and useful vessel, a *Jeremiah 29:11* vessel -- one with a future and a hope.

Are there any contaminants in your life that the Potter needs to remove to, "*. . . complete that good work He began in you?*" Are you hard clay, difficult for the Potter to mold? Don't struggle with Him, yield to Him as the clay does.

When you are ready, the Potter will take your life and make you again. He will knead you, wash you, dip you, and add you back into His original plan and purpose. He loves you! When God looks at you, He already sees the completed work. While you see your present circumstances as impossible, He can look beyond them and see the finished product.

We need to trust God in all things -- especially when He is molding us. Will you let the Potter mold you? Only then can He, "*. . . complete the good work He began in you.*"

Steve Mays, Senior Pastor
Calvary Chapel of South Bay
Torrance, California

August 25

I SWEAR TO TELL THE WHOLE TRUTH . . .

Truth or consequences. A very real issue in our country today. Now in case you think I'm going to launch off into a Clinton/Lewinsky tirade, I'm not. Truth isn't just the President's problem. It's an issue relevant to us all.

There seems to be something in us that is reluctant to be real and honest with one another. We think that holding back the truth might protect people from hurt. Yet when the truth comes out, the discovery of deception only creates deeper hurt. We see it in the hurt and disillusionment that those closest to the president are experiencing right now. Maturity in relationships is dependent on being honest with one another. Paul wrote that when we, *". . . speak the truth in love,"* we grow up in our relationships, we grow up as believers *(Ephesians 4:15).* Job was a guy with problems. But he was also a guy with friends. Friends are great because they can be there to comfort you in your problems. But Job's friends didn't know the whole truth. But the truth is that God sometimes allows difficulties in our lives to test us. So instead of comforting Job, they condemned him. And Job replied to his friends, *"How then comfort ye me in vain, seeing in your answers there remaineth falsehood,"* *(Job 21:34)?*

Truth. Sometimes we're hiding it, trying desperately to keep others from seeing us as we really are. Sometimes we are ignorant of it, not seeing the whole picture. Be real. The truth will set you free.

Steve Edmondson, Assistant Pastor
Calvary Chapel of Fullerton
Fullerton, California

August 26

BACK TO SCHOOL

Here we are again with back to school sales for: shoes, clothes, backpacks, pencils and paper, etc. . . Mom, Dad . . . <u>I NEED THIS</u>!!! And off to the malls we go. Is there any way of getting away from this? NOPE! However, the apostle Peter states this:

"But the God of all grace, who hath called us unto His eternal glory by Christ Jesus, after that ye have suffered a while, make you perfect, stablish, strengthen, settle you."
1 Peter 5:10

Maybe you've been out of school (spiritually) for a while, so gather your supplies, come back, and let the Lord *make you perfect, stablish* you, *strengthen* you, and *settle you* so that you can be that "A" student for Jesus.

"Being confident of this very thing, that He which hath begun a good work in you will perform it until the day of Jesus Christ."
Philippians 1:6

Be thankful, and take a second look at <u>SCHOOL</u>:

S - Service to our Lord Jesus
C - Commitment to Christ
H - Honoring our Savior
O - Obey His Commandments
O - Obedient to God
L - Loyal to Jesus

Mark Maciel, Assistant Pastor
Calvary Chapel of Downey
Downey, California

August 27

THE LORD WEIGHS THE HEARTS

"Every way of man is right in his own eyes,
but the LORD weighs the hearts."
Proverbs 21:2

We fail to take an objective outlook on our actions. Therefore we need to bring every act under God's scrutiny. As
we expose all to Him, we achieve that which lasts for eternity.

"Search me, O God, and know my heart; try me, and know my
anxieties; and see if there is any wicked way in me,
and lead me in the way everlasting."
Psalm 139:23,24

Carl Westerlund, Assistant Pastor
Calvary Chapel Costa Mesa
Santa Ana, California

August 28

WELLS OF SALVATION

"Behold, God is my salvation; I will trust and not be afraid; for the LORD JEHOVAH is my strength and my song; He also is become my salvation. Therefore with joy shall ye draw water out of the wells of salvation. And in that day shall ye say, Praise the LORD, call upon His name, declare His doings among the people, make mention that His name is exalted."
Isaiah 12:2-4

Water. So necessary to sustain life. Such a precious commodity in a dry land like Montana. Yet even more precious, even more necessary than water to our health and life, is our salvation. Since God is our salvation, we cannot let a day go by without drinking deeply of Him. As there is no life without water, there is no life apart from God. Just as our physical thirst proves that we are alive, so our thirst for God proves that we are drawing life from Him.

Now, drawing water out of a well is hard and heavy work. However, when the Lord is our strength then our work, our life, our very existence becomes a joyful experience. Drawing our life from God becomes our joy. When that joy of relationship is within us, we just have to share it with others! Words come gushing forth from our lips in praise, worship, prayer, and telling others about Jesus.

Thirsty? Drink deeply of God every day -- then open your mouth and allow God's Word to flow through you to a dry and thirsty world.

Tom Cox, Senior Pastor
Calvary Chapel of Helena
Helena, Montana

August 29

REMEMBER MY CHAINS

*"This salutation by my own hand; Paul. Remember my
chains. Grace be with you. Amen."*
Colossians 4:18

We come to various circumstances in our Christian experience. We have good times, and we have trials. In trials, we sometimes complain that our lives are too difficult. It would be best in those times to consider the fact that in some parts of the world Christians are in prison for their faith.

Paul never complained about his circumstances. He was serving the Lord, and his calling as a bondslave of Jesus Christ didn't always afford him comfort. He made a simple request to the church in Colosse, *"Remember my chains."*

Les Prock, Senior Pastor
Calvary Chapel North Hill
Milton, Washington

August 30

CALVARY, THE SILENT WAY

"He was oppressed, and He was afflicted, yet He opened
not His mouth; He is brought as a lamb to the slaughter,
and as a sheep before her shearers is dumb,
so He openeth not His mouth."
Isaiah 53:7

Have you ever been falsely accused? You're absolutely blameless, yet someone's mad at you! Or maybe you've been overlooked. You've worked long hours on a project only to see someone else getting all the credit for your hard work! When things like that happen, are you silent, refusing to defend yourself no matter what?

Most of us don't suffer well in silence. If others are abusing or mistreating us we are apt to protest long and loud. We want to make sure that people know we've been treated unjustly. We aren't silent about it. And yet, as this passage in Isaiah so clearly tells us, Jesus, our Lord did just that. He was silent through the most difficult time of His life. In the gospels, we see this very clearly. In *Matthew 26:62-64*, he was silent before Caiaphas, the high priest, speaking only to assert His claim of deity.

In *Matthew 27:11-14*, He was silent before Pilate. *"And He answered to him never a word; insomuch that the governor marveled greatly."* He was silent before Herod, disappointing the king who had hoped to see a miracle or two. *"Then he questioned Him with many words; but He answered him nothing,"* *(Luke 23:9).* And, of course, He was almost completely silent on the Cross, speaking only those few precious words recorded for us in the gospel accounts of His life. Think

(Continued)

about that for a moment -- Jesus, a man without one single, solitary fault -- the perfect Lamb of God without spot or blemish -- was treated like a common criminal by the judicial system of His day. If anyone ever had a right to plead His innocence, it was Jesus. And yet, He didn't. Can any of us make this same claim? In either our silence or our innocence?

Silence is a strength that the Lord desires in our lives, a strength that only He can give. From the perspective of the Cross, "silence" means that you give up your right to yourself. This is the Calvary way. A practice with rich rewards for those who dare to follow it.

How about you? Are you willing to turn yourself over to the Lord? To give up your ambitions, goals, and your will? Can you stand silent when injustice or persecution enters your life? Are you prepared to turn over the control of your life to the one Person who has the perfect plan for it?

Ask the Lord to show you those things you've been hanging on to, and then give them to Him -- once and for all. Clothe yourself in the strength of that new-found silence as you wait in expectation to see what God will do with your obedience. He won't disappoint you.

Take my will, and make it Thine; it shall be no longer mine.
Take my heart, it is Thine own; it shall be Thy royal throne.
Take my love, my Lord, I pour at Thy feet its treasures store.
Take myself, and I will ever be, only, all for Thee.

Steve Mays, Senior Pastor
Calvary Chapel of South Bay
Torrance, California

August 31

AGAIN AND AGAIN

*"I think you ought to know, dear brothers, about the hard time
we went through in Asia. We were really crushed and overwhelmed, and feared we would never live through it. We felt
we were doomed to die and saw how powerless we were to help
ourselves; but that was good, for then we put everything into
the hands of God, who alone could save us, for He can even
raise the dead. And He did help us and saved us from a terrible
death; yes, and we expect Him to do it again and again."*
2 Corinthians 1:8-10

This is much of our life. It describes the many times in our
lives that we do things over and over that we shouldn't.
But again and again He is faithful to us. Even after so many
times of getting into trouble, or being surprised by temptations, GOD is there, again and again. Fulfilling His promise to never leave us or forsake us, He is with us always. It
is in those difficult times we come to the realization that
we are powerless and it is good for us to see this because
then we will cast all of our cares upon Jesus. Unfortunately
we sometimes wait until we have exhausted every way we
know and even ourselves before we get to this place of leaving it with the Lord. But when we do He is there, again
and again. And we know His goodness so we expect Him
to do it again and again. There is a great comfort in knowing GOD'S love is such that He will be there every time for
us no matter what we do or what happens to us. Praise the
GOD of Again and Again!

Stan Denning, Senior Pastor
Calvary Chapel Mid Cities
Paramount, California

September 1

SET YOUR LIMITS

*"My soul is weary with sorrow; strengthen me according to
Your word. Keep me from deceitful ways; be gracious to me
through Your law. I have chosen the way of truth; I have set
my heart on Your laws. I hold fast to Your statutes, O LORD;
do not let me be put to shame. I run in the path of Your
commands, for You have set my heart free."*
Psalm 119:28-32

Sorrow and suffering can bring one of two things; isolation
and hopelessness, or involvement and comfort. Sorrow and
weariness of soul must bring us into closer fellowship with
other believers, and with Jesus Himself. The Word of God
is given to us so that when we are sorrowful we can find the
comfort and freedom that God wants us to have.

It is said that what children need most is the understanding
of boundaries and limits. God's Word fulfills this in the lives
of believers. It brings us freedom because we know where
the limits are, comfort because we know where God is, and
peace because we know God's heart.

Unfortunately, the generation of the 50's and 60's saw any
limits on human expression as a bad thing. In the 80's and
90's, the result was cynicism and self involvement. What
the next generation will bring is anyone's guess, but our
task must be to pray that people would turn to the Word of
God. Let us be known as people who trust in God and His
Word.

Greg Cull, Senior Pastor
Calvary Chapel Shingle Springs
Shingle Springs, California

September 2

GUARDING OUR THOUGHTS

*"Finally, brethren, whatsoever things are true, whatsoever
things are honest, whatsoever things are just, whatsoever things
are pure, whatsoever things are of good report; if there be any
virtue, and if there be any praise, think on these things. Those
things, which ye have both learned, and received,
and heard, and seen in me, do: and the
God of peace shall be with you."
Philippians 4:8,9*

The old saying goes, "thoughts produce acts, acts produce
habits, and habits produce character." Our goal is to have
the character of Christ.

As we think, meditate on spiritual matters; as we obey the
Word of God in our lives, the result will be the fruit of righteousness, and the character of Christ will dominate our
lives.

Neil Matranga, Assistant Pastor
Calvary Chapel of Downey
Downey, California

September 3

DIRTY LAUNDRY

"But now you must also put off all these: anger, wrath, malice, blasphemy, filthy language out of your mouth."
Colossians 3:8

It would be silly to put on dirty clothes after taking a bath. Yet, after being washed from our sin and made new, we can still be guilty of wearing the wardrobe of the old nature.

Better to put off the old wardrobe, along with the old man, and let our Father give us new, clean clothes instead.

Les Prock, Senior Pastor
Calvary Chapel North Hill
Milton, Washington

September 4

FIRST FRUITS

We are all familiar with the story of Joshua's triumph over the city of Jericho. As children, we sang the song "Joshua fought the battle of Jericho. . .and the walls came tumbling down." But the real gem in this story is not the radical removal of Jericho's defenses that we all remember. It is the still small voice of God giving a lifesaving principle that is still critical in our Cross-bearing march into the promised land.

> *"And you, by all means abstain from the accursed*
> *things, lest you become accursed when you take*
> *of the accursed things, and make the camp*
> *of Israel a curse, and trouble it."*
> *Joshua 6:18*

God gave the city into the hands of the Israelites, but He told them to take nothing of the spoils for themselves. Joshua went on to instruct them to bring all of the gold, silver, bronze, and iron into the treasury of the Lord. This is the principal of first fruits. Jericho was God's first victory on behalf of the Israelites in the promised land. They were to take nothing from it. Unfortunately, one of the Israelites named, Achen, did not heed God's warning. He took the spoils and Israel found herself defeated by her enemies.

Why was it so important to establish this principal of first fruits? Because the giving of the first fruits acknowledges two things: (1) God's goodness and (2) His supremacy. It is an act of worship that demonstrates trust in its purest form. The first fruits are just that. They are the first, with no guarantee of more to follow. To give them all away can

(Continued)

only mean that our hope for future provision is in the sovereignty and goodness of God, not in the stash we have stored for ourselves.

In the same way, when we come to the Lord at the point of salvation, He defeats the enemy in our lives and asks us to not take back any of the spoils. How many times do we attempt, as Achen did, to take just one or two things back. We will just hide them in our tent. God will never know. But it becomes a curse to us in just the same way it did to the whole camp of Israel. When we attempt to take back part of the first fruits (our life) which we have given to God, it becomes a curse upon ourselves and those around us; through screams of unbelief and lack of trust in the hand of the Almighty God. If we are finding ourselves in defeat against minor sins, we need to examine our hearts. Could we once again be relying upon ourselves instead of Christ in an area of our life? If so, we have taken back the "first fruits." Fortunately for us, we are under the new covenant which does not require stoning, but instead, submission. We need to do as Christ instructs the church of Ephesus:

". . . You have left your first love. Remember therefore from where you have fallen; repent and do the first works."
Revelation 2:4,5

By giving back to God in whatever area we have taken from Him, trusting Him in the same reckless abandon as when we were first saved, so we can also return to the security of His love. Then we can sit back and watch the walls fall down.

Bob Coy, Senior Pastor
Calvary Chapel Ft. Lauderdale
Ft. Lauderdale, Florida

September 5

HONORING HIS WORD

I was reflecting on how awesome God has been to our fellowship over the years. As I was reading Acts, I came across a message Paul shared with the church of Ephesus:

"And how I kept back nothing that was profitable unto you, but have shewed you, and have taught you publicly, and from house to house, for I have not shunned to declare unto you all the counsel of God."
Acts 20:20, 27

I believe that the Lord has truly blessed us because we honor His Word. Our prayer is that the flock would be diligent in devoting themselves in His Word.

"Study to shew thyself approved unto God, a workman that needeth not to be ashamed, rightly dividing the word of truth."
2 Timothy 2:15

Mark Maciel, Assistant Pastor
Calvary Chapel of Downey
Downey, California

September 6

A COMMITMENT TO GO DEEP

"Oh the depth of the riches both of the wisdom and knowledge of God! How unsearchable are His judgments and His ways past finding out! For who has known the mind of the Lord? Or who has become His counselor? Or who has first given to Him and it shall be repaid to him?" For of Him and through Him and to Him are all things, to whom be glory forever, Amen."
Romans 11:33-36

One of the greatest displays of natural beauty and wonder is the view over the rim of the Grand Canyon. Layers of history are stacked one upon the other. Spanning over a mile are layers upon layers of rock, clay, and fossils; clues to the origins of life that keep archeologists filled with wonder. If they had wanted to study the earth, but only looked at the top layer, they would have missed out on discovering the layers just waiting under the surface. In essence the more we dig, the more we discover.

The same is true in our walk with God. We can get into a rut and limit our understanding of Him. But there is so much more! We need to sharpen our tools, and always be eager to dig for the nuggets of our life in Christ.

After a long and uneventful night, Jesus challenged his disciples to push away from the shore into the deep and there they would make a great catch. Let's make the decision to go to a deeper level with Jesus, too. Let's break the cords of superficiality, and allow His Spirit to lead us into deep water.

Bob Botsford, Senior Pastor
Horizon North County
Rancho Santa Fe, California

September 7

DRIVEN BY APPETITE?

"He that laboureth laboureth for himself;
for his mouth craveth it of him."
Proverbs 16:26

Whether you are willing to admit it or not, everything you do in life is motivated by your appetites. You go to work each day, not because you love getting up early each morning and being bossed around all day, you do it because you have an appetite for money, food, independent living, or nice things. Get the idea? Appetites can be good or bad. Jesus warned us to be careful which appetites we let rule our lives.

"I tell you the truth, you are looking for Me, not because you saw miraculous signs, but because you ate the loaves and had your fill. Do not work for food that spoils, but for food that endures to eternal life, which the Son of Man will give you. On Him God the Father has placed His seal of approval."
John 6:26,27

What "Appetites" are driving your life?

Oh, Lord, give us a hunger for You and Your kingdom!

Mike Sasso, Assistant Pastor
Calvary Chapel of Downey
Downey, California

September 8

OBEDIENCE IS NOT AN OPTION

*"And you have forgotten the word of encouragement that
addresses you as sons: My son, do not make light of the Lord's
discipline, and do not lose heart when He rebukes you, because
the Lord disciplines those He loves, and He punishes
everyone He accepts as His son."*
Hebrews 12:5,6

Will God bless me no matter what I'm doing, just because
He loves me? Can I be disobedient to the Lord and His
commands and still be blessed? What would happen if I
continue to disobey?

The above verses give us the answers. You will not be
blessed, you will be chastised. When you disobey God, and
you walk in disobedience, you will be walking under His
chastening hand. God will be loving, but He will discipline.
It is a relationship between a Father and His child.

We need to clearly set our minds on the fact that obedience
is not an option; it is a command from our Heavenly Father.
He is not waiting for us to decide whether we will be obedient Christians or not. Rather, He is working in our lives,
desiring to manifest His blessings upon us, but know those
blessings depend <u>upon</u> our obedience. God wants us to walk
with Him in obedience. Rejoice when conviction and chastening come, for they confirm that we belong to Him!

Danny Bond, Senior Pastor
Pacific Hills Church
Aliso Viejo, California

September 9

COMMITTED TO THE TASK

"Therefore, since we have so great a cloud of witnesses surrounding us, let us also lay aside every encumbrance, and the sin which so easily entangles us, and let us run with endurance the race that is set before us, fixing our eyes on Jesus the author and perfector of faith who for the joy set before Him endured the Cross."
Hebrews 12:1-3

What a great example Jesus set before us. He was committed to the task set before Him, praise God! Paul wrote to Timothy expressing that same type of commitment.

"I have fought the good fight. I have finished the course. I have kept the faith."
II Timothy 4:7

Today our commitment doesn't seem to be the same. It doesn't take much to get us to turn tail and run. We need to start running towards God and not away from Him. I thank God for His mercies every day. He supplies our every need. Can you imagine this. . .one day we will be caught up in the air and we will spend eternity with the Almighty God our Savior Jesus Christ. Just think, if we had to walk to heaven how many of us would complete the trip? <u>God is good all the time.</u>

Keep on walking.

Glenn Kravig, Assistant Pastor
Calvary Chapel of Downey
Downey, California

September 10

LIAR, LIAR!

"No temptation has overtaken you except such as is common to man; but God is faithful, who will not allow you to be tempted beyond what you are able."
1 Corinthians 10:13

Satan is a liar! In fact, Jesus told us that Satan is the father of all lies. Lying is one of his primary tactics in dealing with men. Paul told us not to be ignorant of his devices *(2 Corinthians 2:11)*, especially in regard to temptation. In this verse we can expose two of Satan's most prominent lies to us.

You are not alone! One of Satan's tactics is to isolate us from the rest of believers. He whispers in our ears things like: "No one is as bad as I am, no one struggles like I do with sin," etc. But this is untrue. Notice scripture says that *". . .no temptation has overtaken us except what is common to man."* The temptations that you are struggling with, are what we are all struggling with. Satan wants to lie to you so that he can make you feel alone, and then you are an easy target for his discouragement -- but you are not alone.

You can make it! Again Satan whispers his lies in our ears things like: "You'll never make it, it's all too much," and on the lies go. If we believe these lies, it destroys our resolve to stay true to God. Yet, they are all lies, for God promised never to let us be in a situation that we could not handle. I challenge you today, to know the difference between the lies of Satan, and the truth of God -- and stick to the truth!

Jim Suttle, Senior Pastor
Calvary Chapel of Roswell
Roswell, New Mexico

September 11

WHOSE IS THAT?

"Jesus answered them and said,
'My doctrine is not Mine, but His who sent me.'"
John 7:16

Something happens to the doctrines of God when they become man's. One, is they leave their rightful owner. Beyond that, man begins to destroy them like everything else he owns. No matter how pure and accurate they once were, they are now a possession rather than a privilege. It is common today to see Christians holding accurate answers, but lacking the fruit intended by them.

By example, Jesus teaches us to give out what we have received, never claiming it as our own. Ask who it belongs to. If it is God's, then we can freely proclaim it from the pages of scripture. We may not be able to answer all man's questions concerning it, but that's the benefit of not owning it. I believe He does! Let man never be amazed at your doctrine, but may he be confounded by your Jesus!

Chris Fredrich, Senior Pastor
Calvary Chapel of Orange Park
Orange Park, Florida

September 12

TRUSTING OBEDIENCE

*"Then He said, 'Take now your son, your only son Isaac,
whom you love, and go to the land of Moriah, and
offer him there as a burnt offering on one of the
mountains of which I shall tell you."*
Genesis 22:2

Abraham put all of his trust in God. I do not know for sure if Abraham understood exactly what God was doing or why he was doing it when God required his son Issac as a burnt offering. Many times, we do not understand what or why God requires something of us. But it is obvious that Abraham feared God. Abraham reverenced God as perfect, just, holy and righteous. He responded to God's command in loving obedience.

As we know, God provided the sacrifice and blessed Abraham, but I also see an unspoken blessing. Abraham not only glorified God by putting his trust in Him, but he also learned to trust God at a deeper level than ever before. Abraham grew to know God in such an intimate and loving way that he could have never experienced had God not tested him and had he not responded in obedient trust.

It is the same for us! We can know God in a more intimate and loving way than we have never known before! To accomplish this, God will lovingly test our obedience, our faith, and our will. The question is, will you respond in obedient trust?

Rick Barnes, Senior Pastor
Calvary Chapel of Wilmington
Wilmington, North Carolina

September 13

RECOVERY

I am often asked my opinion concerning Recovery. In turning to God's Word concerning this, I find in 2 *Timothy 2:24-26* Paul's instructions pertaining to ministers actions toward those that are in need of repentance. The last verse is interesting. *"That they may <u>recover themselves</u> out of the snare of the devil, who are taken captive by him at his will."*

After one has been instructed by teaching, counseling, and examples, a person can then repent and recover themselves out of any hold Satan may have on them.

There are many self-help groups around today. A person may stop a sinful habit in these groups, but remember Jesus died for our sins and He is concerned about the entire makeup of a person. God is not many steps away, but only one—repentance. A person must decide if they want to stop something in their life, or let God completely change their life.

What do you want, partial or total recovery?

Steve Everett, Assistant Pastor
Calvary Chapel of Downey
Downey, California

September 14

VANITY BOULEVARD

"Vanity of vanities," says the Preacher;
vanity of vanities, all is vanity."
Ecclesiastes 1:2

It seems highly unlikely that a man who had it all, that the world deems self-satisfying and pleasurable, would speak words that exhibit such a bleak, dark view of life. Yet ,this is exactly true of Solomon. The word "vanity" speaks of emptiness -- of being void of meaning and purpose, a wisp of vapor, a puff of wind lacking substance. It is a word of despair and disillusionment.

Solomon's quest for purpose and satisfaction started the same way it does for many people today. They start out seeking meaning and fulfillment without God. Multitudes, like Solomon, have the mistaken idea that somewhere, someway, somehow under the sun, life without God holds meaning and happiness; only to come to the same dead end that Solomon did --*"All is vanity and grasping for the wind."* We all need to realize before we step foot on Vanity Boulevard, and discover a dead end, that God is the stuff that makes a man. Without Him, we'll ultimately end up empty.

Joseph Gros, Senior Pastor
Calvary Chapel of Silver City
Tyrone, New Mexico

September 15

CHOOSE TO FOLLOW

"If any of you wants to be My follower, you must put aside
your selfish ambition, shoulder your
cross daily, and follow Me."
Luke 9:23

My pastor says, "It is my conviction that every disciple is a believer, but not every believer is a disciple!"

I understand this statement to mean that a person can have a saved soul, but a wasted life. Yes, they may genuinely know the Lord Jesus Christ, but they are not experiencing the fruitful life that Jesus has planned for them. No, I am not speaking of living a Christian life of flawlessness, because there is only One who has walked in those sandals - - Jesus Christ. But when I consider my shortcomings, all I have to do is remember the Apostle Peter's blunders, and I can be assured there is hope for me.

So what does it mean to be a disciple who has a fruitful life? Here is a basic definition of such a disciple: A disciple of Christ is a disciplined follower of Jesus who chooses to continue learning and applying His teaching in every area of their life because of the grace and love God has freely given to them in Christ.

Rick Kopp, Senior Pastor
Calvary Chapel of the Lewis-Clark Valley
Lewiston, Idaho

September 16

ORDER OF ORGANIZATION

As Fall is now upon us and most of the families have settled back into the routine of back to school, we see that the holidays are right around the corner, again. Looking at this particular time of the year, with all the running around that has to be done, when do we find time to accomplish the things laid before us?

Scripture speaks on the very issue of being organized. In the discourse of the feeding of the five thousand, Jesus shared with His disciples this need. *Matthew 14:13-20* speaks of an order of organization. Especially verse 19: *"And He commanded the multitude to sit down on the grass, and took the five loaves and the two fishes, and looking up to heaven, He blessed, and broke and gave the loaves to His disciples, and the disciples to the multitude."*

First, be still. Second, look up to heaven. Third, do as Jesus directs and you'll find that many things in your life will be accomplished.

Rick Johnson, Assistant Pastor
Calvary Chapel of Downey
Downey, California

September 17

JUST SAY NO!

"For the grace of God that brings salvation has appeared to all men, teaching us that, denying ungodliness and worldly lusts, we should live soberly, righteously, and godly in the present age, looking for the blessed hope and glorious appearing of our great God and Savior Jesus Christ."
Titus 2:11-13

We can, as believers in Christ can say "NO" to ungodliness. With this thought in mind, let's take a look at Samson. He had all the right stuff. Born a Nazarite, ordained to deliver his people from the Philistines, but instead of just saying, No, to temptation, he compromised. His covenant was simply don't drink, don't touch any unclean thing, and never cut your hair. Scripture tells us he conducted his own wedding feast, he retrieved honey from a dead lion's carcass, and then allowed Delilah to cut his hair.

Due to a time lapse in God's judgment, I suspect that after each compromise Samson, no doubt, thought he had gotten away with something. This only propelled him further into sin. Perhaps, he thought, I drink -- no problem. Touch that dead body -- no problem. But one day, he would awaken with no hair and say: *"'. . .I would go out as before, at other times, and shake myself free!' But he did not know that the Lord had departed from him,"* (Judges 16:20).

Consecration can't make up for communion with Jesus.

Mark Carlson, Assistant Pastor
Calvary Chapel Pacific Coast
Westminister, California

September 18

HIGHWAY TO HEAVEN

"And a highway will be there; it will be called the Way of Holiness. The unclean will not journey on it; it will be for those who walk in that Way; wicked fools will not go about on it. No lion will be there, nor will any ferocious beast get up on it; they will not be found there. But only the redeemed will walk there, and the ransomed of the Lord will return."
Isaiah 35:8-10a

The town where my wife and I live and pastor our church is high in the mountains of east central Arizona. In seven minutes, you can be anywhere in town. On most days, traffic problems consist of deer or elk crossing the road or perhaps it is geese and ducks crossing Main Street. The air is filled with the scent of pine and juniper -- it is a wonderful place. In the summer, however, these things change. Tourists come up here to get out of the heat of the desert in which they live. In Payson, there is a major juncture of two highways, one going east and one going north. And everybody that comes into town must make a decision right here, in this idyllic place, which way they are going. As followers of Jesus Christ, we have to make a decision which way we will go every moment of every day. What is God's most celebrated attribute in scripture? It is His holiness, that is what the cherubim speak about every moment around His throne. We, too, are on a highway, and on that highway there are choices to make. The beasts and the lion, (veiled references to Satan) are defeated by our loving Lord and Savior, Jesus Christ.

Curt Mattson, Senior Pastor
Calvary Chapel Payson
Payson, Arizona

September 19

THE CHILL OF LONELINESS

"But Jesus often withdrew to lonely places and prayed."
Luke 5:16

Have you ever thought about how we, as a society, view loneliness? If you do some research — watch TV or movies, read popular magazines, listen to the music on any radio station — you'll quickly learn that we see loneliness as a disease or a punishment that has been inflicted upon us. We drive by trailer parks and convalescent homes, cringing as we imagine the loneliness of those within whom we think are exiled there. We long to have our families home in time for dinner, fearing the empty table. And, of course, our teenagers sit endlessly and wait for the telephone to ring!

Everyone Feels Loneliness
From presidents to peasants, from merchants to mercenaries, the chill of loneliness is a frightening reality. Isolation, rejection, insecurity, and emptiness all seem to define loneliness. Loneliness has taken more lives, driven more people to alcohol and drugs, and troubled more relationships than any other emotion known to man.

Loneliness A Blessing?
I wonder, though, if it's possible that loneliness has been completely misunderstood? Could it be, in God's plan, that loneliness has been allowed for our *good*? Could loneliness, like discouragement and disappointment, be nothing more than God's opportunity to work in our lives?

(Continued)

Alone With God

Throughout the Bible, the Lord has always had one difficult task — to get the children of God alone with Him. But whenever God *did* get people alone and undisturbed, great things happened. Visions were given, His voice was heard, and victories were won.

Do I Run?

What about you? Do you run from being alone? Wherever you are, whatever you are running to, stop, right now, and ask yourself this question: "Could it be that God has allowed loneliness in my life for a reason?" I believe that Jesus desires to bring you to the place where you'll truly realize how deeply you need Him and His love.

Only One Cure

Jesus Christ is the only cure for loneliness, and the only answer to fulfillment. We all enjoy people and relationships, but our relationship with our Lord must come first. Once we realize that *God* is where the loneliness stops, and the fulfillment begins, we can rest in those lonely times, knowing that it's a "God Working" sign that has been put up in our lives, not one that reads "Dead End."

Remember, God uses loneliness to draw you to Himself. It is His desire to establish a richer, deeper relationship with you. *Yield* to this good work He wants to do in your life!

Steve Mays, Senior Pastor
Calvary Chapel of South Bay
Torrance, California

September 20

THE ABILITY OF GOD'S WORD

"The law of the Lord is perfect, converting the soul; the testimony of the LORD is sure, making wise the simple; the statues of the LORD are right, rejoicing the heart; the commandment of the LORD is pure, enlightening the eyes."
Psalm 19:7,8

When the scriptures point out aspects of our lives that need to be changed, we can also count on the Word of God to work upon us and within us to bring about those required transformations. The character of the Word is the basis of the ability of the Word. God's Word is perfect, sure, right, and pure. Consequently, it is able to change lives by bringing spiritual restoration, giving divine wisdom, producing inner joy, and supplying godly understanding.

God wants to set our lives apart for Himself, as well as make them pure. He uses His Word to accomplish such goals. The Lord desires to pour the living water of His Word over our lives through reading, studying, and proclaiming. The results will be the impurities of the world are regularly washed away, and our lives are devoted more and more to His purposes and His glory.

May we each be vessels of the Lord, shaped by His Word to proclaim and to demonstrate what the Word of God is able to do!

Bob Hoekstra
Director of Living in Christ Ministries
Murrieta, California

September 21

WALKING WITH GOD

"And Enoch walked with God; and
he was not, for God took him."
Genesis 5:24

The secret of Enoch's testimony is that he walked with God. The Book of Hebrews tells us that he pleased God and, thus, God took him. There are many people in this world that walk <u>AS IF</u> they were God. They rebel against all authority and will not listen to instruction. Power and pride fuel their souls.

Then there are those who walk <u>FOR</u> God. Many sincere people who are religious fall into this trap. Like those involved in walk-a-thons for worthy causes, the impression left is that God wants me to perform in order to please Him. Many Christians also succumb to this error. Their relationship with God has become distant, stagnant, and works oriented.

What God desires is that we walk <u>WITH</u> Him, heading in the same direction, enjoying sweet fellowship along the way. This is what satisfies the longing in our spirits. Being able to be free from earning God's favor, and reveling in His pleasure.

Tom Dickerson, Senior Pastor
Calvary Chapel North Plainfield
Watchung, New Jersey

September 22

THE LORD WEIGHS THE HEARTS

"Every way of man is right in his own eyes,
but the LORD weighs the hearts."
Proverbs 21:2

We fail to take an objective outlook on our actions. Therefore we need to bring every act under God's scrutiny. As
we expose all to Him, we achieve that which lasts for eternity.

"Search me, O God, and know my heart; try me,
and know my anxieties; and see if there is
any wicked way in me, and lead me
in the way everlasting."
Psalm 139:23,24

Carl Westerlund, Assistant Pastor
Calvary Chapel Costa Mesa
Santa Ana, California

September 23

DO YOU DELIGHT OR DEPLORE?

"I can't stand my life! All I do is suffer. I am always in turmoil. There seems to always be a disturbance happening all around me. I wish I could die!" As you evaluate your life, do you find continual disappointment?

Maybe you're single and at the end of your spiritual rope. You're tired of being alone, and you've had it with God! As far as you're concerned, God doesn't care about you because if He did, He would bring you that spouse you so desperately desire.

Perhaps you have a sickness that periodically rears its ugly head and when it does, you wish you could die! Or maybe your life is filled with worries and concerns. You are worried about your parents because they are older and need constant help, yet you have a family of your own that demands your attention. Perhaps your marriage is shaky right now. You feel spiritually weak from all the battling you've been doing. Let's look at how the Apostle Paul viewed his sufferings:

> "... I delight in weaknesses, in insults, in hardships,
> in persecutions, in difficulties."
> 2 Corinthians 12:10

The word "*delight*" in the original language means, "to think well of, approve, think good, be well pleased, take pleasure, be willing." Do you take pleasure in your hardships? Do I search for a Godly reason in that hardship? Check out why Paul calls his persecutions and hardships a delight in the remainder of verse 10.

(Continued)

"...For when I am weak, then I am strong." Paul saw his weakness as a great opportunity for the Lord to show His faithfulness -- do you? Remember, He'll never, *"...let you be tempted beyond what you can bear. But when you are tempted, He will also provide a way out so that you can stand up under it,"* (I Corinthians 10:13).

In your troubles, hardships, and weaknesses, God wants to show you His strength. He wants to show you that He is able when you are not. He wants to be your strength, your might, and your capability. There are rivers we must cross, valleys we must walk through, hills we must climb, and hurdles we must get over. All of these are necessary for our spiritual strengthening and growth.

Today, if you're saying, "I can't, I just cannot keep on going," the Lord wants you to know that He is your strength. Always keep in mind that He will never call you to do something without first of all providing you with the ability, strength, and spiritual tools you will need to accomplish the task.

D.L. Moody said, "The beginning of greatness is to be little, the increase of greatness to be less, and the perfection of greatness is to be nothing." The Word says that: *"My grace is sufficient for you, for my power is made perfect in weakness. Therefore I will boast all the more gladly about my weaknesses, so that Christ's power may rest on me,"* (2 Corinthians 12:7-9).

May the power of the living God be manifested through you today!

Fidel Gomez, Senior Pastor
Calvary Chapel Tamarac
Tamarac, Florida

September 24

THE GOLDEN YEARS

"And there was one Anna, a prophetess, the daughter of Phanuel, of the tribe of Asher: she was of great age and had lived with a husband seven years from her virginity. And she was a widow about four score and four years, which departed not from the temple, but served God with fastings and prayers night and day. And she coming in that instant gave thanks likewise unto the Lord and spake of Him to all them that looked for the redemption in Jerusalem."
Luke 2:36-38

As we all hopefully continue to grow spiritually in Christ, we also continue to grow older physically and chronologically. As this occurs, the tendency for many of God's people is to allow our increasing physical infirmities to cause a diminishing of our joy and zeal and, tragically, the appearance of bitterness within the hearts of many of His children.

Looking at this remarkable lady named Anna and sensing her "youthful" zeal and excitement, our attention is drawn to the "formula" for her joy and exhilaration.

Please observe the foundations of her "Golden Years." She does not depart from the temple; she serves God; she fasts unto God; she prays day and night; she gives thanks to God; she speaks to all of those around her of Jesus and His coming; she anticipates her redemption and the redemption of her people.

Assuredly, old age will come and with it the lessening of our physical capacities. This may have already occurred

(Continued)

with some of you. Would it not wonderfully benefit us to arrange our "formula" along the lines of Anna's?

On this side of heaven, we too can live out our lives with abundant joy and effectiveness as we: dwell in His "house" regularly; serve Him with love; fast; commune sweetly and personally with Him; have a tender and thankful heart towards the Lord; share our precious Jesus with a sad, needy world; and keep looking up, because He is coming for us soon.

Those approaching "golden years" are rich with possibilities because Jesus Himself has deep, precious and very personal times of fellowship awaiting you there. Maranatha!

Dave Gonzales, Senior Pastor
Calvary Chapel Cerritos
Cerritos, California

September 25

LOOKING AT THE WRONG SIDE OF THE WALL

Often times in our life we run smack, dab right into a wall. We see this wall, as a wall, of restriction, a wall that limits, our freedom, a wall that places limits on "our rights!" Now God must place those walls, hedges, or boundaries in our lives -- not to restrict us, but to protect us.

Just as we set up boundaries for our toddlers, or place boundaries and off-limit places on our teens, so God will generously give us boundaries in our lives. No sex before marriage! Deal honestly in all our business practices! Don't become drunk! These matters are boundaries that God has carefully erected in the believer's life. But here is the key; these are placed there not for restriction, but for protection.

We are simply looking at the wrong side of the wall. On the other side awaits a snarling dog with teeth bared. The teeth of a disease brought on by sexual immorality, the teeth of a serious accident from drunk driving, or the embarrassment and humiliation of a bad business deal. Quit looking at the wrong side of the wall, and start praising Him for each hedge He has protected us with! Satan asked, *"Have you (God) not made a hedge around him (Job), around his household, and all that he has on every side?"* (Job 1:10).

Never let down the hedges in your life that God has grown and groomed up around you. Look what happened to Job when his hedges were cut down to small shrubs!

Brian Bell, Senior Pastor
Calvary Chapel Murrieta
Murrieta, California

September 26

FRIENDSHIP -- A LISTENING EAR

Aren't friends great? Friends are those unique people who will actually listen to you. I love it when my wife and I get a chance to catch up and spend time listening to each other. It's great to have someone who will sit there and listen to all that has happened to you during the day. Someone who loves you and accepts you just the way you are.

Hezekiah was having one of those busier-than-usual weeks. Being king and all, he had lots on his mind. But when the Assyrian army showed up with threats of utter destruction, well, it wasn't turning out to be a very good week. He needed a friend to talk to.

And Hezekiah received the letter of the hand of the messengers, and read it: and Hezekiah went up into the house of the LORD, and spread it before the LORD. And Hezekiah prayed before the LORD, and said, . . . LORD, bow down thine ear, and hear: open, LORD, thine eyes, and see: and hear the words of Sennacherib, which hath sent him to reproach the living God.
II Kings 19:14-16

Hezekiah not only found relief as he cast his cares on the Lord, but God took care of the Assyrians as well. Do you feel a need to talk to a friend? I know Someone who is just waiting for you to call.

Rich Cathers, Senior Pastor
Calvary Chapel of Fullerton
Fullerton, California

September 27

NEVER TOO YOUNG

*"Assuredly; I say to you, unless you are converted and become
as little children, you will by no means
enter this kingdom of heaven."*
Matthew 18:3

In *Matthew 19:14*, Jesus said, *"Let the little children come to
Me, and do not forbid them; of such is the kingdom of heaven."*
Jesus truly wanted the little children to come to Him. He
knew that they would believe in Him by faith. I have heard
many parents say that their child is too young to understand what it is to follow Christ. Corrie Ten Boom was only
four years-old when she gave her life to Jesus. You're never
too young to trust and believe in Him.

Phil O'Malley, Assistant Pastor
Calvary Chapel of Downey
Downey, California

September 28

FIVE INTELLIGIBLE WORDS

"But in the church I would rather speak
five intelligible words to instruct others than
ten thousand words in a tongue."
I Corinthians 14:19

I wonder which five words the Apostle Paul was thinking of when he wrote this? He certainly couldn't solve any great theological debate with five words. Nor could he establish solid scriptural foundation for a great Christian doctrine such as the Trinity or the resurrection.

Paul, being the great Evangelist he was, perhaps, would choose to convey the Gospel plainly. But can that be done with only five words? An acronym comes to mind that the early church used as a secret identity code when they were meeting underground during persecution.

Perhaps you've heard of it . . . "IXOYE." These are Greek letters taken from the first letter of each word in the sentence "Jesus Christ, Son, God, Savior." It simply spells "fish" in the Greek. However, when you break the code these are definitely "five intelligible words!"

Mike Sasso, Assistant Pastor
Calvary Chapel of Downey
Downey, California

September 29

COMMITMENT

"Seek good and not evil, that you may live; and thus may the
Lord God of hosts be with you, just as you have said."
Amos 5:14

There are many who commit their lives to doing evil. They
spend their entire life hurting others and doing no good.
But, if Jesus Christ is your Lord, commit yourself to do good.
Serve your God with all your heart, mind and soul. Begin
by doing good and getting involved in a ministry that will
count for eternity.

Rudy Cardenas, Assistant Pastor
Calvary Chapel of Downey
Downey, California

September 30

GROWING PAINS

My children can sure be finicky at times. For some reason, there is something built into the brain of a child that tells them that chocolate ice cream is an acceptable item of nourishment. But, getting that last spoon of vegetables into their mouths requires only slightly less bravery and effort than it takes to scale Mount Everest.

Two things are observable on the vegetable front. First, consumption of vegetables seems directly proportional to age and learned discipline. The older my children are, the more disciplined they become, the easier vegetable consumption gets. The second lesson is that even if they don't believe it, I, the server of culinary delights, love them as much when I serve them vegetable's as when I'm putting ice cream in front of them. I may have a different reason for serving vegetables than ice cream, but I still love them the same.

Now, as you have suspected these ramblings aren't just about vegetables. It's about life. God is the one who puts things on our plate. As Job learned *(Job 2:9-10)*, *"What? Shall we receive good at the hand of God, and shall we not receive evil?"*

It's really all the same lesson. Maturity and disciplined training *(Hebrews 12:11)* can help us handle the difficult times (the veggies). And God's love never changes. All He does for us is done in love. A great love. An unchanging love.

Steve Edmondson, Assistant Pastor
Calvary Chapel of Fullerton
Fullerton, California

October 1

GRACE OVERFLOWING

*"But Manasseh led Judah and the people of Jerusalem astray,
so that they did more evil than the nations the Lord had
destroyed before the Israelites. And when he prayed to Him,
the Lord was moved by his entreaty and listened to his plea;
so He brought him back to Jerusalem and to his Kingdom.
Then Manasseh knew that the Lord is God."*
II Chronicles 33:9,13

I want you to notice the tremendous contrast in these two verses, for in that contrast we see the magnitude of the grace of God. How would you like to have this first statement about Manasseh said about you?

Maybe you feel like you have done great evil in the sight of the Lord. Don't be discouraged, Paul felt the same way about himself. *In I Timothy 1:15*, Paul tells us *"Here is a trustworthy saying that deserves full acceptance: Christ Jesus came into the world to save sinners of whom I am the worst."*

You have been forgiven a tremendous debt in the Lord. And you didn't have to do a thing to earn it. You can't even come close to earning God's grace, but He gives it to you without charge. And notice, that Manasseh, after he had prayed, was sent back to Jerusalem. Why? Because he had done much harm there, so there was much restoration to do. God takes us, who have done so many things against Him, and uses us as tools of restoration. And notice, it was then that Manasseh knew that the Lord is God.

Curt Mattson, Senior Pastor
Calvary Chapel of Payson
Payson, Arizona

October 2

ANCIENT HISTORY

"I, even I, am He that blotteth out thy transgressions for Mine own sake, and will not remember thy sins."
Isaiah 43:25

A man who was telling his friend about an argument he had with his wife, commented, "I really hate it. Everytime we have an argument she gets historical." The friend replied, "You mean hysterical." "No," he insisted. " I mean historical. Every time we argue, she drags up the past and holds it against me."

Aren't you glad God is not "historical?" When He forgives sin, He forgets it! And that is how we are to act towards one another -- *"Forgiving one another, even as God, for Christ's sake has forgiven you,"* (Ephesians 4:6).

Neil Matranga, Assistant Pastor
Calvary Chapel of Downey
Downey, California

October 3

ARE OUR WAYS GOD'S WAYS?

"I delight in loyalty rather than sacrifice, and in knowledge
of God rather than burnt offering."
Hosea 6:6

Our problems must be solved in a biblical manner. We all might say, "I try," but have you ever heard of "Partial Obedience?" Do we try in the Spirit, and solve our problem in the flesh? God's solutions are completely adequate -- period!

What does God require of us? *Micah 6:8* tells us to "... _walk humbly with your God,"* realizing God's ways should be our ways. *"In conclusion, when all* has *been heard is: fear God and* keep *His commandments, because this applies to every person. For God will bring every act to judgment, everything which is hidden, whether it is good or evil," (Ecclesiastes 12:13,14).*

Lord, may Your Word be a lamp to our feet and a light to our path. God's Word is truth. May we never lean to our own understanding or wisdom, which equals partial obedience. Please read *1 Samuel 15:1-23.*

Glenn Kravig, Assistant Pastor
Calvary Chapel of Downey
Downey, California

October 4

BLESSED ASSURANCE

"Then spake the Lord to Paul in the night by a vision, 'Be not afraid, but speak, and hold not thy peace; for I am with thee, and no man shall set on thee to hurt thee: for I have much people in this city.'"
Acts 18:9,10

Paul had come to a place in his life we will also often come to. It's a place of needing reassurance. The task at Corinth was to be difficult, and Paul had experienced a less than desirable response in Athens from where he had just left. He was humbled by his experience in Athens and now, perhaps, reluctant to be as bold. But the Lord assured him of His presence, and His ongoing blessing and protection.

When we come to this place where we feel our efforts have not been received as we hoped for, remember God is still there, and all His sovereign power is available through His Holy Spirit. We need to just hold on to the promises and continue, despite previous experience and a doubt of the future. I encourage you to *". . . speak and not hold your peace,"* for time is short for all of us, but more so for the unbeliever.

Rick Phelps, Senior Pastor
Calvary Chapel of Lakewood
Lakewood, California

October 5

EXPERIENCE GOD

*"Be still, and know that I am God . . . the LORD of hosts is
with us; the God of Jacob is our refuge. Selah."*
Psalm 46:10,11

"Beware of the barrenness of a busy life!" I saw that quote
and found myself thinking how true it is. Today, most of us
live busy lives. We have schedules and planners, we move
from one thing to the next, and try to squeeze just a little
more into our schedules. We can be so busy, and in the
process become so barren.

Yet, God is calling us to take time and contemplate who He
is. Do you do that? Really, don't read any further until you
ask yourself how much time you really spend thinking about
and knowing God. I am afraid that even the spiritual part
of our lives is often times filled with busyness. We do our
reading, we pray, even intercede for others -- all of which is
good and necessary. But there is so much more for us.

When we stop and just contemplate God, what peace it
brings to our busy hearts. It truly is like an oasis in the
desert. And when we do that, as the Psalmist says, God
becomes our place of rest. O how we need this! The Psalmist ends this Psalm perfectly - Selah, which means stop and
think about it. I challenge you today to find some time to
marvel at God and you will find your life refreshed. Then
peace will settle in your heart.

Jim Suttle, Senior Pastor
Calvary Chapel of Roswell
Roswell, New Mexico

October 6

BEWARE OF COVETOUSNESS

"'Take heed and beware of covetousness, for one's life does not
consist in the abundance of the things he possesses."
Luke 12:15

He then told his disciples about the farmer who had a great increase of crops and so he built larger storage buildings and began to rest in his abundance. God called him a fool for that night his life was to end. He was resting in things that had no eternal value.

Jesus said: "For where your treasure is,
there your heart will be also."
Luke 12:34

There are many Christians today who are buying into the ways of the world. Trusting in their increase. But we are called to live a very simplistic, practical style-life, whether we have much or little. Whatever the Lord does place in our care isn't to be hoarded for our selfish desires, but is to be shared with those in need. As we honor Jesus with all that He has given us, we will be renewed, we will bless others, and we will bring glory to Jesus!

"There is one who makes himself rich, yet has nothing; and one
who makes himself poor, yet has great riches."
Proverbs 13:7

Thomas McCartin, Assistant Pastor
Calvary Chapel North Edwards
North Edwards, California

October 7

HARVEST TIME

"Do you not say, 'There are still four months and then comes the harvest'? Behold, I say to you, lift up your eyes and look at the fields, for they are already white for harvest! And he who reaps receives wages, and gathers fruit for eternal life, that both he who sows and he who reaps may rejoice together."
John 4:35,36

I grew up on a wheat farm in western Kansas. As a farmer, harvest was the most important time of the year. The work was long and hard. Every man, woman, and child had a part in the harvest. Every vehicle was used, even my mother's brand new Lincoln Continental. She would drive it through fields, stop and pop open the trunk. She would then serve us our meals out of it as if it were a chuck wagon. Still, to this day, I get goose bumps when I think of the joy of the harvest. The sacrifices were all worth it.

We have all been called to share in the vision Jesus has for the harvest of hearts. Let's lift our eyes past ourselves, our problems, and our wants. Let us look at the fields for they are white with harvest all over the world. As we join in the harvest, we will rejoice and be filled with the joy of our Lord and Savior.

Jerel J. Hagerman, Senior Pastor
Joshua Springs Calvary Chapel
Yucca Valley, California

October 8

TEARS MUST FALL

"Those who sow in tears will reap with songs of joy. He who goes out weeping, carrying seed to sow, will return with songs of joy, carrying sheaves with him."
Psalm 126:5,6

On Saturday mornings, I often listen to a radio station that plays blues music. While this might not seem very spiritual, one of the things I have learned about the blues is, that singing about having the blues is supposed to make you feel better. Logically speaking, when you make music you will feel better, even if the music relates to how bad you are feeling.

While sin is far more serious than "having the blues," the principle cited in this Psalm is the same. The truth is that we never really understand God's forgiveness unless we have a personal experience with it. Thus, the seed that we sow, is the sorrow and pain that sin causes us. The sorrow it causes helps us to understand how marvelous it is that God desires to forgive, restore and completely cleanse us.

The harvest begins with forgiven sin which turns into joy. This joy is deep, lasting and profound, because it is based firmly upon the work Jesus accomplished for us on the Cross. So, don't be afraid to sow the seeds of sadness, because if we will allow them to remind us of God's goodness, they will soon be followed by songs of joy.

Greg Cull, Senior Pastor
Calvary Chapel Shingle Springs
Shingle Springs, California

October 9

DON'T ISOLATE

"Look not every man on his own things,
but every man also on the things of others."
Philippians 2:4

The body of Christ is given to us by the Lord for our benefit. From fellowship, mutual sharing, and learning, accountability, and support in our walks, through prayer and exhortation: Let's face it, we need each other. I can't begin to tell you of the ruined spiritual lives I have seen in those who have forsaken the body, believing they could walk with God on their own. The Lord sure doesn't think so! Just read *Hebrews 10:23-25.* Are you plugged into the body? Are you involved, attending regularly, and making an effort to know others and have them know you? Your spiritual health and strength rely on it!

Jack Abeelen, Senior Pastor
Morningstar Christian Chapel
Whittier, California

October 10

THE PRINCIPLES OF BLESSING
AND CURSING

"To sum up, let all be harmonious, sympathetic, brotherly, kindhearted, and humble in spirit; not returning evil for evil, or insult for insult, but giving a blessing instead. . . for you were called for the very purpose that you might inherit a blessing."
I Peter 3:8,9

Sowing and reaping is a scriptural principle. If a farmer wants corn, he must plant corn. If we sow blessings, we will reap the blessings of God. The Apostle Paul gives us similar, if not the same, instructions in *Romans 12:21*: "*Do not be overcome by evil, but overcome evil with good.*" Returning good for evil goes hard against the flesh. This is why the Apostle Paul warns us in *Galations 5:16,17*,

". . . But I say, walk by the Spirit, and you will not carry out the desire of the flesh. For the flesh sets its desire against the Spirit, and the Spirit against the flesh; for these are in opposition to one another. So that you may not do the things that you please."

There is no third choice. Paul goes on to tell us: "*Now the deeds of the flesh are evident, which are. . .enmities, strife, jealousy. . .outbursts of anger, disputes. . .*" (*Galatians 5:19,20*). We choose either to obey the Holy Spirit, or to obey the flesh. When we repay evil for evil, it is simply because we have obeyed the flesh rather than the Spirit.

Chuck Trett, Senior Pastor
Calvary Chapel of Henderson
Henderson, Nevada

October 11

ARE YOU A GIVER OR A TAKER?

*"For you remember, brethren, our labor and toil; for laboring
night and day, that we might not be a burden to any of you,
we preached to you the gospel of God."*
1 Thessalonians 2:9

Paul saw himself as a giver and, following his call to serve
Jesus Christ, labored with his hands so as not to be a burden to those to whom he ministered. He also labored so
that the Gospel would be free.

There are some who desire a career in a field where they
can help people. They sometimes look to ministry. Yet
these are the ones not called or chosen, but who serve for a
paycheck. Although the laborer is worthy of wages, the
best test of sincerity is personal cost, not benefit.

Les Prock, Senior Pastor
Calvary Chapel North Hill
Milton, Washington

October 12

LET'S GO FOR A REAL WALK

*"So then, just as you received Christ Jesus as Lord, continue to
live in Him, rooted and built up in Him, strengthened in the
faith as you were taught, and overflowing with thankfulness."*
Colossians 2:6,7

So much of the Christian walk is contained in the verbs of
these verses: received, continue, rooted, built-up, strengthened, taught, and overflowing. *Receiving* Jesus as the Lord
of your life is the first step to an eternity of fellowship with
the God of all creation. Accepting Him as Lord is not a one
time thing -- it is a day to day decision to continue to live in
Him. The more we choose to walk every day with Him, the
more we find ourselves taking root in Him and being *built-
up* into the new creation that He says we are. We find ourselves desiring to be more like Him. More and more we
walk by faith more than by sight, our spiritual legs get stronger, and we find ourselves being strengthened in our faith,
just as we were promised. Through every experience of life,
we are taught by the Holy Spirit to be more like Jesus.

As all of this unfolds in our lives, we begin to thoroughly
enjoy the walk! Thankfulness overflows from our hearts and
lips. This thankfulness is not spiritual etiquette, it is an overflowing, a spilling out that is a result of all that the Lord
pours into our lives. Are you overflowing? If not, then consider the things that God has poured into you since you
have received Christ Jesus as Lord Think on these things
and watch the flow!

Nick Triveri, Senior Pastor
Calvary Chapel Placerville
Placerville, California

October 13

FOLLOW ME

*"Then He said to them all,'If anyone desires to come
after Me, let him deny himself,
and take up his cross daily, and follow Me.'"*
Luke 9:23

Whenever Jesus called people to Himself, He always commanded them to follow Him. The command still stands for us, as believers: Today we must follow Jesus.

He never said to follow a man, an organization, or a church group. Jesus said, *"Follow Me."* That simplifies the Christian life. Things change, people change and times change, but Jesus never changes. He is the same yesterday, today, and forever.

There is a danger of straying or getting lost when following people, places, or things. Continue to follow Jesus and you'll never get lost. He is The Way, The Truth and Life and He's leading you somewhere -- Home.

Keep it simple, Christian -- Follow JESUS!

Jim Misiuk, Senior Pastor
Calvary Chapel of Lake Forest
Lake Forest, California

October 14

DO YOU NEED A QUICK FIX?

*"Surely the arm of the LORD is not too short to save, nor His
ear too dull to hear. Surely your iniquities have separated you
from your God; your sins have hidden His face
from you, so that He will not hear."
Isaiah 59:1,2*

Why doesn't God fix all of the things that are wrong with
the world? Why doesn't God just fix all of the things that
are wrong with me? Okay both of those questions ask a lot,
but couldn't God at least rescue the folks who are starving?
We might do well to consider the answer the prophet Isaiah
gave the people when they asked him.

Many of us despair and we wonder if God even CAN take
away our difficulties. Isaiah states up front that God surely
is not without the power to take away whatever is concerning us, but all too often we are the ones who have turned
away from that power. Our sin is often what stands between us and the freedom we crave.

The reality that I am in the situation I am in because of my
own folly, is a bitter pill for me to swallow. If I blame God
about His injustice, then I will never experience the libera-
tion He has for me. When we can recognize the grace of
God in blessing, and in difficulty, we begin to grasp what
He is doing in us. Let's put no barriers of sin between us
and God. Seek Him instead of relief from our situation.

Greg Cull, Senior Pastor
Calvary Chapel Shingle Springs
Shingle Springs, California

October 15

SHARE THE GOOD NEWS!

*"But ye shall receive power, after that the Holy Ghost is come
upon you; and ye shall be witnesses unto me both in
Jerusalem, and in all Judea, and in Samaria, and
unto the uttermost part of the earth."*
Acts 1:8

We all know that Jesus died for our sins, and if we receive
Him into our heart we will be saved; but how many times
have you shared this truth?

God could have sent angels to preach the gospel, but He
wants <u>us</u> to do it because we have experienced redemption. Angels do not know what redemption is, yet they
rejoice when a sinner comes to the Lord. *Luke 15:10* says,
*"Likewise, I say unto you, there is joy in the presence of the an-
gels of God over one sinner that repenteth."*

Don't be a quiet witness! With the great salvation that God
has given to us, we have the power to be His witnesses.

Manuel Lopez, Assistant Pastor
Calvary Chapel of Downey
Downey, California

October 16

PRINCIPLES FOR A BETTER DAY

"And do not get drunk with wine, for that is dissipation,
but be filled with the Spirit."
Ephesians 5:18

If you are like me, you probably have days when you wake up in the morning and find you are in a great mood and you are ready to take on the world. On the other hand, there are those days you wake up and find you can hardly drag yourself out of bed. Every little thing becomes monumental, and you really don't know how you are going to make it through the day.

In *Ephesians 5*, we are given some help in getting our day started on the right foot. The first thing we need to note is what this is <u>NOT</u> saying. It is not saying that we are to get drunk on the Holy Spirit like someone might while drinking strong wine. But rather, we are to have our senses affected by the Lord's Holy Spirit the same way our senses can be affected by strong drink.

For instance, when you drink alcohol, your eyesight, your hearing, your speech, and your walk, are all affected. The scripture is saying that we are to allow the Holy Spirit of God to affect how we see things, hear things, say things, and how we walk in Christianity.

We can choose to look at this day as an opportunity to be used by the Lord for His glory, to look at people through "His eyes," to listen to people the way the Lord would listen, to guard our speech, and to be guided through the day by His leading. I think of the verse in the old hymn "When

(Continued)

The Roll Is Called Up Yonder" that reads, "Let us labor for the Master from the dawn till setting sun. Let us talk of all His wondrous love and care; then when all of life is over and our work on earth is done, and the roll is called up yonder I'll be there."

May we not stumble through life like a drunk trying to find his way home. Instead, may we have clear direction and purpose each day of our lives until we are called home.

Lord, today we ask that you would fill us with your Holy Spirit. Allow us to look at this day through your eyes and to seek to be an instrument that you can use today and every day. Amen!

Mike Morris, Senior Pastor
Calvary Chapel of the High Desert
Hesperia, California

October 17

SEASONING SALT

*"Let your speech always be with grace, seasoned, as it were,
with salt, so that you may know how you should
respond to each person."*
Colossians 4:6

The taste of salt always leaves us wanting more. When we share with someone, we want it to be so full of grace that people are hungry for more. It is always better to leave people wanting more than wishing for less. It is God's grace and love that reaches out to people's hearts. Let us remember that the answers to all of life's deepest questions and needs are found in the grace which God demonstrated to us through His way of Salvation.

Matt DeWitt, Assistant Pastor
Calvary Chapel Church Planting Mission
Vista, California

October 18

HOW BIG IS YOUR GOD?

"And the LORD said to Moses, 'Has the Lord's arm
been shortened? Now you shall see whether what
I say will happen to you or not.'"
Numbers 11:23

How big is your God? For some of us it could easily be
said that, "Our God is too small." What do I mean by that?
I mean that we limit God in our perceptions of Him. I love
this passage where God tells Moses what He is going to do
in feeding meat to the children of Israel. Moses' response
is one of doubt -- he does not see how it is possible. God's
response to Moses is so good! He asks Moses if His arm
has been shortened. It is a reminder to Moses, and to us,
that nothing is too hard for God.

Lack of understanding like this does a lot of damage. It
keeps us from trusting Him, we live worried lives, we end
up trusting in our paycheck, more than we trust God. We
really begin to doubt that, "Where God guides, God provides." We reverse it to say "Where we can provide, that is
where we will let God guide." Thus we limit God's work
in our lives *(Matthew 13:58)*.

Hey, God is big! His arm has not been shortened, and there
is nothing He cannot do. Are you trusting in Him? Are
you living by sight -- what I can figure out -- or by faith?

Jim Suttle, Senior Pastor
Calvary Chapel of Roswell
Roswell, New Mexico

October 19

RESPONSIBILITY OF THE WORD

*"For I have not shunned to declare unto you
all the counsel of God."*
Acts 20:27

Billboards, news flashes, bumper stickers, t-shirts . . .the world today thrills over the barrage of advertisements flaunting society's worldly desires. But, as Christians, we have a responsibility to share the full counsel of God. Whether it's in the stores or at family gatherings, we need to share the Word. We have the opportunity and resources to advertise the Word through Christian t-shirts, Christian bumper stickers, etc. Let the Word of God have the greater impact!

Mark Maciel, Assistant Pastor
Calvary Chapel of Downey
Downey, California

October 20

STRAINING FOR JESUS?

"Come to Me, all you who labor and are heavy laden, and I will give you rest. Take My yoke upon you and learn from Me, for I am gentle and lowly in heart, and you will find rest for your souls. For My yoke is easy and My burden is light."
Matthew 11:28-30

The RCA building is located on Fifth Avenue in New York. In the front of the building is a gigantic statue of Atlas. This beautifully proportioned, muscle bound guy, is holding up the world on his shoulders. With muscles straining, he is barely able to stand beneath the burden of the world.

Yet, if you go across the street to Saint Patrick's Cathedral, you will see a shrine of Jesus. In this shrine, He is depicted as an eight year-old boy and, with no effort at all, is holding the world in the palm of one hand.

This illustration leaves us with a very simple choice: We can either strain under the burden of the world, or we can give our burden to Christ who can effortlessly hold up your world. All of your straining may seem noble, but don't you think the better option would be to give that burden to Him?

Mark Scott, Senior Pastor
Calvary Chapel of College Park
College Park, Maryland

October 21

OUR GOD IS AN AWESOME GOD!

"If we confess our sins, He is faithful and just to forgive us our
sins and to cleanse us of all our unrighteousness."
1 John 1:9

Our God is an awesome God! How well the adjective "awesome" fits in this sentence. It used to be that you seldom heard the word awesome, but now it has become so common that some even use it to describe pets --"Awesome pooch!" or "Awesome goldfish dude! "

Personally, I like the word best when it is connected to God. Consider these awesome statements that Jesus made to a woman caught in the act of adultery. *"Woman, where are those accusers of yours? Has no one condemned you?"* She said, *"No one, Lord."* And Jesus said to her, *"Neither do I condemn you; go and sin no more,"* (John 8:10-11). God isn't expecting flawlessness, but He does expect us to turn away from our sin and follow Jesus.

Now those are awesome words from an awesome Savior! And they are for you today or any day. They will never lose their validity. The only sin God cannot forgive is the sin that is unconfessed.

So what will we do with these awesome words of Jesus? May we go (free from condemnation) and sin no more!

Rick Kopp, Senior Pastor
Calvary Chapel of the Lewis-Clark Valley
Lewiston, Idaho

October 22

WHERE DO WE GO FOR HELP?

One of the most precious encouragements that the Lord brings to our hearts is that He is our "HELP." He never gets tired of us saying, "HELP."

The Psalmist reminds us that our, *". . . help cometh from the LORD, who made heaven and earth."* To illustrate this wonderful truth, we read, *"Behold, He who keepeth Israel shall neither slumber nor sleep."* The Lord calls Himself, *". . . the LORD God of Israel,"* 108 times. He is the, *"Shepherd of Israel"* and *Psalm 73:1* says, *"Truly God is good to Israel,"* (Psalm 130:7,8) says:

> *"Let Israel hope in the LORD; for with the LORD there is mercy, and with Him is plenteous redemption. And He shall redeem Israel from all His iniquities."*

Yes, our help comes from the Lord, the One Who has promised to help Israel. Whatever your need, call upon Him-- He is our "HELP."

David Hocking
Hope for Today Ministries
Tustin, California

October 23

WORDS OF ENCOURAGEMENT

"Sticks and stones may break your bones, but names can never hurt you." I would imagine that most of us grew up with this gem of bogus wisdom imparted to us by our parents in the midst of those hideous days of elementary school. Those were the days before we were taught that it was not polite to accentuate the most undesirable traits of our classmates through verbal attacks.

Having suffered a debilitating disease just after my fifth birthday, I was forced to wear a brace on my left leg from my hip to the bottom of my foot which required me to wear a platform shoe on my right foot. I spent my first year of grade school being called everything from, "Cripple" to "Monster Foot." Through the unrelenting cruelty of my peers, I discovered that names definitely hurt and have great power.

"The tongue has the power of life and death."
Proverbs 18:21

"The tongue that brings healing is a tree of life,
but a deceitful tongue crushes the spirit."
Proverbs 15:4

As a Christian, I am impressed by the importance of my words. The Bible teaches us that we will be called to give an account for every careless word spoken *(Matthew 12:36)*. The challenge to stay on course with our words is a difficult one, but the key to success lies in *Luke 6:45, "A good man out of the good treasure of his heart brings forth good; and an evil man out of the evil treasure of his heart brings forth evil. For out of the abundance of the heart his mouth speaks."*

(Continued)

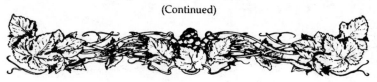

It seems our focus should not be on our words, but rather on our hearts. If we concentrate on purifying our hearts before God, then the words which we utter will be pure. One of the many reasons given for the importance of our speech hinges on the power of encouragement. It is a weapon of warfare that disengages the effects of sin in the life of a believer. Look at *Hebrews 3:13:*

> *"But encourage one another daily, as long as it is called today, so that none of you may be hardened by sin's deceitfulness."*

Through using our tongues to encourage another brother or sister in the Lord, we can bring life where sin is desiring to defeat and destroy. We can look at each individual as either a construction site or a demolition site. Will we use the power of life or death in the words we speak?

As exciting as it is to be able to edify and build up the body of Christ, I must say that it takes a second seat to an even greater accomplishment. Look at *Proverbs 23:15,16:*

> *"My son, if your heart is wise, My heart will rejoice; indeed, I myself; yes, my inmost being will rejoice when your lips speak right things."*

When my heart is wise and I speak right things, I can rejoice with the inmost being of God. Now, my smile appears through speaking what is right, by building up and not tearing down, by making sure that my tongue brings only life, never death.

Gennarino Desterfano, Assistant Pastor
Calvary Chapel Ft. Lauderdale
Ft. Lauderdale, Florida

October 24

THE HOUSE THAT GOD BUILT

David was a man in love with his God. He was known as a man *". . .after God's own heart."* At one point in his life, after having conquered most of his enemies *(2 Samuel 7:1-2)*, David was lounging around his fine palace and beginning to feel a little guilty. After all, he was living in a fine cedar house, while God's place of meeting with His people was nothing but a tent. And who had helped him conquer all those enemies? It had been God! So David began to talk with the prophet Nathan and told him that he intended to build a great house for God. It seemed right to Nathan at first, at least until God began to speak *(1 Chronicles. 17)*.

I don't think God was offended with David's idea. But David had it wrong. It was <u>God</u> who was going to build a house for David. In fact, God began to remind David that everything in their relationship had been based on what God had done for David, not what David had done for God. It was God who had raised David up from being a shepherd to being a king.

That's the way it is with our relationship with God. It's never been based on what we've done for Him, but only on what He's done for us. Have you been so worried and concerned that God is somehow not pleased with what you do for Him? You've got it all wrong. No one could love you more. He *wants* to bless you. Stop worrying and start receiving all that He has for you. Stop striving. Be still.

Rich Cathers, Senior Pastor
Calvary Chapel of Fullerton
Fullerton, California

October 25

HAVE YOU HEARD THE GOOD NEWS?!

"Be very careful then how you live; not as unwise but as wise,
making the most of every opportunity
because the days are evil."
Ephesians 5:15,16

All of us have experienced the joy of possessing good news and desiring to share it with someone before we burst from utter excitement. That's weak in comparison to the <u>good news</u> we possess in knowing Jesus Christ and the eternal hope of heaven that He gives. We need to wake <u>each day</u> praying, "Lord, please bring one person across my path today with whom I can share the blessed good news of the gospel!" Then, be ready to share!

Tim Hearron, Assistant Pastor
Calvary Chapel of Downey
Downey, California

October 26

WHERE ARE THE NINE?

"Ten lepers lifted up their voices, and said, 'Jesus, Master, have mercy on us.' And when He saw them, He said unto them, 'Go show yourselves unto the priests.' And it came to pass, that, as they went, they were cleansed. And one of them, when he saw that he was healed, turned back, and with a loud voice glorified God, and fell down on his face at His feet giving Him thanks."
Luke 17:13-17

". . .I will make darkness light before them, and crooked things straight. These things will I do unto them, and not forsake them."
Isaiah 42:16b

In our do-it-yourself world, we are prone to view our dark spots and crooked places as projects for self-help, therapy, or blaming others, etc. Notice how emphatic the "I wills" appear. Jesus can and will. . .!

". . . He (Jesus) is a rewarder of them that diligently seek Him."
Hebrews 11:6b

Ed Cornwell, Assistant Pastor
Calvary Chapel Costa Mesa
Santa Ana, California

October 27

AN ORDINARY DAY

*"And the Angel of the Lord appeared to him in a flame of fire
from the midst of a bush. So he looked, and behold, the bush
burned with fire, but the bush was not consumed. Then Moses
said, 'I will now turn aside and see this great sight,
why the bush does not burn.'"*
Exodus 3:2,3

Have you ever wondered what would have happened if
Moses hadn't turned aside to see this great sight? Would
someone else have lead Israel out of Egypt? Would it have
been another 40 years? Well, Moses did turn aside and the
rest is miracles.

This was an ordinary day for Moses, and yet, God made it
the most wonderful day in his life!

So, let's keep our eyes and ears open. And remember, we
serve a God who speaks to people from burning bushes and
uses fugitive shepherds to display His mighty works.

Jeff Stewart, Senior Pastor
Calvary Chapel Pomona Valley
Pomona, California

October 28

COUNTING THE COST

The other day I went to get a haircut and the lady that cut my hair ended up being a Christian. She was so starved for fellowship (her husband not being a believer) that she got excited about the things of the Lord and kept talking and cutting, talking and cutting, talking and...well, you get the picture. When we were through I looked more like a Marine than a Pastor! When I got to church people asked me why my hair was so short. As I pondered my answer I recalled the scripture in *2 Samuel 24:24* where David says, *". . . I will not offer burnt offerings to the Lord my God with that which costs me nothing."* I had been praying for more opportunities to serve the Lord and give of myself for my Master. Little did I know I would literally be giving of myself . . . and my hair for the Lord!

Brethren, there are many ways to serve the Lord. Don't be surprised if you find yourself in unique situations in your service for the King. Whatever price you pay, (hair loss or not!) it sure is worth it when we think of all the Lord has done for us. It's great to be in the Lord's army. Yes, Sir!

Louie Monteith, Senior Pastor
Calvary Chapel Norco
Norco, California

October 29

SINK OR SWIM

Jesus was led into the wilderness to be tempted by Satan *(Matthew 4:1-11)*. Although He was tempted three times, He was tempted by three distinct temptations. I'm reminded of the ship Titanic. Upon its maiden voyage, there was such an arrogant confidence and glory given to this ship that one shipmate was even quoted saying, "God Himself couldn't sink this ship." Where I have not noticed much attention is on the sister ship Britannic. The Britannic sank also, although by a distinct cause of its own. It was the fiery heat of a deliberate explosion that rendered this ship to its demise.

Our lives are much the same in the sense that Satan attempts to sink us spiritually using distinct temptations. So we must be careful not to become arrogantly self-confident, lest we (sink) or fall. We must also be careful not to focus too much on our past sin failures, lest we become vulnerable in some other distinct area of our lives. For such reasons, we should avoid ever having confidence in our own strength to overcome temptation. For God gives us victory to overcome temptation, not on our own strength, but by our faith in His Son Jesus Christ, all for His glory *(1 John 5:4,5)*. Let's keep our focus on the Savior rather than the sin.

Following the Titanic sinking, its sister ship was simply renamed Britannic rather than its originally intended name GIGANTIC. Remember, it's much better to be humble than to be humbled.

Steve Edmondson, Assistant Pastor
Calvary Chapel of Fullerton
Fullerton, California

October 30

GOD'S GIFT

As I was out getting some early shopping done for Christmas gifts, I was thinking of those family members I love and how I wanted to get them just the right present. Then I thought of how God gave us the best gift ever -- the Lord Jesus Christ.

As you give gifts to your loved ones this year, remember God's tremendous gift to you.

Oh, how He loves us!

Kelley Taylor, Senior Pastor
Calvary Chapel of Everett
Everett, Washington

October 31

THE THINGS THAT THE WICKED DO

*"Oh let the wickedness of the wicked come to an end; but
establish the just; for the righteous God
trieth the hearts and reins."*
Psalm 7:9

Today, known as Halloween, a day in which evil runs rampant, it is sad that many people in our own community, neighbors, family, and friends are not aware of the evil associated with this day that is dedicated to Satan.

It's not just passing out candy and treats, but rather seeking evil and sacrifice to the devil; a day in which Satan is glorified and uplifted. However, the children of God are not to be fooled, but rather to expose the darkness and provide a refuge for our community.

Today, instead of glorifying Satan, we can celebrate our Lord and Savior Jesus Christ because He has triumphed over evil!

*". . . having wiped out the handwriting of requirements that
was against us, which was contrary to us. And He has taken it
out of the way, having nailed it to the Cross. Having disarmed
principalities and powers, He made a public spectacle
of them, triumphing over them in it."*
Colossians 2:14,15

Mark Maciel, Assistant Pastor
Calvary Chapel of Downey
Downey, California

November 1

PRAYER, THE DECIDING FACTOR

"And the King said: "What do you want me to do Nehemiah?"
And Nehemiah said, "So I prayed to the God of
heaven and I said unto the King. . ."
Nehemiah 2:4

First: Nehemiah brought everything before the Lord. He prayed about everything.

Second: Prayer was his first response in every situation. We need to follow that pattern. God, help us to be instant in prayer and to let prayer be our first response in every situation we face.

"Call unto Me and I will answer thee and show thee great and
mighty things which thou knowest not."
Jeremiah 33:3

John Henry Corcoran, Assistant Pastor
Calvary Chapel Costa Mesa
Santa Ana, California

November 2

MORE LIGHT

"And when they say to you, 'Seek those who are mediums and wizards, who whisper and mutter,' should not a people seek their God? Should they seek the dead on behalf of the living? To the law and to the testimony! If they do not speak according to this word, it is because there is no light in them."
Isaiah 8:19,20

Some Christians today are always searching, looking, and seeking to satisfy their hunger for more light and more experiences -- outside of the Word of God. The only problem is, that you will never know if what you are doing is of God or not. Waiting to see if any fruit is born out of that experience is foolish. The Lord tells us that we are to seek after His Word, for if we look outside His Word for direction, we are not going to find more light, but darkness!

Instead of seeking to have our ears tickled, let's seek to have our hearts conformed to His Word. If you want more light, then go to the source, Jesus Christ, and not to the one who disguises himself as an angel of light! In *John 1:1* we are told of Jesus that, *"In the beginning was the Word, and the Word was with God, and the Word was God."* Thus, we should be seeking after the Law and the Testimony, and not experience. If you want to draw closer to God and have more of His light in your life, then draw close to Him according to His Word -- not outside of His Word where there is only darkness!

Joe Guglielmo, Senior Pastor
Calvary Chapel of Manitowoc
Manitowoc, Wisconsin

November 3

OH, GIVE THANKS!

Giving thanks to the Lord is not a suggestion, it's a command in scripture. There is so much for us to be thankful for, isn't there? One of the ways we come before His presence is with thanksgiving, which is actually an offering from the heart of redeemed saints. Thanking God is not only a command, it is also good. Thanking God from a pure heart is more pleasing to Jesus than a heartless, meaningless ritual.

Our Lord Jesus expressed thanks for the provision of food; He thanked Abba at the Passover for the cups of wine that symbolized sanctification, instruction, redemption and praise. Remember how Jesus responded with an additional blessing to the leper who expressed thanks for the work of God in his life?

Rather than laughing at dirty jokes (or telling them!), our lips are to be filled with thanks. The Levites were to start every day thanking and praising the Lord. As we grow up in Christ through the Word and the power of His Holy Spirit, the result is an inevitable overflow of thanksgiving.

Oh! Thanks to our God for His victory through Jesus Christ our Lord; for His triumph in Christ that makes Him known in our lives. As we stand in awe of our wonderful Savior and His infinite love for us, may our hearts respond today, tomorrow and forever with thanks to the glory of God!

Ray Viola, Senior Pastor
Koinonia Fellowship
East Rochester, New York

November 4

CHAIN OF FOOLS

*"For although they knew God, they neither glorified Him as
God nor gave thanks to Him, but their thinking became futile
and their foolish hearts were darkened. Although they
claimed to be wise, they became fools."*
Romans 1:21,22

Sometimes I begin to wonder how it was that the men and
women of old gradually turned away from God. So soon
after the flood, people were living as though it had never
occurred, even though every living human was a direct
descendant of Noah, the only Godly man on the planet at
that time! How does that happen?

Have you ever found yourself feeling as though your relationship with God has become somewhat stale? Your desire for His presence just isn't as strong as it once was!

Heed Paul's warning! It begins so subtly! Maybe you find
that it embarrassed you recently to give thanks for your
food in a public place. Or you realize that you've begun to
take pride when complimented for a job well done when,
in the past, you would have acknowledged HIS involvement!

Every good gift comes from Him! Acknowledge Him as
God! Give thanks for the breath you breathe, the gifts He
gives, and the abilities you enjoy! Better to grow in WIS-
DOM, then to gradually become a fool.

Robert Fountain, Senior Pastor
Calvary Chapel of Miami Beach
Miami Beach, Florida

November 5

SING UNTO THE LORD

*"I will praise the name of God with a song and I will
magnify Him with thanksgiving."*
Psalm 69:30

I like how personal King David is in this Psalm; more than
<u>we</u> will praise, he says, *"I will praise."* He wasn't the type
of person who would come to church looking to be entertained. He would always come with a purpose -- to worship his Lord.

How would he worship? *"With a song."* Worship songs are
so beautiful and express so much. God has blessed the
church with many gifted musicians and singers to lead the
body in praise. All the ingredients are present, so let's make
sure we come with that personal intention to praise Him!

Let us also sing songs of *"Thanksgiving."* These songs testify to God's work in our lives, how He answers our prayers,
and it shows our awareness of His touch. We also sing our
thanksgiving to Him for His sustaining grace, mercy, and
provision.

Mike Stangel, Senior Pastor
North Shore Christian Fellowship
Haleiwa, Hawaii

November 6

SOWING SEEDS OF COMPASSION

"Now as He approached the gate of the city, behold, a dead man was being carried out, the only son of his mother, and she was a widow; and a sizeable crowd from the city was with her. And when the Lord saw her, He felt compassion for her, and said to her, "Do not weep. And He came up and touched the coffin; and the bearers came to a halt. And He said, "Young man, I say to you, arise!" And the dead man sat up, and began to speak. And (Jesus) gave him back to his mother. "
Luke 7:12-15

One of the qualities that draws mankind to Jesus is His compassion. That which looks beyond any faults or failures and sees and feels one's need and does something about it. This is what we see in the story of Jesus raising this widow's dead son.

First, it says, ". . . *the Lord saw her.*" This is the first step in sowing seeds of compassion -- one must look. We need spiritual eyes to see. Second, we must allow ourselves to feel. It says, ". . . *He felt compassion for her.*" If we fail to be touched by people's suffering, then we are no different than the world. Third, we must take action. Having seen and felt, Jesus then brought relief to this woman. His compassion took action and her suffering was gone.

Today, you too will have opportunities to show God's compassion -- the result is that God will be glorified.

Scott Vincent, Senior Pastor
Calvary Chapel of Edmonds
Edmonds, Washington

November 7

PATIENTLY WAITING

"The LORD is my portion, saith my soul; therefore will I hope in Him. The LORD is good unto them that wait for Him, to the soul that seeketh Him. It is good that a man should both hope and quietly wait for the salvation of the LORD."
Lamentations 3:24-26

Who can blame us for getting excited when the LORD is our portion? The word portion originates from the casting of lots to determine the inheritance of the Tribes in the Promised Land. It speaks of hope, a future, a life in terms of a place of fulfillment and rest. We may grow anxious at times in our present captivity of this world, but a reminder that the LORD Himself is our future gives such peace.

How we yearn for what will be! Even so, we can enjoy a foretaste now. God is good to those who wait for Him, a rewarder of those who diligently seek Him. Too often, it is God who is waiting for us, seeking us as we are miles away doing our own thing wondering why God doesn't seem to be blessing.

How good it is to have a quiet soul, tranquility, and peace. It comes from knowing the future is secure, anticipating that glorious appearing. The wait will be definitely worth it!

Steve Miller, Senior Pastor
Calvary Chapel of San Jacinto
San Jacinto, California

November 8

JUST ASK -- THERE'S MUCH MORE!

As Paul was working his way through Asia Minor, he came across a group of men who were disciples of the Lord. They had been brought to the Lord under the ministry of a preacher named Apollos. Paul asked them:

> *"Have ye received the Holy Ghost since ye believed?"*
> *And they said unto him, "We have not so much as*
> *heard whether there be any Holy Ghost."*
> *Acts 19:2*

This is certainly odd, for a group of disciples to not have heard of the Holy Spirit! Many would have us believe that we are immediately filled with the Holy Spirit the very moment that we believe, asking Jesus into our heart. Yet here was a group who had already believed, and Paul sensed something missing. In fact, after he lays hands on them, we read that:

> *". . .the Holy Ghost came on them;*
> *and they spake with tongues, and prophesied."*
> *Acts 19:6*

We need to guard ourselves from the mentality that says that we've received all we're going to need. There i̲s more, beloved. The life of the Spirit is one characterized by an overflow of love, joy, peace, patience, self-control, and more. Has your walk been dragging lately? Jesus offers an outpouring of the Holy Spirit to those who thirst. Come and drink *(John 7:37-39)*.

Rich Cathers, Senior Pastor
Calvary Chapel of Fullerton
Fullerton, California

November 9

SPIRITUAL CONDITIONING

*"Devote yourselves to prayer, keeping alert in it with
an attitude of thanksgiving. . ."*
Colossians 4:2

Proskartereo is a Greek word made up of two root words: *pros* meaning "towards," used intensively, and *kartereo* meaning "to be strong." Together they mean "to be strong towards," translated here *"devote"* yourselves.

If I said this morning we're all going to go out and run a mile in under eight minutes, some could make it because they are "strong towards" running, while others would drop out because they have not conditioned themselves in this way. In Colossians 4:2, Paul exhorts us to be strong toward prayer. How many Christians are spiritually flabby, out of shape, unconditioned, and weak in that which is of primary importance to their growth and the health of the body.

What's your spiritual condition? Devote yourself (be strong towards) prayer, keeping alert in it with an attitude of thanksgiving.

Bill Stonebraker, Senior Pastor
Calvary Chapel of Honolulu
Honolulu, Hawaii

November 10

A LIFE VERSE!

"Trust in the Lord, and do good; dwell in the land and cultivate faithfulness. Delight yourself in the Lord; and He will give you the desires of your heart. Commit your way to the LORD; trust also in Him, and He will do it."
Psalm 37:3-5

Do you have a life verse? I do and I think everyone should. God wants us to trust Him, to do good, and cultivate faithfulness! Cultivate is an agricultural word which means to work and till the soil, taking the rocks out of it and getting it ready for the owner to grow something in it. After you have done this, we are called to delight. Tell God what is on your heart, believe that He heard your prayer and then commit it to Him, like a farmer waiting for the harvest. Not only does it take hard work and faith, it also takes trust. You can't see that seed growing until it breaks out of the soil and hits the light. Faith is the assurance of things hoped for, the conviction of things not seen.

One verse and look at how many things we can glean from it. What is your life verse? Where do you draw upon when you need an answer? Today, find a verse and live it.

Bill Richard, Senior Pastor
Calvary Chapel Encinitas
Encinitas, California

November 11

GOD'S PRESENCE IS WITH ME

"The Lord replied, 'My presence will go with you, and I will give you rest.' Then Moses said to Him, 'If Your presence does not go with us, do not send us up from here.'"
Exodus 33:14,15

I have been in the ministry for many years now and I still experience those "Monday Morning Blues." I want to give up, quit the ministry, and find a 9-to-5 job. "It isn't worth it, Lord! I think I heard You wrong when You called me to be a pastor. Let's call the whole thing off, okay?" As seems His way, He gently leads me back to Exodus where I read again about Moses; how this man also struggled with his call and the ministry to which the Lord chose him. I am encouraged to know that God's presence is with me and that only through Him can I find much-needed rest. I love Moses' response, *"If Your presence does not go with us, do not send us up from here."* Through this beautiful passage, I am also reminded of Jesus' comforting words in *Matthew 11:28*:

"Come to me, all you who are weary and burdened, and I will give you rest."

Remember that the Lord is our rest and our much-needed strength!

Bob Ortega, Senior Pastor
Calvary Chapel of Las Cruces
Las Cruces, New Mexico

November 12

VETERAN'S DAY

"I thank my God, making mention of thee always in my prayers, hearing of thy love and faith, which thou hast toward the Lord Jesus, and toward all saints."
Philemon 1:4,5

Throughout scripture, we read of God doing some awesome works. But it takes obedient individuals to hear the call to serve. Our nation will be remembering Veterans Day soldiers who served our nation. These people fought for the freedom we now enjoy.

Let's take time to pray for those veterans and thank them for their service to our country.

Rudy Cardenas, Assistant Pastor
Calvary Chapel of Downey
Downey, California

November 13

SOVEREIGN ENDURANCE

"He will endure as long as the sun, as long as the moon, through all generations. He will be like rain falling on a mown field, like showers watering the earth. In His days the righteous will flourish; prosperity will abound till the moon is no more."
Psalm 72:5-7

When I was in elementary school, my father sold new cars for a couple of years. When he would bring home the books with the pictures of next year's models in it, we would marvel at how futuristic they all looked. They came out with what they called "concept cars" each year as well. They would have all of the devices and features that were sure to be included in cars 20 years in the future. It is comical to look back at some of those cars and realize that we thought this was the future. We simply don't know what will last, and we don't know what is coming tomorrow.

I thought about all of this while I read this Psalm. In vs. 7, Solomon declares that God's prosperity will abound till there is no more moon. God alone understands what is forever, and we have committed ourselves to his judgment. What God has for us in heaven is more permanent than we are capable of understanding. What He has for us here and now is more stable than we are able to fully understand. Let us look to His Word as always being reliable and true, and understand that even when all else changes, God stays the same.

Greg Cull, Senior Pastor
Calvary Chapel Shingle Springs
Shingle Springs, California

November 14

KINGDOM KEY

"And ye shall seek me, and find me,
when ye shall search for me with all your heart."
Jeremiah 29:13

There are many seekers in this world, but few finders; many hopeful, but few realizing hope fulfilled. In this world, we seek money through info-mercials and the lottery only to be disappointed. We seek youth through plastic surgery and diets only to have youth elude us. The house on the hill; only to have it fall in the ocean. We seek God through "seeker friendly churches" that tell us what we want to hear in an entertaining sort of way. The result is like spiritual cotton candy; lots of sweet fluff, but no substance. The only way to find God is to seek Him with your whole heart, undivided in purpose and principle. If we seek God with our whole heart, He will be found and upon being found everything else in our life will fall into its proper place.

"But rather seek ye the kingdom of God;
and all these things shall be added unto you."
Luke 12:31

Cary Wacker, Assistant Pastor
Morningstar Christian Chapel
Whittier, California

November 15

COMBING THE FIELDS TOGETHER

*"I do not pray for these alone, but also for those who will
believe in Me through their word; that they all may be one, as
You, Father, are in Me, and I in You; that they also may be one
in Us, that the world may believe that You sent Me. "And the
glory which You gave Me I have given them, that they may be
one just as We are one: "I in them, and You in Me; that they
may be made perfect in one, and that the world may know that
You have sent Me, and have loved them as You have loved Me."*
John 17:20-23

It was a typically frigid Canadian winter day. Jessica, a
little 4 year-old, wandered away from home and was lost.
The family called all the people of the community together
to set out looking for little Jessica. But, unfortunately, each
person searched *individually.*

Soon it was dark and, still, no Jessica. Finally, someone
suggested they join hands and form one long line and comb
the grass fields *together* instead of individually. But it was
too late. By the time they found Jessica, she was curled up,
frozen to death. Someone cried out in anguish, "If only we
had joined hands before!"

Jesus prayed for our oneness in John 17. It was His death-
bed prayer that *we* would be one. Why? So that the lost
might be found. The fields are white unto harvest! May
we comb them together, as one.

Mark Scott, Senior Pastor
Calvary Chapel of College Park
College Park, Maryland

November 16

ABIDING IN CHRIST

"I am the vine, you are the branches; he who abides in Me,
and I in him, he bears much fruit,
for apart from Me you can do nothing."
John 15:5

Many people are arrogant, prideful and self-sufficient, especially when we have a job, money, and everything is going our way. We even believe that we own the whole world
and we forget to give thanks to God, because everything
comes from God. We sometimes think that because of our
knowledge we are who we are!

But let me tell you something -- without Christ, you and I
are nothing, and we can't do anything.

Manuel Lopez, Assistant Pastor
Calvary Chapel of Downey
Downey, California

November 17

WHOSE BOOK IS IT?

*"All scripture is God-breathed and is useful for teaching,
rebuking, correction, and training in righteousness."*
II Timothy 3:16

"Mommy, whose book is this?" The question came from a little girl who had just discovered a black, dusty, leather bound volume on a table. The mother looked up and smiled, "Why, that is a Bible, God's book." "Well," said the little girl, "why don't we send it back to Him because we don't use it around here." The innocence of a child sometimes probes deeply into our lives.

Have you discovered what the Bible has to say about your life? Why not start today and discover why the Bible is the world's bestselling and best-loved book? Teddy Roosevelt once said, "A thorough knowledge of the Bible is worth more than a college education." Read it and discover guidelines for living.

Glenn Kravig, Assistant Pastor
Calvary Chapel of Downey
Downey, California

November 18

SPEAKING THE TRUTH

*"In this you greatly rejoice, though now for a little while, if
need be, you have been grieved by various trials, that the
genuineness of your faith, being much more precious than
gold that perishes, though it is tested by fire, may be
found to result in praise, honor, and glory at
the revelation of Jesus Christ."*
1 Peter 1:6,7

In Biblical times, gold was not refined as it is today, with
chemicals leaching away the impurities. The smelter would
heat a large vat of ore until it was molten and glowing red.
The heating caused the impurities to rise to the surface where
they would be scraped away. The process would be continued again and again, until finally the smelter would be able
to see his reflection in the refined material.

God's Word says that our faith is more valuable than gold.
That's certainly different than most men's perspective!
Mankind spends a lot of time seeking to amass riches like
gold, while God's use for gold is to pave His streets in
heaven! *(Revelation 21:21)*. In other words, in God's
economy, gold has all the worth of asphalt.

The Father desires to refine us so that our faith, which is far
more valuable than gold, would be found to bring glory to
Him when Jesus returns. The part of the picture with the
most impact is the smelter looking into the vat and seeing
his own reflection. God wants to look into our lives and see
His reflection. Part of the refining process comes in the form
of trials -- some big, some small.

(Continued)

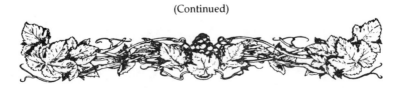

I was talking to a high school girl a very short time ago. We stood in front of a friend of ours who is in a wheelchair due to a degenerative disease. Barring some miraculous act of God, he will likely be going to see Jesus in the next few years. . . and here she was complaining about a broken fingernail! Her trial was little, his was big.

Our faith may be tested by fire, but on that day when Jesus returns there will be a loving God looking into our lives and seeing His reflection in us.

That must be why James could write, *"My brethren, count it all joy when you fall into various trials."* (James 1:2).

May our trials make us better, not bitter. Let them always drive us closer to Jesus, instead of further away.

Brian Michaels, Senior Pastor
Rocky Mountain Calvary Chapel
Colorado Springs, Colorado

November 19

HOW TO ACTIVATE THE PROMISES OF GOD

"If any man will come after Me, let him deny himself,
take up his cross and follow Me."
Luke 14:27

1. Deny self. . .Be God-centered.
2. Take up your cross . . .Total submission to the Father.
3. Follow Jesus Christ.

If you are feeling defeated this morning, then let Luke 14:27
speak to your heart. This, friend, is how God's promises to
you are activated. This is the key to a victorious Christian
life.

John Henry Corcoran, Assistant Pastor
Calvary Chapel Costa Mesa
Santa Ana, California

November 20

IS THE POWER IN THE POTHOLE?

"Search me, O God, and know my heart; try me, and know my
anxieties; and see if there is any wicked way in me,
and lead me in the way everlasting."
Psalm 139:23,24

It's your morning commute. You're driving down the road, sipping on your coffee, humming a worship song in your head, when suddenly you hit a pothole. The coffee goes up . . .the coffee comes down! Has this ever happened to you?

When something like that happens, we usually get a bit upset. Our anger is often directed at the pothole. However, did you ever consider that the pothole was simply revealing the contents of your mug? We blame the pothole, but if there had been no coffee in the mug, then there would be nothing to spill.

Many of us have certain people in our lives who rouse our anger. They say things that bother or do things that annoy us. When our paths cross, our "mug" is jolted and out flows bitterness, criticism, hostility, etc. These "pothole" people cause anger to spill from our hearts and we blame them for it. "I wouldn't be so mad if he wasn't so. . ."

Are they just exposing what is already in the heart? When your life is jolted by a person or circumstance, whatever is on the inside comes out. What spills from your heart when you hit the potholes of life?

Todd Lauderdale, Assistant Pastor
Calvary Chapel of Murrieta
Murrieta, California

November 21

CHASTENED AND CHERISHED

"And you have forgotten the exhortation which speaks to you as to sons: 'My son, do not despise the chastening of the Lord, nor be discouraged when you are rebuked by Him; for whom the Lord loves He chastens, and scourges every son whom He receives.'"
Hebrews 12:5,6

What a remarkable thing God does with us! In our time of greatest depression, confusion and hurt, our tendency is to cry out to God and ask why. We want everything to be rosy and nice, yet the Lord is brutally honest when it comes to chastisement. No amount of positive confession can make His chastisement go away! If we look closely at the text, we see just how beautiful the Lord is, and how He is exactly Who He said He would be to us.

We see in verse 5, God calls us His sons (I am sure you can take it to mean daughters, too)! This is wonderful in and of itself that the Lord would call us His sons, and care enough for us to reach His hand down to correct us. He says clearly that He loves us enough to chasten us. It does not necessarily mean we have done something wrong; on the contrary, we may have done everything right! This is God's way of refining us and conforming us into the image and likeness of Jesus. He wants to make disciples out of us. He wants us to be partakers of His holiness *(Hebrews 12:10)*. This does not come without some suffering.

The neat thing about this chastening is that it proves we are sons and daughters of God. He has not left us illegitimate. Irresponsible parents leave children to fend for themselves.

(Continued)

God is not irresponsible. His correction is to prove that we are His children. It is not punishment, but training. This is a normal experience for children. The well-trained are usually more mature in their relationship with God. Someone who thinks that they can get through life without the chastening is an unfortunate person!

We should not be discouraged. We should be encouraged that God would allow certain things to come along into life that would enable us to be corrected for the glory of God. We should never look at chastisement as anything other than opportunity to learn as much as we can about God and ourselves. We should embrace it, be partakers of it, and see the peaceable fruits of righteousness.

Someone once said that the vine dresser is never closer to the vine than when He is pruning it. Oh, if we could only embrace that and realize that the creator of the universe is touching us and conforming us! How different will we then see our affliction!

Kirk Thompson, Assistant Pastor
Calvary Chapel of Philadelphia
Philadelphia, Pennsylvania

November 22

PRESERVING PRAYER

"Praying always with all prayer and supplication in the
Spirit, and watching thereunto with all perseverance
and supplication for all saints."
Ephesians 6:18

As Paul gave to the Ephesians the encouragement to put
on the whole armor of God in their warfare with the devil
(Ephesians 6:10-18) in the above verse, he emphasized persevering prayer. One of the greatest areas of stumbling for
most Christians is prayerlessness; let alone, prayer that is
persistent and persevering. Yet, God would have us press
ahead, stick with it, be courageous, and not fail as we seek
victory in Him. To persevere means to be constant and
focused, to be ready at all times. How is your prayer life?
God looks for the persistent to bless and calls us to be so.
Just check out Jesus' parable of the unjust judge, *(Luke 18:1-*
8). Let's pray some more.

Jack Abeelen, Senior Pastor
Morningstar Christian Chapel
Whittier, California

November 23

WHEN GIVEN THE OPPORTUNITY, GET AWAY!

"And the apostles gathered themselves together unto Jesus, and told Him all things, both what they had done, and what they had taught. And He said unto them, Come ye yourselves apart into a desert place, and rest a while: For there were many coming and going, and they had no leisure so much as to eat. And they departed into a desert place by ship privately."
Mark 6:30-32

Jesus wanted to get away with His disciples where there would be no hustle and bustle of activities. Jesus wanted to carve out time with the Apostles in teaching and reflecting in a place where they would not be distracted.

There is a time when the Lord will make opportunity of us to get away and spend quiet time with Him. Men's and women's conferences are an opportunity. There is nothing like getting away from the routine for the purpose of being taught from the Word. With just a Bible or note pad in hand, or nothing at all, but you and the Lord. It is always an incredible time. How many times do we really get a chance for a couple of days to do that? If Jesus saw this as important for His men, and took the initiative to provide it, how much more important is it for us to take the opportunities that He provides a time to separate ourselves and be with Him. It is just what the soul and spirit needs.

Kent Nottingham, Senior Pastor
Calvary Chapel, Tallahassee
Tallahassee, Florida

November 24

HOLY VANDALISM!

"Some men came, bringing to Jesus a paralytic, carried by four
of them. Since they could not get him to Jesus because of the
crowd, they made an opening in the roof above Jesus and,
after digging through it, lowered the mat the paralyzed
man was lying on. When Jesus saw their faith,
He said to the paralytic, 'Son, your sins are forgiven.'"
Mark 2:3-5

Have you ever been reckless in your life? Have you ever
taken big risks? There is one kind of recklessness that is
acceptable to God . . . recklessness in knowing Him.

How much do you want Jesus? How much do you crave
His touch, His Word, His healing? Let's be willing to take
big chances for God! Let's determine to recklessly abandon
ourselves to Jesus that we might receive the reward!

Mike Sasso, Assistant Pastor
Calvary Chapel of Downey
Downey, California

November 25

LABORERS OF LOVE

*"Then He saith to His disciples, 'the harvest is plenteous, but
the laborers are few. Pray ye, therefore, the Lord of the harvest,
that He will send forth laborers into His harvest.'"*
Matthew 9:37,38

Harvest -- The Bible refers to this word 67 times! It means
"the act of reaping or gathering a crop."

Jesus used this term when explaining to His disciples that
there are many souls ready to be saved! What was lacking?
Laborers!

*"The harvest is plenteous, but the laborers are few. Pray ye,
therefore, the Lord of the harvest, that He will send forth
laborers into His harvest.'"*

Today the fields are white, ready for the harvest, but the
problem remains the same. A lack of laborers! We have
such a great opportunity to be involved daily in the Lord's
work. So prepare yourself, through prayer, to do the work,
because God will use you!

Neil Matranga, Assistant Pastor
Calvary Chapel of Downey
Downey, California

November 26

O' GIVE THANKS!

*"O' give thanks unto the LORD; for He is good: because His
mercy endureth for ever. Let Israel now say, that His mercy
endureth for ever. Let them now that fear the LORD say, that
His mercy endureth for ever. I called upon the LORD in
distress: the LORD answered me, and set me in a 'high place',
They compassed me about; yea, they compassed me about: but
in the name of the LORD I will destroy them."
Psalms 118:1,2,4,5,11*

This could have been a scripture that comforted the 967
Jews at Masada as the 10th Roman Legion surrounded
them. Patrick Henry said, "Is life so dear and peace so sweet
as to purchase at the price of chains and slavery? Forbid it,
Almighty God! I care not what course others may take, but
as for me, give me liberty or give me <u>death</u>!" We know that
this is the choice the Jews took. All committed suicide! They
failed to believe the whole Psalm, *"The Lord is my strength
and song and is become my salvation" (Psalm 118:14).*

May we, no matter how hard it gets or how dark it looks
<u>hold on</u>. For it's easier to die and to give up than to <u>live for
Him</u>. *"For the Lord is on my side; I will not fear: what man can
do unto me?" (Psalm 118:6).*

May this Thanksgiving be our celebration and thanks for
the Lord strengthening in us. For He is good and His mercy
endures forever. Thanks Lord!

Jeff Johnson, Senior Pastor
Calvary Chapel of Downey
Downey, California

November 27

SPIRITUAL HOUSE CLEANING

*"Do you not know that you are a temple of God, and that
the Spirit of God dwells in you."*
I Corinthians 3:16

When King Hezekiah came to the throne, he faced some overwhelming tasks *(II Kings 18)*. There were enemies on every side. What was Hezekiah's priority? The first month of his reign, he ordered the temple to be purged and purified in order to reestablish the nation's worship with Jehovah. This should also be our priority.

The first thing Hezekiah did was to open the front doors of the temple, allowing the brilliance of the sun to reveal the clutter and dirt. We all need to open the front door of our spiritual life to God. He knows what's inside anyway, but it takes the glare of His holy presence to show the extent of our spiritual dirt. We need to remember that God sees everything and we need to see what He sees.

God's work doesn't deserve halfheartedness. Hezekiah asked the priests and Levites to consecrate themselves and to give the job top priority. Do not be neglectful *(II Chronicles 29:5-11)*. What is God asking of you today?

Glenn Kravig, Assistant Pastor
Calvary Chapel of Downey
Downey, California

November 28

DISCOURSE FOR DISASTER

"For I say, through the grace given unto me, to every man that is among you, not to think of himself more highly than he ought to think; but to think soberly, according as God hath dealt to every man the measure of faith."
Romans 12:3

Matthew 23:1-39 is a discourse in which Jesus pronounces seven woes upon the Scribes and Pharisees. He denounces them because they:

Shut the door of the kingdom in men's faces *(vs.13)*
Corrupted proselytes, those converted to Judaism *(vs. 15)*
Reversed the truth regarding the oath *(vs. 16-22)*
Inverted values *(vs. 23-24)*
Boosted rituals *(vs. 25-26)*
Externalized religion *(vs. 27-28)*
Swaggered about their superior goodness *(vs. 29-32)*

Have we heard of any churches or religions that do this? And what about us, as believers?

Rick Johnson, Assistant Pastor
Calvary Chapel of Downey
Downey, California

November 29

KEYS TO COPING

*"Grace and peace be multiplied to you in the knowledge of God
and of Jesus our Lord, as His divine power has given to us all
things that pertain to life and godliness, through the knowledge
of Him who called us by glory and virtue, by which have been
given to us exceedingly great and precious promises, that
through these you may be partakers of the divine nature, having
escaped the corruption that is in the world through lust."*
2 Peter 1:2-4

I can't believe there are so many out of control people in the
world. It seems like all I do all day is talk to people who are
struggling -- careening through their lives -- claiming that
Jesus is the center point of their reality. Their lives show
that they're not doing what the Bible teaches!

Either the Word is true or it's not! Either the Bible is the
Word of God, or it's the biggest lie in the universe. It gives
me great peace to know that whatever problems start to
roll down the hill towards me I can hold on to these facts:

1. God knew about it in advance;
2. He has a plan to deal with it;
3. His plan is clearly laid out in His Word;
4. His ultimate goal is my maximum benefit; and
5. If I do what I can do to follow His plan, He will take
   care of every detail and, in His timing, move me from
   focusing on my problem to seeing God's benefit for my
   life.

Whatever happens, don't let the enemy hold you down. It's
so incredible to realize that the Lord is able to use the most

(Continued)

painful situations to draw us closer to Him and to His purpose for us. The more painful the situation the more capable He is to use it. The key issue to fellowship with Christ and our fellow believers is that whatever He brings our way is intended to cause growth and maturity. Humbling ourselves is the best opportunity for immediate growth, however, other forms of difficulty are equally as useful in turning us into the servants He has called us to be.

Isn't it bizarre how every day, as a Christian, you have to start from scratch. No matter how spiritual you were the night before, you wake up each morning just as carnal as you could possibly be. Only when I spend time praying, reading, and walking in the Spirit, do I have the potential to become a spiritual giant.

"It's a wild world, and it ain't about to get no tamer, so keep your hands on the wheel, your eyes on the road, and remember -- there's a war goin' on!"

Tony Scott, Assistant Pastor
Calvary Chapel of Pasadena
Pasadena, California

November 30

THE WRATH OF GOD

*"For the wrath of God is revealed from heaven against all
ungodliness and unrighteousness of me, who suppress
the truth in unrighteousness."*
Romans 1:18

In *Romans 1:18,* Paul declares that the wrath of God is revealed from heaven against all the unrighteousness of men,
who hold the truth in unrighteousness. The wrath of God
is usually associated with the Old Testament because of the
Noah flood, Sodom and Gomorah, etc. Yet, the wrath of
God is also very much a part of the New Testament. We
must understand that God's wrath is an absolute part of
His nature, just as much as love is. God's holiness demands
the wrath of God and His wrath is a reminder of His holiness.

No man can charge God with being unfair or cantankerous.
His wrath is used, at times, as chastisement to drive man
back to Himself, such as David when he fell into adultery.
Man has been under God's wrath since the fall and has been
in continuous rebellion against the revealed and expressed
will of God, which is to repent from his sins by accepting
Jesus as Savior.

The wrath of God is towards the ungodly and unrighteous.
The ungodly are those who are in a wrong relationship with
God by not having their sins forgiven, which is the obstacle
between God and man. Consequently, they are also unrighteous, which refers to being in a wrong relationship with
one's fellow man. Man cannot be right with man until he is
right with God. Man has held the truth of God in

(Continued)

unrighteousness, pressing it down and changing it to a lie.

God must execute His wrath on sin. We have one of two choices: a person can choose to have God's wrath on him for his sinful nature and be damned for eternity, or he can accept the provision that God has made in His Son Jesus Christ. God not only placed our sins on Christ, but He became literal sin that you and I might be made into the righteousness in Him. Jesus drank of the cup of God's wrath as He cried out, *"My God, My God, why has Thou forsaken me?"* In *Psalm 22:3*, He gives the reason: *"But thou art holy."*

As a parent's discipline is used to cause the child to see his wrong and turn from it, so the wrath of God is used to cause men to reflect on himself and sin. God and His Word, which is a form of love, will cause us to accept His concern and love for us. Being man and God at the same time, Jesus reconciled us back to God by paying the debt on man could pay. Come and kiss the Son lest He be angry with you and you perish senselessly.

Xavier Ries, Senior Pastor
Calvary Chapel of Pasadena
Pasadena, California

December 1

LET THE LIGHT SHINE

*"I am the light of the world; he who follows Me shall not walk
in the darkness, but shall have the light of life."*
John 8:12

Jesus is having a dramatic dialogue with the religious leaders who opposed Him and were seeking to get Him. He
would often use various examples that were around to draw
a picture for the people to see. Here Jesus was using a common sight to all Jews of the time. They had a nightly ceremony that took place in the temple courts. Each evening
the priests would light two huge candelabras - called
menorahs (a multibranched candleholder). The huge
menorahs would then light the whole temple area for the
priests to continue to work in through the night.

It is in reference to this ceremony that Jesus says, *"I am the
light of the world; he who follows Me shall not walk in the darkness, but shall have the light of life."* It is interesting to note
that Jesus didn't say that He was the light of Israel, but the
"world." That means that the person that is living in the
middle of nowhere has a Savior that had died for his sins
and the Creator of the universe seeks to come into his life
whether he was born in the year 32 A.D. or in the year 1998
A.D. That is just amazing to me!

During the years the children of Israel wandered in the wilderness, the Shekinah glory of God lit the Tabernacle. Because of the sinful practices of the people, there came a time
when the visible presence of God departed from the Tabernacle. Today, God reveals Himself to man through His Son,
Jesus Christ, and He desires that His light would shine

(Continued)

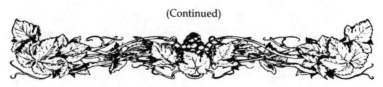

through His children.

The world we live in is a very dark place, and people are wandering around with no direction for their lives. The question we must ask ourselves is, "In what way can I allow the light of Jesus Christ to shine through me today?" Let's not hide that light, but let it shine brightly through us for the world to see.

"Now no one after lighting a lamp covers it over with a container, or puts it under a bed; but he puts it on a lamp stand, in order that those who come in may see the light."
Luke 8:16

Mike Morris, Senior Pastor
Calvary Chapel of the High Desert
Hesperia, California

December 2

WISE UP

"When they (the wise men from the East) had come into the house, they saw the young child with Mary His mother, and fell down and worshipped Him. And when they had opened their treasures, they presented gifts to Him:
gold, frankincense, and myrrh."
Matthew 2:11

It really is true as the song goes, *"Wise men still seek Him."* The Bible teaches that wisdom begins with the fear of the Lord.

Notice the sequence of events here, and how it pertains to us. First, they positioned themselves close to Jesus. Jesus said, *"Come unto Me."* Second, they saw Jesus for who He is and, consequently, fell and worshipped Him. A thankful, surrendered life is overflowing with seeing Jesus for Who He Is -- the Saviour! The reason people don't understand why we worship so much is often because they have never seen Him for who He is.

Lastly, they opened up and they presented gifts. Let's not simply come close to Jesus this morning to merely see what He is like. Let's open up the treasury of our hearts, present Him with our lives, our thanks, and our best. Let's sing today, let's worship our Saviour!

Mike Stangel, Senior Pastor
North Shore Christian Fellowship
Haleiwa, Hawaii

December 3

FOR THOSE WHO ARE OVERWHELMED

Psalm 61 is God's prescription for those who are over-whelmed. Face it, apart from all of the difficulties that we encounter along the way, life tends to be quite overwhelming in and of itself . My question for you today is: When life gets tough, should there be a significant difference between a disciple of Christ and a nonbeliever?

Of course there <u>should</u>. Even within the body of Christ, what separates those who conquer from those who fail? Is it not the individual's response towards Christ and his perception of the situation? What do you do when you are overwhelmed? David, the man of God, would reply:

> *"Hear my cry, O God: attend unto my prayer."*
> *Psalm 61:1*

Isn't that what <u>we</u> are supposed to do, *(Hebrews 4:14-16)*? In Romans 12:12, we are exhorted to be *". . .instant in prayer."* David said, *"Lead me to the Rock that is higher than I."*

Secular counseling will tell us that <u>we</u> are supposed to be the rock. But the truth is that <u>Jesus</u> is the Rock to whom we turn *(I Corinthians 10:4)*. Only He can put out the fires of life and calm the raging sea of adversity. Do you believe that today? Do you believe that with all your heart?

You see, Jesus is a Risen Savior . . . that is a fact! *(I Corinthians 15:5-7; Acts 1:3)*. However, if your prayer life is clouded with doubt and unbelief *(Hebrews 11:6)*, I'm afraid you are doing nothing more than wishing for things to take a turn for the good. Is Jesus your Rock today? If so, the

(Continued)

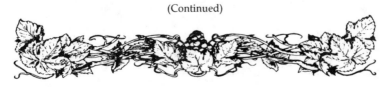

gates of hell shall not prevail against you, *(Matthew 16:18)*. We must hide in our heart these precious truths *(Psalm 119:11)* or some of us will be found "believing in vain" *(I Corinthians 15:2)*.

No, Jesus is not a crutch . . . He's more! He's our Shelter and Strong Tower *(Proverbs 18:10)*. May God's grace teach us how to lean upon our Saviour. He's accessible every second *(Ephesians 2:18)*. He cares for you *(1 Peter 5:7)*. Because we know that, I mean really know that, we can sing praises to Him forever *(Psalm 61:8)*.

Remember, when overwhelmed, first, do what you usually do last: Pause (Selah) -- everything is going to be just fine *(Romans 8:28)*. You are surrounded by an Immovable Rock *(Psalm 125:1-2)* and His Name is Jesus *(Revelation 19:16)*.

Ray Viola, Senior Pastor
Koinonia Fellowship
East Rochester, New York

December 4

JESUS IS COMING SOON!

*"In My Father's house are many mansions; if it were not so, I
would have told you. I go to prepare a place for you. And if I
go and prepare a place for you, I will come again
and receive you to Myself; that where
I am, there you may be also."*
John 14:2,3

Jesus promised to come again. You can be sure He will keep
His promise. *"I will come again and receive you to Myself; that
where I am, there you may be also."*

It has been said that Christ is coming as:

the Jeweler after His jewels *(Malachi 3:17)*
the Harvester for His wheat *(Matt. 13:30)*
the Merchantman for His pearls *(Matt.13:45)*
the Nobleman for His subjects *(Luke 19:12)*
the Shepherd for His sheep *(1 Peter 5:4)*
the Kinsman for His Ruth *(Ruth 4:14,15)*
the Bridegroom for His bride.

He is coming to the Wedding before He comes to the war
(Revelation 19). He will come as the Battler at Armageddon,
but first as the Bridegroom Divine.

Bill Stonebraker, Senior Pastor
Calvary Chapel of Honolulu
Honolulu, Hawaii

December 5

ONE HOUR

When we look at time in increments, it seems like we never have enough of it. We make statements such as "I don't have a second to spare" or "I just don't have time." But if we look at an hour as being a commitment or a part of our lives, we will always have time.

Jesus dealt with this same problem. It had to do with His disciples. It was concerning their commitment to prayer. Jesus said to them, *"My soul is deeply grieved to the point of death; remain here and keep watch with Me."* Jesus returned to His disciples and found them sleeping and said to them, *"So you men could not keep watch with Me for one hour?"* This happened two more times. Jesus warned them:

> *"Keep watching and praying that you may*
> *not enter into temptation."*
> *Matthew 26:38-45*

Is prayer a matter of time with you, or is it a commitment? May we never hear Jesus say to us, *"Are you still sleeping and taking your rest?"* Battles are won on our knees not on our backs.

Glenn Kravig, Assistant Pastor
Calvary Chapel of Downey
Downey, California

December 6

POSITIONED "IN" CHRIST

"These things I have spoken to you, that in Me you may have peace. In the world you will have tribulation; but be of good cheer, I have overcome the world."
John 16:33

Notice the "in's." Having a correct relationship with Jesus is positional. If we place ourselves "in" Him, ("in" His teachings, "in" His will, "in" His purposes), we then can experience His promises. According to this verse, *peace* is the key. As you read your Bible, you'll find hundreds of promises, most being dependent upon the recipient being positioned "in" Jesus.

However, we must also notice the alternative. If we do not position ourselves "in" Jesus, then we are automatically positioned *". . .in the world where you will have tribulation."* Why do that to yourself?

Jesus is offering you peace. Why not take Him up on His offer?

Rick Coburn, Senior Pastor
Calvary Chapel of Dallas
Piano, Texas

December 7

FOR THEY INTENDED EVIL AGAINST YOU

"For they intended evil against You; they devised a plot which they are not able to perform."
Psalm 21:11

Often times, we find ourselves ruled by the fear of others. We are afraid of what others may do to us. This can keep us from stepping out in faith, it can also keep us from loving others as we should. How many times have you wanted to do something, serve in a ministry, or go to an event only to find out the person you fear is involved or going to be there. Instead of being able to serve or go to the event, we avoid the very things that God has called us to do.

But in these verses, we find that there is no reason for us to fear man. People may be planning revenge against us or they may be bitter toward us, but it is so important to remember that God is in control of our lives. Nehemiah was such a great example. Sandballat and Tobiah were always seeking to destroy the work of rebuilding the wall of Jerusalem. At one point, they were attempting an assassination plot against Nehemiah. Nehemiah put His trust in the Lord and continued the work that God had called Him to. When Nehemiah did that, God became His shield and protected him from the plots of the enemy.

Remember, the enemy can only do what God allows him to. Be bold and be strong in your faith, for God will not allow them to perform the evil plot they have devised against you.

Chuck Lind, Senior Pastor
Calvary Chapel Olympia
Olympia, Washington

December 8

WARNING, WARNING, WARNING!

Earthquakes, floods, wars, tornadoes, hunger, killings, missing persons, abduction, sex for sale; we hear these broadcasts throughout each day on television and the radio. We can't help but be alarmed at the ugliness of our society, however we are given a challenge by Paul in *Ephesians 5:16,17*:

> *"Redeeming the time, because the days are evil.*
> *Wherefore be ye not unwise, but understand*
> *what the will of the Lord is."*
> *Ephesians 5:16,17*

Brothers and sisters, we are living in evil days (Sodom and Gomorrah), and we have a responsibility to be bold in our FAITH, letting people know about our Savior Jesus Christ! Knowing this, what are you doing to be a witness for Him?

Mark Maciel, Assistant Pastor
Calvary Chapel of Downey
Downey, California

December 9

STUDY!

*"Do your best to present yourself to God as one approved,
a workman who does not need to be ashamed and
who correctly handles the word of truth."*
2 Timothy 2:15

While reading her Bible on a public bus, a belligerent man confronted a bashful Christian. He boldly asked if she believed everything in the Bible. She said she did. He then said, "If you believe EVERYTHING, then explain to me how Jonah lived for three days in the belly of a whale!" The woman answered, "I don't know, but I believe he did." The man became more agitated. "Lady, you should be able to explain what you believe!" She quietly repeated her inability to know exactly how Jonah survived, but noted she would ask him once she got to heaven. Sarcastically, the rude guy asked, "And what if Jonah didn't make it to heaven?" "Then you ask him," was her reply!

Sometimes we won't be able to answer every question, but we are told to study!

Neil Matranga, Assistant Pastor
Calvary Chapel of Downey
Downey, California

December 10

IT'S ALL A MATTER OF PERSPECTIVE

"When the disciples saw Him walking on the sea, they were troubled, saying, "It is a ghost' And they cried out for fear. But immediately Jesus spoke to them, saying, 'Be of good cheer! It is I; do not be afraid.' And Peter answered Him and said, Lord, if it is You, command me to come to You on the water.' So He said, 'Come.' And when Peter had come down out of the boat, he walked on the water to go to Jesus. But when he saw that the wind was boisterous, he was afraid; and beginning to sink he cried out, saying, 'Lord, save me!' and immediately Jesus stretched out His hand and caught him, and said to him, 'O you of little faith, why did you doubt?'"
Matthew 14:26-31

Our view of Jesus Christ will determine whether we sink or swim in this life. Seeing Him vaguely or sporadically will make problems seem insurmountable, yet how much greater is He than our problems! If He could control the wind and waves, feed the multitude with a few loaves and fishes, He certainly could handle the daily problems that would pop up in their lives. Truly, your view of Jesus will determine whether you experience victory or defeat.

A penny can block out the sun if you hold it close to your eye. It's all a matter of perspective. A problem held too close and too tightly can make it seem as though the Lord is no where around. What's your perspective? *"Commit your way to the Lord, trust also in Him, and He shall bring it to pass,"* (Psalm 37:5).

Bill Stonebraker, Senior Pastor
Calvary Chapel of Honolulu
Honolulu, Hawaii

December 11

WAKE UP CALL

"He awakens me morning by morning. . ."
Isaiah 50:4

This verse in the Old Testament was actually a prophecy concerning the type of devotional lifestyle Jesus (who is our example in all things) would have here on earth.

It has been estimated that during an average life span of 75 years a Christian will spend:

> 23 years sleeping
> 19 years working
> 6 years traveling (rush hour?)
> 6 years eating
> 7 1/2 years dressing and personal hygiene
> 6 <u>months</u> in devotions

If we are truly being led by the Spirit, we are being led to cultivate the love relationship with Jesus.

". . .Rise up, my love, my fair one, and come away!"
Song of Solomon 2:10

Mike Stangel, Senior Pastor
North Shore Christian Fellowship
Haleiwa, Hawaii

December 12

IT'S TIME TO CHOOSE

*"I'm going to put an end to all people, for the earth is filled with
violence because of them. I am surely going to destroy both
them and the earth. So make yourself an ark of
cypress wood, make rooms on it and coat it
with pitch inside and out."*
Genesis 6:13,14

*"Go into the ark, you and your whole family because I have
found you righteous in this generation."*
Genesis 7:1

Wow! This story sounds like it could fit today's world,
doesn't it? In this current generation, which category do
you fit into? Those being destroyed or the righteous ones
who are being saved?

"The Judge is standing at the door."
James 5:9b

Dan Marks, Assistant Pastor
Calvary Chapel of Downey
Downey, California

December 13

JOY OF LIVING

"Therefore do not worry about tomorrow, for tomorrow
will worry about its own things. Sufficient
for the day is its own trouble."
Matthew 6:34

What are you concerned about today? What are you living for today? So often we are focused on the future. We are thinking about what we must do tomorrow, or the next day. We live for the weekends! But in so doing we miss what God has for us today. We forget that today is a day especially designed and created by God. *"This is the day the LORD has made; we will rejoice and be glad in it,"* (Psalm 118:24).

Simply put, we miss the joy of living this day with God. For some of us, this is so "normal" we don't know anything else. But in this awesome passage in Matthew, God says, *". . .seek Me first,"* and the idea is to make that the concern of our hearts today. This does not mean to seek Him first and then, second, seek the concerns of the world. No, what it means is to make your priority, your focus today, the Lord. Then get this — He will take care of your concerns — He personally will handle your worries. But instead we live in worry and stress.

I encourage you today — let your heart be focused on the Lord. As someone said it so well, let God carry your worries — He will be up all night anyhow!

Jim Suttle, Senior Pastor
Calvary Chapel of Roswell
Roswell, New Mexico

December 14

THE KINDNESS OF OUR KING

"Now it came to pass in the thirty-seventh year of the captivity
of Jehoiachin, king of Judah, in the twelfth month, on the
twenty-fifth day of the month, that Evil-Merodach king of
Babylon, in the first year of his reign, lifted up the head of
Jehorachin, king of Judah and brought him out of prison. "
Jeremiah 52:31

What were you like when you first came to the Lord? Were
you clean, neat, and pretty without fault to your name? Were
your thoughts, attitudes, and actions totally pure? Were
you already kind to everyone? No? I don't think any of us
can make that claim.

Like Jehoiachin, the king of Judah who spent thirty-seven
years imprisoned by the Babylonians, most of us have come
out of some type of prison or another. The enemy had held
us captive. We needed to have the Lord replace our "filthy
rags," -- our old thoughts, and destructive habits. We definitely needed some improvements.

Eventually, though, the Holy Spirit worked in our lives and
we changed. We began to read the Bible, attend church,
and some of us became involved in one ministry or another.
We put aside the old life-style and actually preferred to fellowship with other believers in God's house. We were different than when we started our walk with Jesus.

But a funny thing happened after we changed. We began
to look upon the unsaved with contempt. We shook our
head at their language, could not believe their materialism,

(Continued)

and eventually without even realizing it, we developed an ATTITUDE. We forgot that it was the Lord Jesus who took us out of the same prison these people were in. We overlooked the fact that He had accepted us just as we were . . . no strings attached.

Instead, we began to believe that we had always been a proper child of God. WE began to decide which person would or would not be suitable for the kingdom of God. Or THAT person would never come to church, or THIS person would never get saved. We began to set restrictions on the unsaved, limiting salvation to the people we were comfortable with. And we also set restrictions on what God could do in the lives of such people.

Will you remember this about the church of Jesus Christ? God is the only one responsible for changing the lives of His people -- not you -- only God. And Jesus loves each person just as they are, He only desires that they come to Him. Your responsibility is to bring people to the Lord -- to take them by the hand and lead them toward Him. Don't worry about their appearance or their qualifications. No one is exempt. Just bring them, each and every one.

God will do the rest. He'll speak to them, He'll change them, and He'll bless their lives. You have only to love each person with His agape love, and He'll be more than glad to supply you with that. Love them, and let your King bring them out of their prisons.

Steve Mays, Senior Pastor
Calvary Chapel of South Bay
Torrance, California

December 15

LOOKING AHEAD

As we can see today, the enemy is alive and working. Not only is he working to blind the minds of unbelievers, he is also trying to discourage the lives of believers. A great verse for us to keep in mind during those times is found in the book of *Philippians 3:13*:

"Brethren, I do not count myself to have apprehended; but this one thing I do, forgetting those things which are behind and reaching forth unto those things which are before."

Paul knew that times of failure would come. How we need to keep our eyes to the sky! I challenge you this morning to memorize this scripture and place it within your heart.

Louie Cruzado, Assistant Pastor
Calvary Chapel of Downey
Downey, California

December 16

FREE BUT NOT CHEAP

"...the free gift of God is eternal life in Christ Jesus our Lord."
Romans 6:23b

"For by grace you have been saved through faith; and that not
of yourselves, it is the gift of God."
Ephesians 2:8

These scriptures point to the fact that our salvation is a free gift of God. There are no so called acts of righteousness we can perform to earn our salvation, no financial agreements we can negotiate to purchase our atonement, no personal sacrifices deep enough to gain us entrance into heaven. In short, there is absolutely nothing man can do to secure his salvation. Salvation is a free gift offered to man by God.

While our salvation is free, this does not suggest that the price to obtain our salvation was cheap. The fact is our salvation was extremely costly. The cost at which our salvation was purchased was the life of the Son of God. Peter in his first epistle writing about the cost of our redemption says: *"Knowing that you were not redeemed with perishable things like silver or gold from your futile way of life inherited from your forefathers, but with precious blood, as of a lamb unblemished and spotless, the blood of Christ,"* (1 Peter 1:18,19).

The next time you think about the free gift of God, also remember the price it took to obtain it.

Ron Terrall, Assistant Pastor
Calvary Chapel of Downey
Downey, California

December 17

FAILURE

In *Matthew 14:22-33*, the disciples were in a boat at night in the middle of a storm. Jesus comes to them walking on the water, and of course they were terrified. We then see Peter stepping out of the boat at our Lord's beckon and walking on the water to come to him. Peter began to be afraid and started to sink. He called out to Jesus and was saved immediately.

Most people center on Peter's failure to keep his eyes on Jesus. But we need to look closer at this passage especially verse 31. *"And immediately Jesus stretched forth His hand, and caught him, and said unto him, O thou of little faith, wherefore didst thou doubt?"*

- Jesus catches him first
- Our Lord then corrects him
- If Peter had little faith, then the others who never got out of the boat probably had much less

Lesson: Do we center on our failures, or on others, or do we see God's hand ready to catch us <u>first</u> and then show us where we went wrong?

Steve Everett, Assistant Pastor
Calvary Chapel of Downey
Downey, California

December 18

FOCUS

*"As they ministered to the Lord and fasted, the Holy Spirit said,
'Now separate to Me Barnabas and Saul for the work
to which I have called them.'"*
Acts 13:2

Guidance . . . God's will for our lives . . . it seems that so
often, that this is one thing we really struggle with. Hopefully we want God's will in our lives, if you don't, quite
honestly, you probably don't understand what a loving Father He is, and how His will is the very best for your life.
But if we do want God's will, how do we find it? In our
passage today we will see a couple of issues that help with
this. The rest of the book of Acts, and history itself shows
us that this decision in *Acts 31:2* is of God. So how do we
apply this to our lives?

First, they ministered to the Lord. So often when we need
guidance, we do spend time with the Lord, but it is all focused on us. We are praying for wisdom and circumstances,
but how often do we minister to the Lord. This is such an
awesome picture. To just make God our focus, to care about
Him and not us.

Secondly, they fasted. They denied themselves. Fasts can
take all kinds of forms, but the root of it is to deny ourselves, to put our personal needs down in order to focus
more freely on God. So in this atmosphere, where God was
the focus, and the personal needs were pushed into the back-
ground, God guided in a powerful and clear way. And I
believe, if we in a similar way focus on God and deny ourselves, God will guide us.

(Continued)

So what am I saying, if you want to know God's will then you need to jump through these "hoops" to find it? Absolutely not! This is not a way to manipulate God, this is saying simply that if we are focused on God, and not majoring on ourselves, that we are in a better place to hear from God, and in such a place, I believe we will find God's will for our lives.

So minister to the Lord today, don't major on yourself and in such a place, just trust your life into His capable hands.

Jim Suttle, Senior Pastor
Calvary Chapel of Roswell
Roswell, New Mexico

December 19

I WILL WORK A WORK IN YOUR DAY

"Behold ye among the heathen, and regard, and wonder marvelously: for [I] will work a work in your days, [which] ye will not believe, though it be told [you]."
Habakuk 1:5

God was telling Habakuk about how there will be a work, an awesome work, in his days which he may not believe. What is so awesome is that we are living in these very days. God truly desires to do that awesome work in our lives, and through our lives, that will blow people's minds.

Just as Peter, Paul, James, Matthew, Mark, Luke, John and others had their day, it is now our turn to have our day to watch the MASTER at work. He will use people like us and the circumstances around us to bring His glory to the Kingdom!

Mark Maciel, Assistant Pastor
. Calvary Chapel of Downey
Downey, California

December 20

PERFECT PEACE

"You will keep him in perfect peace, whose mind is stayed on
You, because he trusts in You."
Isaiah 26:3

We live in a world that has become increasingly stressed
out and uptight. The everyday pressures of life, try to rob
us of our peace. In *Isaiah 26:3*, we have a beautiful promise
that the Lord will keep those whose minds are stayed on
Him in *"perfect peace."* The literal Hebrew translation is, *"You
will keep him in peace, peace."* That's appropriate, because
scripture tells us that there are two different kinds of peace
He wants us to walk in.

The first is *"Peace with God,"* (*Romans 5:1*). This peace occurs
when a person surrenders their life to Jesus Christ as Savior
and Lord. The second is the *"Peace of God"* (*Philippians 4:7*).
This is a practical peace that guards our hearts and minds
against the everyday pressures of life.

But, the peace of God won't automatically fill your heart
once you make peace with Christ. Christians can still worry
and have anxiety. The Apostle Paul exhorted us to, *"Let the
peace of God rule in your hearts,"* implying that His peace will
rule when we allow it to! However, the peace of God will
never rule in our hearts until we first learn to trust God in
everything. We are commanded in scripture:

"In everything give thanks for this is the
will of God in Christ Jesus for you."
1 Thessalonians 5:18

(Continued)

You won't thank God in everything until you first learn to trust God in everything. But trusting God in everything is impossible unless we believe these three things about Him.

God Is Sovereign: God is aware of and is in control of absolutely everything that touches our lives. Nothing happens in my life except what God allows for His purpose.

God Loves Me With All Of His Heart: This He proved on Calvary *(Romans 5:8)*. God's word clearly teaches that His sovereignty and love always work together for my ultimate good *(Romans 8:28)*.

God Has Infinite Wisdom: God is wiser than we are. We accept this in principle, but not always in practice -- especially when we don't understand what's happening in our lives. God is working for our ultimate good to give us a future and a hope *(Jeremiah 29:11)*.

So when anxieties and fears begin to rise up within you, remember these things, and believe them with all of your heart. Then follow these instructions:

"Be anxious for nothing, but in everything by prayer and
supplication, with thanksgiving, let your
requests be made known to God."
Philippians 4:6

Phil Ballmaier, Senior Pastor
Calvary Chapel of Elk Grove
Elk Grove Village, Illinois

December 21

TURN OFF THE NOISE

"Truly my soul silently waits for God; from Him comes my salvation. He only is my rock and my salvation; He is my defense; I shall not be moved."
Psalm 62:1,2

As we are silent before God, we see Him work. We must turn off the noise of our striving and fighting, so that we can wait for Him to meet our need. He not only provides salvation from sin, but also He is our deliverer in life difficulties. Let's get quiet before Him.

Carl Westerlund, Assistant Pastor
Calvary Chapel Costa Mesa
Costa Mesa, California

December 22

CHRISTMAS PAST, PRESENT, AND FUTURE

It's funny how nostalgic this time of the year can be. Somehow our memories are jazzed to think of Christmas's past. We used to sing a song years ago at Christmas time. The first line went something like, "You need Jesus more than once or twice a year." What a true and poignant message! How would any of us make it in this chaotic world, in such a chaotic time, without the Christ of Christmas?

My prayer for you is that you will allow the Prince of Peace to live peaceably in your heart now, and throughout the coming year. May you come to know Him more than you ever have before.

Bil Gallatin, Senior Pastor
Calvary Chapel of the Finger Lakes
Farmington, New York

December 23

JESUS "OUR REASON FOR EVERY SEASON!"

The 10 Christmas Commandments

I. Thou shalt not leave "Christ" out of Christmas, making it "Xmas." To some, "X" is unknown.

II. Thou shalt prepare thy soul for Christmas. Spend not so much on gifts that thy soul is forgotten.

III. Thou shalt not let Santa Claus replace Christ, Thus robbing the day of its spiritual reality.

IV. Thou shalt not burden the shop girl, the mailman, and the merchant with complaints and demands.

V. Thou shalt give thyself with thy gift. This will increase its value a hundred fold, and he who receiveth it shall treasure it forever.

VI. Thou shalt not value gifts received by their cost. Even the least expensive may signify love, and that is more priceless than silver and gold.

VII. Thou shalt not neglect the needy. Share thy blessings with many who will go hungry and cold unless thou are generous.

VIII. Thou shalt not neglect thy church. Its services highlight the true meaning of the season.

IX. Thou shalt be as a little child. Not until thou has become in spirit as a little one art thou ready to enter into the kingdom of Heaven.

X. Thou shalt give thy heart to Christ. Let Him be at the top of thy Christmas list.

Anyone keeping these commandments is sure to have a blessed Christmas.

Brian Bell, Senior Pastor
Calvary Chapel Murrieta
Murrieta, California

December 24

CHRISTMAS EVE

When we love someone, we seek to express that love by giving to them meaningful gifts.

"God so loved us that He gave His only begotten Son."

That is what Christmas is all about — love and giving. This is why giving is such an important part of our celebration of the holiday.

Chuck Smith, Senior Pastor
Calvary Chapel of Costa Mesa
Costa Mesa, California

December 25

CHRISTMAS GIVING

In *Luke 1:35*, we see Mary as a type of believer:

> *"The Holy Ghost shall come upon thee and the power of the Highest shall overshadow thee: therefore also that Holy Thing which shall be born of thee shall be called the Son of God."*

God <u>gave</u> His Son and Jesus <u>gave</u> His life and the Holy Spirit came to live in us as we believed.

Now, Mary in *Luke 2:7*:

> *". . .and she brought forth her first born son."*

So now, God desires that we, being born of God bring forth His Son to a dying world.

Give Christ at Christmas!

Jeff Johnson, Senior Pastor
Calvary Chapel of Downey
Downey, California

December 26

TRAIN UP A CHILD

*"Train up a child in the way he should go: and when
he is old, he will not depart from it."*
Proverbs 22:6

As parents, we have a responsibility before God in the way
that we raise our children. Certainly this includes raising
our children to know and serve the Lord *(Ephesians 6:4)*.
But this means more than just reading Bible stories to them.
As parents, we ought to be setting the right example for our
children to follow. Children have an inborn desire to be
like their parents *(Proverbs 17:6)*, and like it or not, they're
going to copy much of what they see in us.

But this verse appears to go beyond just teaching them about
Jesus. Another translation is, *"Train up a child according to
their way."* In other words, each of our children are unique.
Each child has their own blend of personality, talents, and
calling. For the parent, our responsibility is to study our
children and raise them in a way that builds on who they
are. Your child can't live to fulfill the dreams of what you
wanted to be, but they can live to fulfill the dreams that
God has for them.

We've got someone who can show us how to do all this.
There is no better example for us to follow. And when it
comes to knowing just who you are, what you're like, and
where you're going, no one knows better than your Father.
Teach us Lord!

Rich Cathers, Senior Pastor
Calvary Chapel of Fullerton
Fullerton, California

December 27

STANDING BEFORE GOD

"So Moses' father-in-law said to him, "The thing that you do is not good. Both you and these people who are with you will surely wear yourselves out. For this thing is too much for you; you are not able to perform it by yourself. Listen now to my voice; I will give you counsel, and God will be with you: Stand before God for the people."
Exodus 18:17-19

Moses is experiencing a crisis. There aren't enough hours in the day, nor does he have enough strength to do what he's trying to do. What was he trying to do? Help people. But it was too much.

He gets great advice from Jethro, his father-in-law. In verse 19, Jethro says first *". . .stand before God for the people."* You see, Moses had been standing before the people for God. He had it backwards. To really be of service Moses had to first stand before God.

Are there people you would like to help? Then realize today that to be helpful to them, you must first stand before God and allow Him to minister to you.

Jeff Stewart, Senior Pastor
Calvary Chapel Pomona Valley
Pomona, California

December 28

DON'T BE DECEIVED

"Be sober, be vigilant; because your adversary
the devil, as a roaring lion, walketh about,
seeking whom he may devour."
1 Peter 5:8

Jesus emphatically warns us that we are susceptible to deception *(Mark 13:5-6)*. He says that many will come seeking to deceive us. Reading our newspapers reveals how many "Saviors" are promoting themselves as the answer to our life's problems. "The new you" and "Revolutionize your life" are just a few of the many hooks that are trolling for your attention.

Ed Cornwell, Assistant Pastor
Calvary Chapel Costa Mesa
Santa Ana, California

December 29

FIRST LOVE!

*"To the angel of the church in Ephesus write: The One who
holds the seven stars in His right hand, the One who walks
among the seven golden lampstands, says this: 'I know your
deeds and your toil and perseverance, and that you cannot
endure evil men, and you put to the test those who call themselves apostles, and they are not, and you found them to be false;
and you have perseverance and have endured for My name's
sake, and have not grown weary. But I have this against you,
that you have left your first love. Remember therefore from
where you have fallen, and repent and do the deeds you did at
first; or else I am coming to you, and will remove your
lampstand out of its place — unless you repent.'"
Revelation 2:4,5*

Found within three verses are three critically important ingredients to keep your first love alive with the Lord.

1. <u>Remember</u> therefore from where you have fallen. In any
relationship, this can happen when one of the partners stops
working at the relationship. We are called to remember what
did we do when we first fell in love. In this case, what did
we do when we first fell in love with the Lord?
2. <u>Repent!</u> This means to turn around. Turn around and
do the things you used to do again. It's not too late to re-
kindle that first love.
3. <u>Do the deeds you did at first</u>! Do those things again! Get
radical for the one you love! Show Him you care by spending time with Him in conversation.

Bill Richard, Senior Pastor
Calvary Chapel Encinitas
Encinitas, California

December 30

WALK IN HIS FOOTSTEPS

"Who is among you that feareth the LORD, that obeyeth the
voice of his servant, that walketh in darkness, and hath no
light? Let him trust in the name of the
LORD, and stay upon his God."
Isaiah 50:10

The obedient walk is not usually the easy walk. The path
that seems so dark and lonely, is many times the well-trod-
den of the holy Son of God, who beckons us to lean on
Him and follow Him to the place of everlasting light.

John Van Scott, Assistant Pastor
Calvary Chapel of the Finger Lakes
Farmington, New York

December 31

GOD OF CHRISTMAS PAST

"Then I looked, and behold, a Lamb standing on Mount Zion."
Revelation 4:1

Well, another Christmas season has passed. And, hopefully, yours was not characterized by stress and debt, but by joy and thankfulness as you took time to reflect on the birth of our Lord!

God, in His Word, had promised to send a Messiah. The Old Testament is full of promises. And He fulfilled His promise on that first Christmas. Every December, we celebrate His fulfilled promise.

God has also given us the promise that Jesus will come again. One day, He will descend from heaven and stand on Mount Zion. Our King will establish His kingdom here on earth! That is His promise, and God has a reputation for keeping His promises.

Are you stressed? Are you struggling? Is the sinful condition of our world grieving your heart? Remember, it won't last forever. Jesus is coming back! Because He promised He would.

"Surely I am coming quickly."
Revelation 22:20

Todd Lauderdale, Assistant Pastor
Calvary Chapel of Murrieta
Murrieta, California

INDEX

INDEX

INDEX

INDEX

INDEX

INDEX